P9-DMV-371

SUPPOSE....

You were the only man alive on the Martian space station, and its orbit was deteriorating...
Your dead wife tapped on the window...
Your plane flew into another world...ours...
A little bird hung over murderers' heads, and testified...
A red-eyed thing from another world howled in the night for you...
But your salvage operation on a distant planet was doing all right, after all...

That would be OK, wouldn't it?
And when you consider that there are 12
more stories in here that are as full of
promise as tomorrow, that will entertain
you and cause you to thrill to the
possibilities they uncover...the latest
from **L. Ron Hubbard's Writers of The
Future Contest®** ... And when you consider
that the illustrations for these stories
were done by the winners in the first
year of **L. Ron Hubbard's
Illustrators of The Future Contest** ...

HOW CAN YOU RESIST?

WHAT'S BEEN SAID ABOUT THE *L. RON HUBBARD Presents WRITERS OF THE FUTURE* ANTHOLOGIES

"These stories represent the best of the fresh talent in the field..."   GENE WOLFE

"Opening new trails into the worlds of SF..."   JACK WILLIAMSON

"What a wonderful idea—one of science fiction's all-time giants opening the way for a new generation of exciting talent! For these brilliant stories, and the careers that will grow from them, we all stand indebted to L. Ron Hubbard."   ROBERT SILVERBERG

"There's an explosion of talent in these pages."   ROCKY MOUNTAIN NEWS

"Highly recommended for the majority of SF collections."   BOOKLIST MAGAZINE

"All the stories are provocative, imaginative, and entertaining..."   DELAND (Florida) NEWS

"A double success for science fiction fans—it encourages new talents in the field, and it provides readers with some very good stories."   BUFFALO (New York) NEWS

"...these stories present imaginative situations and solid literary skill."   THE OTTAWA (Canada) CITIZEN

"... recommended as literally being the best, the very best, available to the public today."

MIDWEST BOOK REVIEW

"Writers of The Future *brings back some of the science fiction reminiscent of* Twilight Zone *and* The Outer Limits. *But it also brings a modernized innovativeness and mystery unmatched by its forerunners."*

THE UTAH STATESMAN

"... not only is the writing excellent ... it is also extremely varied. There's fantasy and adventure fiction ... humor ... and mainstream SF ... Don't miss this anthology. There's a lot of hot new talent in it."

"... the best-selling SF anthology series of all time."

LOCUS MAGAZINE

"... packed with raw talent ... a must buy for everyone who wants to write science fiction."

FANTASY REVIEW

"... drop whatever you're doing and run to the nearest bookstore. This book is more than worth the effort."

THE LEADING EDGE

"This is a remarkable collection ... in its content and scope." THE JOHNS HOPKINS UNIVERSITY NEWS–LETTER

"The varied style and consistent quality lead to a reading experience beyond belief." PLANETARY PREVIEWS

"... an exceedingly solid collection, including sf, fantasy and horror ..." THE CHICAGO SUN–TIMES

"If you buy only one paperback in the SF field this year, make it this one." MEMPHIS COMMERCIAL APPEAL

QUANTITY DISCOUNTS

The L. Ron Hubbard Presents Writers of the
Future anthologies are available at special
quantity discounts when purchased in bulk
by schools, organizations, and special-interest
groups such as SF clubs and writing workshops.

Write or call for more information:
DIRECTOR OF PUBLIC INFORMATION,
Bridge Publications Inc., 4751 Fountain Avenue,
Los Angeles, CA 90029.

Or call toll-free 1-800-722-1733, or 1-800-843-
7389 in California.

L. RON HUBBARD

PRESENTS

WRITERS
OF THE
FUTURE

VOLUME VI

L. RON HUBBARD

PRESENTS

WRITERS

OF THE

FUTURE

VOLUME VI

The Year's 18 Best Tales from His
Writers of The Future
International Writing Program
Illustrated by the Winners in His
Illustrators of The Future
International Illustration Program

With Essays on Writing and Illustration by
L. RON HUBBARD
BEN BOVA
ALEX SCHOMBURG
FRANK KELLY-FREAS
ALGIS BUDRYS

Edited by Algis Budrys
Frank Kelly-Freas, Director of Illustration

Bridge Publications, Inc.

COPYRIGHT © 1990 BY BRIDGE PUBLICATIONS, INC.
All Rights Reserved.

No part of this book may be used or reproduced in any manner whatsoever without written permission except in the case of brief quotations embodied in critical articles or reviews. For information, address Bridge Publications, Inc., 4751 Fountain Avenue, Los Angeles, CA 90029.

Kansas City Kitty: Copyright © 1990 Michael L. Scanlon
Red Eyes: Copyright © 1990 Stephen Milligan
Winter's Garden: Copyright © 1990 Sharon Wahl
A Foreign Exchange: Copyright © 1990 Matthew Wills
Dancing with Dinosaurs: Copyright © 1990 Charles D. Eckert
Water: Copyright © 1990 John W. Randal
A Branch in the Wind: Copyright © 1990 Bruce Holland Rogers
Riches Like Dust: Copyright © 1990 Scot Noel
Blueprint for Success in Art: Copyright © 1990 Alex Schomburg
Eulogy for Lisa: Copyright © 1990 Jason Shankel
The Dive: Copyright © 1990 James Verran
Flutterbyes: Copyright © 1990 Jo Etta Ledgerwood
The Magician © 1990 Michael I. Landweber
Science in Science Fiction: Copyright © 1990 Ben Bova
The Bookman: Copyright © 1990 David Ira Cleary
The Vintager: Copyright © 1990 James Gleason Bishop
Mothers of Chaos: Copyright © 1990 Pete D. Manison
The Children of Crèche: Copyright © 1990 James Gardner
The Scholar of the Pear Tree Garden: Copyright © 1990 Annis Shepherd
Under Glass: Copyright © 1990 David Carr
Illustration on page   7: Copyright © 1990 Peggy Ranson
Illustration on page   31: Copyright © 1990 Timothy Winkler
Illustration on page   56: Copyright © 1990 Kevin Dzuban
Illustration on page   74: Copyright © 1990 Derek Hegsted
Illustration on page   94: Copyright © 1990 Allison Hershey
Illustration on page 108: Copyright © 1990 Beryl Bush
Illustration on page 119: Copyright © 1990 Kelly Faltermayer
Illustration on page 128: Copyright © 1990 Daniel S. Oman
Illustration on page 153: Copyright © 1990 Kelly Faltermayer
Illustration on page 196: Copyright © 1990 Jeff Fennel
Illustration on page 220: Copyright © 1990 Ruth Thompson
Illustration on page 235: Copyright © 1990 Jeff Fennel
Illustration on page 280: Copyright © 1990 Timothy Standish
Illustration on page 295: Copyright © 1990 Kevin Hopkins
Illustration on page 310: Copyright © 1990 Ruth Thompson
Illustration on page 325: Copyright © 1990 Timothy Standish
Illustration on page 364: Copyright © 1990 Allison Hershey
Illustration on page 382: Copyright © 1990 Timothy Winkler
Cover Artwork: Copyright © 1989 L. Ron Hubbard Library

This anthology contains works of fiction. Names, characters, places and incidents are either the product of the author's imagination or are used fictitiously. Any resemblance to actual events or locales or persons, living or dead, is entirely coincidental. Opinions expressed by non-fiction essayists are their own.

ISBN 0-88404-504-8

Library of Congress Catalog Card Number: 84-73270
First Edition Paperback 10 9 8 7 6 5 4 3 2 1

Printed in the United States of America
Cover Artwork by Frank Frazetta

WRITERS OF THE FUTURE, ILLUSTRATORS OF THE FUTURE, and the Writers of The Future logos are trademarks owned by L. Ron Hubbard Library.

CONTENTS

ACKNOWLEDGEMENTS

The judges for L. Ron Hubbard's Writers of The Future and Illustrators of The Future Contests serve at a cost in time and attention taken from their own prestigious careers. In the Contest year of this anthology, they were, for the Writers of The Future Contest:

Gregory Benford	Ben Bova
Algis Budrys	Ramsey Campbell
Anne McCaffrey	Larry Niven
Frederik Pohl	Andre Norton
Robert Silverberg	Jerry Pournelle
John Varley	Jack Williamson
Roger Zelazny	

For the Illustrators of The Future Contest, they were:

Edd Cartier	Leo & Diane Dillon
Bob Eggleton	Will Eisner
Frank Frazetta	Frank Kelly-Freas
Jack Kirby	Ron & Val Lakey-Lindahn
Paul Lehr	Moebius
Alex Schomburg	H.R. Van Dongen
William R. Warren, Jr.	

Serving as the instructor in the WOTF invitational writers' workshop at Sag Harbor, Long Island, was Tim Powers.

Our cover illustration is "Leaping Lizards," by Frank Frazetta, an original commissioned painting. Mr. Frazetta's career as a master of his field has spanned decades and aroused worldwide admiration for his works. The art may be seen at the L. Ron Hubbard Gallery, 7051 Hollywood Boulevard, Hollywood, California.

Introduction
by
Algis Budrys

Welcome to the sixth volume in this series. It's chock full of stories which we think are clearly fun to read. Every year is different; yet every year is the same in bringing you the excitement not only of reading the stories but of knowing that in the years to come, some of these names are going to be very well known. Perhaps all of them.

L. Ron Hubbard's Writers of The Future Contest is now very much a tradition in the field. Ninety writers have been brought forward, over the years, and introduced to the reading public. A gratifying number of those have gone on to publish novels, or otherwise distinguish themselves, and as the years pass, more and more of their colleagues will join them. It is with great pride that we say this, and the sure knowledge that L. Ron Hubbard was right—something like the Contest was very much needed.

With the best good will in the world, the conventional media cannot devote themselves to the needs of the novice writer more than a fraction of the time. At L. Ron Hubbard's Writers of The Future, it is all we do, and the latest set of results is waiting for your perusal in these pages. We think you will agree they are, as usual, remarkable.

This year, for the first time, we have added something new . . . the results of L. Ron Hubbard's Illustrators of the

Future Contest. My friend, Frank Kelly-Freas, has produced a crop of winners that bids fair to stand tall in science fiction and fantasy illustration for years to come. In fact, several of these novice artists have already achieved regular publication since winning in the Contest.

For more about this, see Kelly's and my essays toward the back of the book. Meanwhile, why don't you start sampling the results?

—Algis Budrys
Editor

Kansas City Kitty
by
Michael L. Scanlon

About the Author

Michael L. Scanlon has been perfecting his craft for a long time; ten years. Meanwhile, he has been working as an office temporary in the Seattle area, and also participating heavily in science fiction fandom—the hard core of science fiction lovers, who get together at conventions or otherwise display their unusually strong liking for the field. He was invited to be Fan Guest of Honor at Vikingcon, in Bellingham, as a matter of fact.

A 1986 attendee at Clarion West, he seems to have more than gotten the hang of it; "Kansas City Kitty" is a very tight, very professional story. We're very glad to have it.

About the Illustrator

Peggy Ranson was born in Memphis, Tennessee, and attended school there through the freshman year at Memphis State University, when she quit to go to work and never went back. Eventually she moved to New Orleans, working on graphics. Although she had been reading science fiction since the age of twelve, and was aware, vaguely, of science fiction conventions, she waited until she discovered, one day, that the office of the World Science Fiction Convention was three doors down the hall, before doing anything about it. Designing *the New Orleans Convention program book was the start of it all; since then she's discovered other conventions, art shows, and amateur magazines; now she's trying for the step up to professional publication.*

We were jumped by MiGs over the Kenai Peninsula, and one of them got lucky. I saw the missile coming on the radar and announced it.

I was still watching the radar scope when the warhead went off. One minute the screen was full of blips, ours, theirs, and the garbage we were throwing out, and the next, it went white all over.

"Brace," I yelled when the screen blanked, and hunkered down in my seat, trying to prepare for the blast.

Berentson, the tail gunner, shouted and then everything went to hell. *KC Kitty* lurched, and tilted nose down. A roar came in past my headphones, punctuated by squeals of overstressed metal.

The whole plane started to shudder. The vibrations grew until I was sure she was going to come apart in midair. I tried to remember the bail-out sequence.

"Hang on," Captain Subota's voice came over the intercom. I prepared for the order to jump for it, but it didn't come. An eternity passed in the next twenty or thirty seconds. Gradually the vibration lessened, and it felt like we were leveling off.

"Damage report," Captain Subota spoke again. I began to think we might make it, after all. I hadn't been looking forward to bailing out over the North Pacific. Our only hope of survival then would be rescue by a Russian gunboat. The Captain had saved us again.

McGregor, the copilot, reported in. One engine was out, he said, and there seemed to be damage to the tail control surfaces.

"Manion?"

"I'm all right, Captain," I said. "All the electronics are out."

"I suppose that includes the radar. How about the radio?"

I looked at the blank screen in front of me. "The radar's out, all right, Captain. I'll check the radio."

While I fiddled with knobs and switches, I heard the Captain try to raise Berentson. After the third or fourth try, the tail gunner's voice came on the circuit, slow and weak.

"Cap—Captain?" There was only static for a moment. "Captain, I'm sorry I screamed."

"That's all right, Berentson," Captain Subota said. "How are you feeling? What's your situation?" The Captain spoke with a soothing undertone.

More static. "Not—not so good, Captain. My shoulder hurts."

"What's wrong with it?"

"I can't see." There was a pause, then "I'm blind." A hint of hysteria crept into Berentson's voice.

"Easy, now," the Captain said. "Were you wearing your antiflash goggles?"

"Y—Yeah."

"Then the blindness is temporary." I know he mentally added the word *probably*. "Is there anything else wrong?"

The line was empty of anything but static for so long I wondered if Berentson had lost consciousness. Then, "My side's wet. I think it's blood." Pause. "It's cold in here, too."

I felt myself smile for a moment when I heard that. Berentson always complained about the cold in the tail gunner's compartment. "Cold as a drill instructor's smile,"

Illustrated by Peggy Ranson

was the expression coined one night at the NCO club. The smile faded. I wondered how bad the injuries were.

"Hang on, Pat," Captain Subota said. "We'll be back at the field before long, and you'll get a week in the hospital."

After a weak agreement from Berentson, the Captain switched back to me. "Get anything running, Manion?"

"No, sir." I thought for a moment, "I mean, the transmitter may be working, but I'm not receiving anything. No radar at all," I added.

"Can you get us a course back?"

I looked at my small-scale chart. "TAC's got a strip at Juneau."

"Too short."

"Can't we set down there? They'd have a field hospital, at least."

"I want a bomber base with crash crews, not a frontline fighter strip. Tactical Air Command doesn't know bombers."

"There's Langley RCAF base outside Vancouver." I looked south on the chart, peering at the symbols.

"I want to go to McChord," he said. "Vancouver was socked in when we took off, probably still is. Tacoma is only a few minutes farther south." He paused. "I want to get Berentson into a hospital, but I also want to get the *Kansas City Kitty* into a repair shop."

"Roger, Captain. McChord it is." They might break up the crew if the *Kitty* couldn't be repaired. I eyed the instruments that still worked. "Come to 94 degrees magnetic, at least until I can shoot the stars and get us a more accurate heading." I thought for a moment. "What about the rest of the squadron?"

McGregor spoke up. "No sign of them. No MiGs, no squadron, no nothing. Except the cloud."

"Cloud?"

"We turned enough to see behind us. There's a glowing cloud where the missile went off." Subota's voice sounded strained.

"There should be a cloud—" I started to say, but McGregor cut me off.

"*It's still glowing*." His voice had an edge of hysteria. It was the first time he'd ever sounded like that.

"All right, McGregor," Captain Subota said briskly. "Manion, get us a fix so we can get back home."

"Yessir," I said. When the Captain set his mind to something, there wasn't much to do about it. That was why he was the Captain. In between course computations, I caught glimpses of the cloud. It wasn't like anything I'd ever seen before. Writhing like an amoeba, glowing with its own light, it receded into the distance as we flew south.

I shot the stars, gave a course correction to the Captain, and tried not to think about our chances. It all depended on how badly damaged the *KC Kitty* was. B-45F's were tough. I've seen them come back all in pieces. I've also seen them go down with hardly a hole in them.

I wondered if Berentson was going to make it. I hoped so. Except for McGregor, we'd been together over three years. That was a long time during a war. It wouldn't be the same if we lost Berentson so soon after Garcia.

Even if that happened, even if Berentson died or left, there was still Captain Subota. He *was* the *Kitty*. He kept bringing her back, no matter what happened. I liked him. Not the same way I liked Berentson, but more than any of the other officers I'd served under.

We'd really caught it this mission.

Maybe the Captain was right about how long Berentson would be in the hospital. We were all going to have to have antirad treatments, that was for sure. At least that meant two weeks off the flight line.

That gave me something better to think about. Two weeks off from the war. I could get away from base after the first week of treatment. Maybe I could go camping, or try to go someplace on the ocean shore.

I stopped thinking about whether we would get back, and considered what I would do when we did. As I daydreamed, I tried to repair what I could. Navigation would only take a few minutes every so often, and I didn't even have the radar to watch. Maybe I could get a radio working, cannibalizing parts from other equipment. I lost track of the time.

"Manion?" Captain Subota's voice crackled over the intercom.

"Yessir." I cleared my throat. The image of Pat and I reliving this mission over pitchers at the NCO club vanished from my mind.

"I need a navigational check."

I calculated our location. "We're just north of the Olympic Peninsula. We'll be at McChord in under an hour."

McGregor spoke up. "We're low on fuel."

"How bad?"

"We're riding on empty."

"We have enough," Subota snapped. "We're low, but we'll make it, just." There was a pause. "How about the radar?"

I shook my head, then realized how tired I was, and spoke over the intercom. "Sir, the radar's shot. I've been working on the other equipment." Not expecting anything, I started searching up and down the bands on the set I had been working on.

I got static, and twice, fading hints of some sort of transmission. "Captain, I think that I've got one of the sets working."

"Good. Send a message."

"Sir, I have a receiver apparently working. I don't know about a transmitter." The Captain expected miracles, I guess. He usually did, but then he performed them, too.

"Give it a try, anyway. Send a message, ah, saying that we are damaged and low on fuel, but coming in for McChord, and that we want priority for landing." He barely hesitated before describing the situation we were in.

I got out the coding equipment and composed the message, then sent it.

"Repeat the message at ten minute intervals. Now, do we need a course correction?" Repeating the message wasn't standard radio procedure, but I figured we wouldn't get chewed out too much under the circumstances. I reached for the Morse key and began to send it again. We might need it. Our IFF transponder could be out, and local interceptor crews were real touchy since Tacoma got atom-bombed.

After giving the Captain a course correction, I went back to work on the radio. A test picked up more little snatches of broadcast, but nothing I could identify. What was really strange was the music. More than once, the tuner drifted through what sounded like civilian radio broadcasts. As far as I could tell, though, they were nowhere near the CONELRAD frequencies.

Fiddling with the radio, navigating, and sending out our emergency message kept me from thinking about much except that it was almost over. Subota was bringing us back again, and I was actually looking forward to the debriefing and then some sleep. Broken clouds rolled under us as we flew on.

Both the Captain and McGregor spoke at the same time, so I didn't make out what they were saying at first.

"—all the lights! Look at 'em! Where—"

I looked out and saw a carpet of lights spreading out before us. At first, I didn't understand what it was. Then the hair stood up on the back of my neck, and I felt goosebumps on my forearms. I've seen pictures. It was the lights of a peacetime city. Split-second glimpses showed roadways, buildings, houses streaking under us.

"Manion. Manion!" The Captain was as close to shouting as I've ever heard. "Shut up, McGregor. That's an order."

"I'm here, Captain." I answered finally.

'What's on the radio?" he snapped.

"Garbage," I said. "Sorry, sir. There's a fair bit of radio traffic, but the tuner keeps drifting, and it's all real faint."

"Keep trying." His voice sounded strained.

McGregor shouted. "MiGs! Both sides of us."

I looked at the shapes pacing the *Kitty*, shivered, then thought about it and got mad at McGregor. There couldn't be MiGs here. The Soviets don't have any aircraft carriers, and their nearest bases were up in Alaska. When we got back, I was going to talk with the Captain about McGregor. We didn't need someone like him on the crew.

"They're an escort. Not MiGs."

"Bullshit. Sorry sir, but we don't have any fighters like that."

"They have American markings. Keep yourself under control, McGregor. They're probably experimental models." Did the Captain sound the faintest bit uncertain? "So now we have an escort," he mused. "Can you raise them?"

"I'll try, sir." I selected the TAC Intercept frequency and tried voice transmission. "Charlie Romeo Seven Three Four to escort aircraft," I said. "We have radio troubles. Please respond if you are receiving our signal." I switched frequencies and tried again.

McGregor spoke up. He was trying to stay calm, but you could tell that he was not holding up too well. "Captain, number four engine has quit."

"Shut down opposite engine."

"Shut down," McGregor echoed as the noise level dropped on the other side of the *KC Kitty*. "We're out of fuel, sir."

"Manion, even if they aren't listening, keep sending. Tell them we are out of fuel and will have to make a forced landing. In the meantime, I will try to signal them by hand. McGregor, pick out a level enough stretch to put her down."

I could feel the *Kitty* change direction and lose altitude. I looked down. There was too much below. We could try to set the *Kitty* down on one of those impossibly wide streets, but there were obstructions everywhere. Huge streamlined light poles lined the roadways. I looked up, saw an open expanse. "There," McGregor said. "Twelve o'clock, dead ahead."

"No," the Captain murmured. "That's Boeing Field." As he said the words, I recognized the site. The Boeing crater was one of the earliest atomic bomb sites on the West Coast. I'd seen it plenty of times before, outbound and coming back.

It was different, somehow. In the seconds of our approach, I saw buildings in a style I'd never seen before.

If Captain Subota had any qualms about landing at an airfield which had been destroyed years before, he didn't show them. He put the nose of the *Kitty* down and swung her around on a final approach. Our escorts followed us.

The landing was a blur. The landing gear came down just as the fuel finally ran out. We were about a hundred feet off the runway, and my stomach clenched like a fist. The only sound was the wind whipping around the *Kitty*. Captain Subota flew like he was part of the plane. We drifted down so gently we didn't even bounce.

I saw impossibly large planes parked to our right as we rushed by. "Give me a hand with the brakes," Captain

Subota muttered to McGregor. The nose of the *Kitty* bounced up and down as the brakes were applied.

The *Kitty* slowed and finally came to a stop. For a moment, everything was silent, and we sat there without moving. I found that I was panting, tried to breathe more slowly.

"What is going on?"

"Eh, Captain?" McGregor said. I blinked and pulled my oxygen mask off. My sweat added an accent to the smell of the bombardier's station.

"What the *hell* is going on?" The Captain almost never used profanity. "We're sitting on the ground on a runway which was destroyed years ago. We were escorted in by jets we don't have and the whole city of Seattle is lit up like— like a carnival!"

Vehicles drove up as he was talking. A fire truck I could recognize, and the ambulance, too. There were also cars with revolving lights on the roof. They were like so much of the surroundings, familiar in purpose, strange in design. Men in various uniforms climbed out of the vehicles.

I unbuckled myself and started to open the hatch. "What are you doing, Manion?" Subota snapped.

"I was going to—" I started to answer him, but he interrupted.

"You were going to go out? Not until I've thought for a moment. We don't know who those people are." His voice sounded strained. The men outside were gathered into a cluster, conferring about something. One on the outskirts of the huddle stared up at the cockpit. He made waving motions, as if we should come out. I mentioned him to the Captain.

"They don't seem unfriendly, Captain."

"All civilians. Just police, no troops. Why?" He seemed to be talking to himself. "All right. We'll go out and meet with these people. Let me do the talking, Manion."

By the time we were down on the concrete, two men stood next to the *Kitty*. They watched as we stepped down to the concrete. McGregor and I stood on either side of Captain Subota and faced them.

One of the men was obviously a fireman. The other wore a uniform with badges marked "Security." He glanced at the other man for a moment, then spoke to us in Russian. Out of the corner of my eye I saw Captain Subota stiffen.

"Mih nee paneemayoo pa-rooskee," I said, and repeated it in English. "We don't speak Russian. You'll have to get a translator," I added. I was confused. Why were they speaking Russian, when they had English-language patches?

Both the fire fighter and the security man started at my answer. "You're American?" the fireman said, and the other looked toward the tail end of the *Kitty,* toward the USAF markings there.

"Yes," I started to reply, when Captain Subota motioned me to silence.

"Please identify yourselves, gentlemen." He spoke casually, but there was hardness in his voice.

"Sir?" The security man spoke. "Excuse me, but we would like to ask the same of you." A badge above his breast pocket caught the light. "Barrett," it read. He continued.

"Is this Air Force business? The interceptors radioed the tower that a silent bogie was coming in." A frown appeared on Barrett's face. "We called McChord Air Force Base. They know you're here." He cocked his head. "If you gentlemen would like to accompany me, we can wait somewhere more comfortable."

Subota shook his head. "We'd rather not. Could I see some identification?" he repeated. Barrett frowned again, then pulled a little leather folder out of his pocket. He flipped it open, stepped forward and handed it to Subota.

The Captain studied it for a moment, then handed it to me.

I stared at the badge and identification card. They identified him as Charles Barrett, an employee of Boeing, holding certain clearances. It was written in English, and had a color photograph of Barrett in one corner. I suppose it was as authentic as anything else around here. I didn't know any more. I handed it back.

Captain Subota looked at Barrett for a long moment, then nodded slowly, as if to himself. "I'm Captain Subota, this is Technical Sergeant Manion and Lieutenant McGregor. Sergeant Berentson is in the tail turret, and is injured."

The fireman spoke into a walkie-talkie and the ambulance rolled up to the *Kitty*, coming to a stop by the tail. Attendants sprang into action, pulling out a gurney and running up to the turret.

"Manion," the Captain said, "they may need help getting in." He looked at me and I started towards the tail. The ambulance crew figured out the emergency exit before I got there, though. One of them stood on the gurney while the others braced it. He was easing Berentson out.

Blood covered the upper half of Berentson's coverall, but I saw her hand move as the ambulance crew put her on the gurney.

"Your injured crewmember is a woman?" Barrett seemed surprised. "I thought—"

"What?" Subota asked.

"Is this an Air Force mission? Or are you from some movie set? I've never seen a plane like that," Barrett said, pointing over our heads at the *Kitty*. His expression was troubled, but he recovered quickly. "If this is classified, tell me, and I'll make suitable arrangements, sir."

"Classified?" Subota echoed. "We were on a normal bombing mission. Wartime security—" Barrett interrupted him.

"Sir? A bombing mission, you say?" He looked

thoughtful for a moment, then his expression hardened. "The Air Force will want to speak with you." He paused. "Boeing prosecutes use of its facilities under false pretenses. I don't know what is going on, but if you would like to make a statement, we can go to the security office."

"What is going on here?" Out of the corner of my eye, I could see Captain Subota looking at me. "Mister Barrett, when we left on our mission, this place," I waved a hand to encompass Boeing Field, "was a bomb crater. Seattle was blacked out, and—" The siren on the ambulance cut me off. It raced into the darkness, lights flashing.

As the noise of its passage died, I turned back to Barrett. Captain Subota spoke before I could. "Sergeant, let me do the talking."

"No, Captain." I swallowed. "With all due respect, sir, I think we need some plain talk. We have got to have *facts*." I waved my hand at Barrett. "We haven't told him anything. He hasn't told us anything."

I spoke to Barrett before Subota could respond. "When we left, we were at war with the Soviet Union. Are we still?"

"Still?" he said. "We've nev—" Subota interrupted him.

"Manion, *shut up*," he snapped. I wondered why he didn't formally make it an order.

I turned to face him. I clenched my fists, trying to regain control. Captain Subota stiffened and McGregor backed up a step. "*Sir!*" I almost shouted, then continued in a lower tone. "The *Kitty* isn't going to get off the ground without help. Berentson is on her way to the hospital; we don't know how bad off she is," I took a ragged breath. "We need help."

I'd never disobeyed the Captain before. Maybe I was going to lose my stripes. It didn't seem that important any more. We stood facing each other for what seemed like an eternity I heard a fading echo of a siren, wondered briefly if it was the ambulance Pat was in.

"Mutiny," Captain Subota mouthed, not loud enough to be a whisper. I don't think anyone else heard.

"No, sir," I mouthed back, but couldn't think of anything else to say to him. I was trying to figure out what had happened to us.

I spun to face Barrett again. "What year is this?" He had been studying our little tableau, and the question seemed to take him by surprise.

"1989," he stammered.

I looked at him, then shook my head. "Not far enough," I muttered. Everyone was staring at me now. "Not far enough in the future," I addressed myself to Barrett and the fireman. "There should still be some signs of the Boeing crater."

A sideways glance showed shocked expressions on Subota's and McGregor's faces. I couldn't blame them. It was quite a shock, suddenly being in the future. A suspicion was growing in my mind. We might be in for a worse shock.

"Mister Barrett, we left Fairchild Air Force Base on a bombing mission against the Soviet supply dumps around Nome, Alaska, on March 28, 1971." I heard a sudden intake of breath from Captain Subota. "I asked before if we were still at war with the Soviet Union. Are we?" I thought I knew the answer.

Barrett studied me with a peculiar expression on his face. His moustache twitched. "We have never been directly at war with the Soviet Union," he said slowly. "Even the cold war is slowing down, with *glastnost* and *perestroika*." I didn't recognize the terms, which didn't surprise me much.

The fireman was staring off into the distance with a dreamy look. "A parallel world," he half whispered to himself. Everyone turned to stare at him. He became aware of

being the center of attention, gave a little grin of embarrassment, then shrugged and spoke again.

"I, ah, read a lot of science fiction," he mumbled.
Nobody laughed, and he continued with more confidence.
"You," he said, nodding toward Subota, McGregor and I,
"are from another Earth, like ours, but one where the
United States went to war with the Russians."

"You aren't at war with the Soviets," Subota murmured. "Never have been."

The fireman shivered. A towing tractor drove through
the circle of vehicles and headed for the nose of the *KC
Kitty.* Captain Subota snapped a glance at it, then turned to
Barrett.

"What's that doing here?"

The security man looked puzzled at the question. "To
take your plane to a hangar."

Captain Subota looked off into the distance, then at Barrett. "How soon can you get us repaired and refueled?" I
looked at the Captain when he spoke, getting the first idea
of what he intended to do.

"There will have to be an investigation first. The Air
Force will want to talk to you and examine your plane, and
then there's the FAA, and. . . ." Barrett shrugged.

Before he could add anything, Captain Subota turned
and walked quickly back to the hatchway leading up into the
KC Kitty. He paused, gripping the handles.

"I'll get the logbook. That should help speed things
up," he announced, hoisting himself up into the fuselage.
He climbed out of view, and I wondered what he was up to.
His face appeared briefly behind the cockpit windshield,
then ducked from view.

Barrett shook his head. "Your captain will be in for a
disappointment, I think. The investigation is going to take
days, maybe even weeks."

I walked over under the belly of the *KC Kitty,* looked

up through the hatchway. Captain Subota was busy attaching wires to a little box. "Captain," I spoke softly. "Barrett says we won't be free to go for days, maybe more." As I said the words, I felt a sense of relief.

"We don't have days. We have to go *now,* and hope that it's still there." He spoke through gritted teeth.

"It?"

"The cloud." He looked down at me, and in the near darkness I felt rather than saw his eyes fix me with an intense stare. "Don't you see? The bomb had something to do with our being here. That glowing cloud it left, it's got to be a way back, our way back."

I didn't feel as certain. "But—"

"Get Barrett over here," he said, finished with whatever he was doing and starting down to the hatchway, carrying the box with its attached wires.

I backed away from the hatch and saw Barrett and the fireman still facing McGregor. They seemed to be trying to talk to him, but he was just shaking his head.

"Mister Barrett," I called over to him. "The Captain would like to see you." He walked over just as Captain Subota got to the hatch and dropped through to the pavement.

"Yes, Captain Subota?" Barrett squinted at the box and wires Captain Subota held.

"This is a deadman's switch. We carry a single 25-kiloton atom bomb. That would be enough to smash half of downtown Seattle from here." The Captain spoke slowly, measuring his words. "Keep your hands away from your gun," he added, as Barrett moved forward, one hand moving almost unconsciously to the holster on his hip.

I tried to conceal my surprise. Thinking about how the Captain had chosen his words, I decided he hadn't quite lied. We *do* carry a single atom bomb or a high-explosive blockbuster. We'd dropped our bomb during the mission, but Barrett didn't know that.

Captain Subota ordered McGregor to bring him Barrett's gun and get aboard the *Kitty* to keep a lookout. Barrett watched the Captain while McGregor took him the pistol. As McGregor climbed up through the hatchway, Barrett spoke.

"What do you want?" Beads of sweat glistened on his forehead in the light of the headlights, but his voice remained steady.

I looked away from our little tableau. The crowd was out of sight, peering around the parked vehicles. The other security men were behind their cars, guns drawn. A walkie-talkie on Barrett's belt crackled a burst of static.

"I want JP-4, aviation fuel. Our tanks topped off." The Captain thought for a moment. "How fast could you get a crew out here to install a radio?"

"Install a radio?" Barrett stared at the Captain. "Why—"

"Because ours is out," Captain Subota snapped. "How fast?" He waved the phony deadman's switch. "Use your walkie-talkie to get the fuel out here. *Now.*"

Barrett took the walkie-talkie off his belt. He called his dispatcher and explained the situation. The walkie-talkie crackled as the dispatcher asked questions and Barrett answered. He listened to a final question. "He has no further demands, Dispatch." He looked at the Captain. "Do you?" he asked coldly.

Captain Subota shook his head. "Just the fuel. And the radio." His lip quirked a little. "I'm sorry to have to do this, but I want to leave here as fast as I can."

The fireman looked up at the *KC Kitty* with fear and awe. "A fuckin' nuke, on a deadman's switch." He shivered again. "Jesus," he whispered.

I stepped closer to Captain Subota, away from the fireman and Barrett. "Sir," I said in a low voice, pitched not to carry to the two of them. "This isn't right."

"We haven't got time to do the right thing, Manion," he replied as quietly.

"There's no guarantee that the cloud will still—" he cut me off.

"There's no guarantee in anything, Sergeant, but it's a chance we have to take. It's our only way of getting back." He spoke as if it were more than a chance, that it had to be, because he desired it.

A sudden burst of speech on Barrett's walkie-talkie interrupted us. Both Barrett and the fireman leaned in towards it, straining to make sense of the words. Suddenly, the fireman straightened up. He looked up at the *KC Kitty*, and backed away a couple of steps.

Then he looked at us. "Your," he waved a hand at the tail of aircraft, "ah, tail gunner. At the hospital, they found out she was—she'd been exposed to radiation." He looked horrified at the thought. "Th—that's why you're getting the fuel."

Barrett had continued to listen to the hand-held radio while the fireman spoke. Finally, it stopped, and he addressed us. "Captain, your fuel should be arriving momentarily. Another car will bring a radio set." He paused. "The tower is at 125.2 Megahertz," he added.

"Megahertz?" I repeated.

"Uh, megacycles," the fireman said.

Barrett looked puzzled, but didn't comment. Captain Subota peered into the darkness, looking for the fuel truck. A muffled shout made us glance up at the cockpit of the *Kitty*. McGregor pointed into the distance. A pair of headlights were coming down the runway.

"You should tell everyone to move back," Captain Subota said to Barrett. The security man looked startled, then nodded and waved a hand to motion the onlookers back while he spoke into the walkie-talkie. The fire truck rolled slowly away, then stopped. The security cars remained where they were.

The tank truck rolled to a stop behind the *Kitty*. Two men got out with slow caution and stood beside it. "Manion, show them where the filling ports are, and tell them to hurry."

I walked under the *KC Kitty*'s wing. The two men tensed when they saw me coming. I raised my hands to show I was unarmed, then pointed out the fueling ports. "Here, and the same place on the other wing. The Captain wants you to hurry." They didn't answer, just went to work with a nervous intensity.

When I got back to the front of the *Kitty*, the fireman cleared his throat, then spoke to me. "When did, ah, the war start, on your world?" He thought for a second. "I mean, on your Earth?"

The question surprised me. I glanced at the Captain, but he was peering off into the darkness, as if to see any obstacles to our departure. "I don't know. 1955 or '56, I think. They sank some of our ships, or we helped the Hungarians, I don't remember how it started. It was a long time ago." I shrugged.

He looked like he wanted to ask more questions, but a pickup truck arrived, bringing the radio. It was the size of a small suitcase, and was self-contained. At the Captain's directions, the men in the truck set it out on the runway and left. I got it and put it in the *KC Kitty*. It made the already crowded nose compartment claustrophobic.

"—ower calling unidentified grounded aircraft. Tower calling unidentified grounded aircraft. Come in, unidentified grounded aircraft." The set didn't take any time to warm up. The speaker responded instantly when I flipped the switch.

"This is Charlie Romeo Seven Three Four, on the south end of main runway," I said into the microphone.

"Is this the person in charge?" the voice asked.

"Negative." I peered out the plexiglass nose. "Captain Subota is, ah, unavailable at the moment." The Captain was keeping an eye on both Barrett and the refueling crew. When he glanced up, I made motions toward my ear and mouth, to show that we had a working radio, and pointed toward him, to indicate the tower wanted to speak to him. He shook his head.

McGregor called down from the cockpit. "Tell the Captain we're topped off. All tanks show full, including the auxiliary." I rogered him and activated the microphone again. "Tower, Captain Subota should be able to talk to you shortly." I hooked the radio into the intercom, so the Captain could speak directly to the tower.

I dropped through the hatch to the pavement. The impact made me stagger, and I realized how tired I was. "Captain, McGregor says all the tanks are full, and I've got the radio hooked up."

He nodded once, then fumbled one-handed with Barrett's revolver and swung the cylinder out, dropping the cartridges onto the pavement. That done, he shook the pistol to snap the cylinder back into place, and extended it to Barrett.

The security man looked at the empty pistol, then at Captain Subota's face. The Captain gave a little shrug. "I'm sorry it had to happen this way."

Barrett reached out to take his gun back, but didn't say anything. Captain Subota continued to look at him for a moment longer, as if trying to think of another way to apologize, then shrugged again. "Clear the runway, we're taking off," he said, finally, waving his free hand in a shooing motion. Barrett and the fireman left, not running but not waiting around, either.

As the Captain got ready to climb up into the hatchway, I caught his attention. "What about Pat—Sergeant Berentson?" I asked, afraid of the answer.

He stopped and looked me in the eyes. "We're going to have to leave her,' he said slowly. "She is a casualty of the mission. She'll be all right here, I'm sure of it," he added. I continued to stare at him. He dropped his gaze and hoisted himself into the fuselage. When he was inside, he reached down to give me a hand up.

I looked at the hand and then at his face. "I don't want to go, Captain."

He pulled his hand back a bit, cocked his head and stared at me. After a moment he realized he had the phony deadman's switch in his other hand and set it down.

When he spoke again, his voice was low and earnest. "You are the navigator. We can't get back without you." He paused, as if searching for words. "We've been on a lot of missions together, James. I need you." He held out his hand again.

After a moment, I took it. I still didn't want to go, but I did owe the Captain for all the times he'd brought us back safely.

The tower was on the air as soon as we started our engines. "Charlie Romeo Seven Three Four, this is Boeing Tower. You are advised you will have Air Force escort when you take off. Your flight path is not to pass over populated areas. We repeat, the Air Force interceptors have orders to shoot you down if you attempt to overfly Seattle. Do you copy?"

"We copy, Tower," Captain Subota sounded almost happy again. "Are we cleared to take off? We will be flying out over Puget Sound and the Olympic Peninsula, headed north." He paused. "We'll avoid Seattle. Advise the Air Force accordingly."

Another voice came on the air. "Charlie Romeo Seven Three Four, we copy your transmission to the tower. This is Easy Leader. Come twenty degrees to the west as soon as you lift off.'' I looked up through the nose canopy to try and see the escort, but the cloud cover was still low.

The tower gave us clearance to take off. The Captain followed Easy Leader's instructions and turned left as soon as we were airborne. As we rose slowly into the air, the fighters came down to meet us, two of them so close we were almost touching them, others farther away.

They didn't do anything, just matched our speed and course. Once we were away from Seattle, the two on our wingtips even moved out and gave us some room. I guess they didn't know what else to do. After a while, a huge aerial tanker matched our course and the fighters took turns getting fuel from it.

The Captain changed course as I navigated, trying to bring us back to the place where we nearly died. The roar of the engines was almost soothing, and I started to drowse and think about what lay at the end of our trip. The cloud probably wouldn't still be there. Even if it was, it may not have had anything to do with our finding ourselves in this world.

I wondered what this world was like. It didn't seem so bad. It wasn't at war. That was something. I was just a kid when the war started. I've seen movies and read books, but I can't imagine what peacetime is like. Something like being on furlough, but permanent, I guess.

I hoped Pat would be all right back in Seattle. It wasn't as if she were dead, I'd just never see her again. I'd miss her, though. We'd had some good times, on leave and just horsing around on base.

The radio woke me up. ''Charlie Romeo Seven Three Four, this is Easy Leader. You are about to enter Alaskan airspace. Please advise your intentions.''

The Captain spoke smoothly. ''Easy Leader, we are about to enter a search pattern. We are searching for a glowing cloud.'' I was glad that the Captain was telling the truth to them. He continued. "If you have radar and notice any strange blips nearby, we would appreciate being vectored to them." I had to hand it to the Captain. Trying to recruit our escort showed his determination.

"We copy, Charlie Romeo Seven Three Four." Easy Leader sounded almost surprised.

By my reckoning, we were at the location where the missile almost got us. I switched the radio off the intercom and told the Captain. He banked the *KC Kitty,* and we began a slow search spiral out from the spot. The Captain told me to advise the fighters what we were doing, and I did. All I got back was a laconic "We copy."

While the Captain and McGregor flew the *KC Kitty* and looked for the cloud, I looked too, but I also listened. Easy Leader had switched frequencies and was talking with Elmendorf Air Force Base. A flight was being readied to relieve him and his men.

Dawn lightened the sky. It was still too early to be daylight, but the stars were fading and you could almost sense the clarity of the air. Solid cloud cover stretched out underneath us, a soft-looking floor to the universe that was the *KC Kitty* and her escort. Small bumps in the cloud floor showed the mountain tops of the Kenai Peninsula below us.

The *KC Kitty* banked suddenly. I switched to the intercom just in time to hear the Captain and McGregor whooping in joy. I looked out the nose canopy and saw a bright patch in the distance. It was the wrong direction for the rising sun. The cloud was smaller than when we left it, but it was still far larger than the *Kitty.*

As the *KC Kitty* rushed towards the cloud, I found myself staring at the brightness of it until I blinked back tears. I had lived through seven years of war. My best friend lay in a hospital bed far south of here. I was going back to a world of endless war and death.

Captain Subota and McGregor were still shouting up in the cockpit. The cloud grew until we were only seconds away from it. The edges of it were in constant movement.

I checked the straps on my harness, making sure they were tight. Parachute, survival kit, a chart of the Kenai Peninsula. All there. "Good-bye, Captain," I said, and bailed out.

The *Kansas City Kitty* plunged into the cloud and vanished, leaving only an afterimage. As I drifted down to a new world and an old friend, I wished Subota and McGregor the best of luck.

Red Eyes
by
Stephen Milligan

About the Author

Stephen Milligan is 25, and is a computer-aided designer. He is also a performing pianist. He is a red belt
in Tae Kwan Do, and "a pretty fair sabre fencer." Other than
that, he's a fairly ordinary single male who once sat down
and wrote a short-short story a day, when he was sixteen. He
has that restless urge to write. "Red Eyes" is his first sale;
we strongly believe there will be many others.

About the Illustrator

Timothy Winkler was born in 1964 in Nashville, Tennessee, where he graduated from Hillwood High School in 1982.
At Hillwood, his commercial art teacher, Shirley Fincannon,
was influential in his decision to pursue a career in art.

Beginning in 1981, he began winning competitions and
appearing in gallery showings. In 1986, he began a career
doing illustrations for dissertations, theses and articles for various researchers in the Univerity of Tennessee's Life Sciences
Program. He has resided in Knoxville since 1985.

When a rusted-out red VW
bug pulled into the parking lot of Mt. Moriah
Baptist Church, I thought its occupant must
be on the way to worship until the passenger door swung
open in invitation. I didn't have a thumb out, or a sign cut
out of a box with an arrow and a city magic-markered on
it, but some people will stop to give a man a ride just
because he looks tired and a long way from anywhere.

The driver was a blonde girl, maybe seventeen, butter-
scotch blonde, dressed in baggy jeans and a loose black T-
shirt whose fit, though it was impossible to tell for sure, was
consistent with the possibility of a nice figure. Darkly
arched eyebrows peeked over her aviator sunglasses as she
looked me over, and I hazarded a glance at my reflection in
the rear side window. The curvature elongated my face, and
this combined with my week's worth of beard to make me
look like a scruffy Dali saint, eyes the color of weathered
teak. She gave a little nod, entering a verdict of harmless.

"Going south?"

"Yes," I said. It felt like south, and a little west.

"Hop in. My name's Sarah." She wrestled an electric
blue Gibson guitar case thick with hand-painted Grateful
Dead emblems into the back seat to make room for me.

"David," I said, and I knocked the worst of the dust
off my jeans and backpack before I got in. "You're a musi-
cian."

"Yep. I'm a folkie, old Bothy Band and Renbourn and
Fahey tunes, and my own stuff whenever I can slip it past."

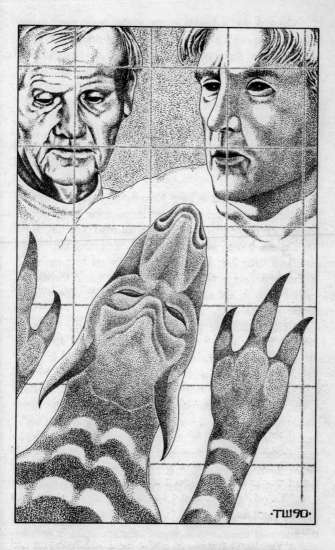

Illustrated by Timothy Winkler

The VW was a deathtrap, and as she drove Sarah cheerfully pointed out particulars in its state of decay. The stickshift had been replaced with a Budweiser beer tap; a piece of coat hanger which stretched between the accelerator cable and a bolt in the well-ventilated floor served as a gas pedal; the brake had to be levered off the floor with the toe after each use.

"Body's so rusted out the only thing holdin' the front and back ends together's the roof," she said. On hard bumps, the car bent like an accordion. "What's the destination?"

I have mastered a long Kerouac-style rap for people who want me to justify my lifestyle, all about seein' Amurica and the existentiality of the eternal road, cruising down life's highway with my consciousness streaming out behind me, but I liked her; she didn't seem put off by whatever it is that puts people off about me, and I had a feeling she wouldn't buy it. She confirmed this by waving off my explanation.

"Don't mean to pry. When I was fifteen, I thought hitching to LA with three dollars, a guitar, and no change of clothing was 'romantic.' It got old pretty quick, but I wrote some good songs."

She wasn't really that much of a talker, but neither am I, and she wound up carrying the conversation. It was funny watching the miles roll back so quickly after all that walking, the farms slipping by too quickly to really see them. In ten minutes we'd gone further than I'd walked all afternoon. When the road turned a little to the west, she pulled down the sun visor, and taped to the inside was a yellowed picture, a Polaroid of a huge family assembled on a wide front porch, young men bearded and older men potbellied in testimony of the plump women's culinary skills, a willowy girl that might have been a younger Sarah balancing on the railing, an American flag hanging limp from a slanted pole over their heads.

"Know where you're going to stay tonight?" she asked.

"I hadn't really thought about it. I like walking at night; I thought I'd go a little further after you drop me off." I could tell she thought this was strange, but that maybe I was just trying to let her know that I didn't expect her to offer to put me up for the night. "I know I don't look it, but I've got plenty of money," I said, knowing that if she'd really spent any time hitching she'd understand the wisdom behind this. "I'll find a motel when I get tired."

"Well, we don't have many muggers down here, but we do have rednecks." She eyed my I ♥ NY sweat shirt. "You may not believe it in this day and age, but you might want to button up your jacket over that shirt. Y'all ain't in the most enlightened part of the States."

She wanted to go to Eastman Conservatory next year, but was worried about getting in, she told me. She'd spent the summer up north, and said that at heart she felt like a foreigner, now. My sweat shirt and lack of a drawl convinced her I was a fellow alien; she named a few of the places she'd seen; Saratoga Springs, Bennington, the Fulton Chain of Lakes, and we talked about the ones I admitted to knowing.

"Blue water and open fields, that's what I liked about New York," she said. "The clay colors all the lakes and streams red down here. And everythin' is cut out of the forest. Every town, every farm, every road. It can be claustrophobic. All the roads are like this." She waved at the moving walls of green, deepening as the sun went down. I tried to see it the way she described, tunnels hewn through living emerald: the subterranean kingdom of Carolina, with rivers of blood and drawling redneck gnomes, waiting to pounce on innocent, helpless New Yorkers, but my imagination wasn't up to it.

We passed a sign that said New Hope Fire District. I've seen a lot of places with names like that. New Hope, North Carolina. Charity, Wisconsin. Freedom, Florida. Providence, Rhode Island. Never had the places themselves seemed particularly appropriate to the names, but I thought it would be satisfying if there was a Self, in Wyoming, maybe, where all those people who set out to find themselves wind up.

Like the sun breaking free of clouds, the prickling of excitement which had been building in me all day bloomed into full-blown déjà vu. And the attendant fear I had forgotten in Sarah's cheerful company expanded in my chest.

New Hope was one of those towns that had no obvious reason for being there. It was a little way off the old Highway 86. There were two cubes of concrete in the lot of Kemple's Mobil station which probably once supported one of those five-story-high signs that are supposed to lure travelers off the highway; after nine or on a Sunday, the weary motorist would have found Kemple's closed and might have wound up in the Shadowood Motel (WELCOME, Air Conditioning, Heated Pool, Color TV, Visa & Mastercard, VACANCY) for the night. The new NC86 ran a few miles east and wasn't as heavily trafficked now that 15-501 was completed. Somehow the town had managed to hang on until the boom in nearby Research Triangle Park sent the land prices anywhere within reasonable driving distance back up to a respectable level. It was still the kind of place adults came to get away from it all and the kids left for pretty much the same reasons. I had been in New Hope about eight months before for less than ten minutes, guest of a truck driver who was taking back roads to avoid weigh stations.

As we passed by the houses and shops, the thing in my head that's not really much like a compass swung slowly until due west felt right; my head felt better if I thought in that direction. Sarah pulled into the Mobil station, overshot the pumps, and had to back up. "Brakes," she muttered. "Couldn't stop a runaway tricycle." She pointed down the road. "I live just outside of town."

"South?" I asked.

"Well, closer to west, actually."

I weighed the possibility of getting her to take me out that way against the probability of her getting suspicious, and my own growing hunger. I wanted to face what was ahead on a full stomach.

"I've changed my mind. I think I'll spend the night in town, get up early tomorrow."

"That's probably your best bet," she said.

"Thanks again for the ride."

"Don't mention it."

She paid for the gas, climbed into the car, and drove off into the twilight like the end of a bad movie, waving once out the open window without looking, and that was Sarah, with her music and her big family and her past hitchhiking days and her fondness for blue water and open spaces. Another human being I could expect never to see again, one of the thousands I had encountered in the last two years, never quite penetrating the surface tension which is common to all brief, chance acquaintances, which protects us from the necessity of recognizing each other as complete persons.

Once, a month before, I had described what I was looking for to a boy in the Blue Ridge Mountains in West Virginia, and on seeing my money his face had been overcome by the artless deadpan of the hick putting one over on the city slicker. He said he knew exactly what I wanted and where it was, and that I could see it that very night.

Where he had gotten hold of a lemur I did not want to imagine; a zoo somewhere was missing one, evidently. He had shaved it from nose to tail, leaving a carefully clipped bit like an arrowhead at the tip (his own artistic addition, certainly no part of my description). He had dyed its skin black, painted markings on it with phosphorescent paint, and done something to make the round ears look pointed. The forward-looking saucer eyes were already red, as I had described, though he had no way of knowing or adjusting the fact that they were a shade too dark. The pupils were round and tiny in the flashlight's beam. Despite its size, about that of a three-year-old child (when I pointed this out the boy swore that it was the offspring of the very creature I sought, and would grow to the size of a large man), it was a frightening creature to behold, with its human expression on that inhuman face, and its scrawny, weirdly jointed body. Later that night, actually in the morning just before dawn, I snuck back to the house and found the blanket-draped cage where the boy kept the animal. I used the blanket to catch and carry it, and fifty miles down the road I set it loose in the woods.

It bit me on the forearm and slashed my face with its claws before it ran away. Before that I was feeling guilty about not taking it into D.C., well off my planned route, to turn it over to someone at the zoo. The cuts took a long time to heal, and still left were a row of faint white lines I could see on those rare mornings when I had a chance to shave; reminders of how foolish I can be.

There was a barbecue across the street from the Mobil station, a shoebox-shaped wooden building painted red and adorned with a neon sign which said "P ul's B rbeque Restaur nt"; perhaps someone would soon return to dispense with the remaining "a." Another sign stood in the gravel parking lot, an arrow covered with yellow light bulbs which were supposed to light in sequence from tail to tip, but due to a majority of dead bulbs instead twinkled in a spastic pattern. A noisy exhaust fan bulged like a parasite from the side wall. It didn't look like a good place for a last meal; but that thought was morbid and unwarranted, especially since alternatives were nonexistent.

None of the dozen or so people inside the dim building looked like they were Paul. Behind the half-wall which separated the kitchen from the dining area, an obese black woman bustled over a smoky, hissing grill. A plump, attractive girl in jeans and a bowling shirt with "Paul's" scripted across it slipped off her stool, picked up a pad from beside the register and led me to a corner booth by one of the only two windows. I squinted at a grease-stained paper menu and ordered a shredded pork sandwich with hushpuppies and a Coke.

"Ain't got no Coke," the girl said. "The damn machine busted this mornin'. Y'all want a beer?"

"What do you have?"

She looked at the ceiling and recited as if she read it from the water-stained pressboard. "Got Bud on tap. Bottles we got Bud, Miller, Miller Lite, Schlitz, uh, Coors. . . ."

"Draft Bud is fine."

"A Bud man, huh?" She smiled and wrote it down. "Y'all stayin' with someone in town? I just wondered 'cause I didn't see y'all drive up."

"No, I was just passing through, but I think I'll stay the night, now. I heard of something I might be interested in from the guy who gave me a ride in."

"Oh yeah?" She looked skeptical. "Not much interestin' goin' on around here that I know of."

"Well, I heard there have been some strange things seen in the woods around here. Some kind of a big animal with weird eyes." I fixed her with a sharp look. "A bear maybe, or a big wolf."

She shook her head. "Not that I heard about. And I

heard about most everythin' 'round here.'' She winked, an effort which involved her whole face.

"I'm with the government," I said. "Department of the Interior. I'm an ecologist. You're sure you didn't hear anything about it? It might have been a while ago."

"Nope," she said. "Hey, I'd better put your order in. Y'all don't want to sit there all night."

Maybe I should, though, I thought, despite her denials. Like waking up and knowing it is raining before you hear the drops on the roof or knowing over which horizon the sea lies, I could feel the presence, somewhere far beyond the back wall of the restaurant, out in the darkening Carolina countryside. "It must have been the next town over he was talking about," I said, and she went back to the half-wall and handed the slip of paper to the cook, then resumed her perch on the wooden stool by the cash register.

Out through the window, night fell, stars came out. No moon tonight, I remembered. Lights came on in all the houses up the street. More people came into Paul's, by two's and four's. My beer came, followed by my food, and I drank and ate slowly.

Two years; I should have given up long ago. Eight weeks before, when the driving force vanished, I should have quit. If only I could have found some way to want what these people wanted, four-wheel drive and satellite dishes and two dogs, relatives visiting for Christmas and Easter. Or I could have bought into one of the other dreams I had seen, a new BMW every four years and 2.6 perfect kids, a wallet full of credit cards, maybe. A mobile home would be nice, with plastic pink flamingos to sit on whatever piece of real estate was presently my front yard. But I never could forget home, never could understand the way things worked here, the way people worked. Those soft yellow squares of light across the street might as well have been as distant as the hard points above.

I finished, left a good tip, and paid at the cash register. I asked the waitress which road went west, and she said, "Main Street here, old 86, that crosses New Hope Road at the traffic light, and New Hope Road runs just about west all the way to Greensboro." Outside it was cold, and I turned up the collar of my jacket and thought about getting something out of the backpack to put on under the sweat shirt. The door to Paul's swung open again almost before it closed after me, spilling sounds of frying grease and clinking silverware, a rectangle of light, and a beer-bellied, balding man into the night. He squinted at the change of lighting, saw me, and walked over.

"You a friend of Sarah's?" he asked. "I saw you get out of her car...."

"Just met her this afternoon," I said politely, wondering if he could be a boyfriend; it seemed unlikely. "Are you a relative?"

"Neighbor," he said. For a second I thought that was all he had to talk to me about. "I heard you tellin' Lynn about how y'all was with the government," he said finally, giving his belt a futile heave.

"Did you hear what I asked her about?" I said. He nodded, not even feigning embarassment over his eavesdropping.

"Y'all don't look like a man from the government, mister," he said, studying me. I shrugged, to say maybe I'm not, and how many government ecologists have you seen anyway, and what's it to you? He continued his scrutiny, and I wasn't in the mood for harassment, so I started to walk. He kept pace with me, though, and when he spoke again his voice was a notch more serious.

"This thing y'all are lookin' for with the weird eyes. Do y'all know what it is?"

I stopped. "You've seen it."

He looked away, then back, and nodded.

"You know where it is?"

"Maybe. . . ."

"Take me there. Where is it?"

"Y'all ain't from no government."

I unzipped the small pouch on my backpack and brought out one roll of money, and then took the other one from the inside pocket of my jacket, the big one I had gotten from a salesman up in Montana I didn't like to think about any more. "This is important to me," I said.

He looked hard at the rolled-up tens for a few seconds, but then he said, "Y'all can keep the money. It's in my shed. And it's all yours."

His name was O'Dell, and he had a 1954 Ford flatbed with a bumper sticker that read "My Wife, Yes, My Dog, Maybe, My Gun, Never!" The pressure in my head was getting stronger, and adrenaline was making me jumpy, so I had a hard time concentrating on the story he was telling me.

". . . last year, thought it was a bear. But as soon as I shot it I knew it was somethin' else. God, that howl, like somethin' dead with a cold hurricane blowin' through its skull. I'm almost used to it by now, but that first howl I'll take to my grave.

"When I was just outta high school a bunch of my friends and me all drove out to Oregon at the beginnin' of the summer, then we took the ferry up to Alaska, and worked on a fishin' boat all summer. Made damn good money. Come August, everybody else went home, but I went out to the highlands for two weeks with this old Indian I met. Heard the wolves howlin' to each other. Indian said they was talkin' 'bout the Caribou. Anyway, that's almost like how it sounded, like a whole pack of wolves. Only I thought instead of Caribou, it was talkin' 'bout me." He spoke calmly enough, but drove like a maniac, sending the truck careening around corners I could barely see in the weak headlights. The woods opened occasionally for farms. Mailboxes flashed by irregularly. He pointed out Sarah's family's place as we went by, an unpainted farmhouse, every angle out of true, which looked as if it had been assembled from a cheap kit by a giant toddler with underdeveloped motor skills. I recognized the porch from the picture.

O'Dell's was an even less inspiring dwelling, single story, white aluminum siding, black fake shutters, a plastic lamp post with a few ears of Indian corn tied to it in anticipation of Halloween and a bulb that flickered and dimmed oddly, all of this illuminated in a sweep of the headlights as we turned into the driveway. A pair of retrievers, one Golden and one Labrador, put forth a volley of barks and made abortive attacks on the tires of the truck, then retreated back into the darkness.

He didn't have to show me to the shed. I could hear the noise as soon as he shut off the engine. Not the wounded howl O'Dell had described, but the hunter's snarl, a cat's purring grown loud and mean as an approaching tornado.

I froze in the seat. The night wheeled smoothly, and I grabbed the window frame for support. This was crazy, this wasn't something I wanted to or should be doing.

"Hey, you all right?" O'Dell asked. He walked around to my side of the truck and opened the door. "It's okay; I got him fenced in."

"It," I said automatically. "He's an it." I got out of the car and followed him to the shed. It was a lean-to with nothing to lean against, a rickety slope-roofed wooden construct about eight feet by four. It didn't look nearly strong enough for what O'Dell said it contained. The door fitted badly, and around the edges I could see weird blue flashes and hear a sharp crackle above the snarling.

"Wait a minute," said O'Dell and jingled a set of keys, holding them up to the moonless sky, which had clouded over during the ride, to find the one he wanted, and opened the padlock. He lifted up on the latch to make the door clear the ground, and dragged it open.

I had been face to face with it once before. For a split second, with my heart trying to leap out through my mouth, I had looked into its face, and for months I needed only to close my eyes to bring back the afterimage and taste the panic. I could feel the sweat starting on my back, my forehead.

It threw itself at the electric wire as I entered, and for the first time I smelled the sharpness of ozone and the tang of singed hair. It fell after a moment to the wooden floorboards, bounced up and threw itself again at the crisscross of wires, which I now saw wound around white porcelain insulators bolted to the walls and ceiling of the shed. A jury-rigged electric cage. Now I understood how he had held it all this time. It kept coming at me and hitting that wall of white pain and falling back, until finally it started pacing back and forth and at last just sat and stared at me, red eyes all the articulation of hate it needed.

O'Dell stood by, watching it with a faint, detached sadness, like a man contemplating a piece of plumbing in need of expensive repair. I could barely stand. It felt as though my nerves would pull out through my skin the way the roots of running weeds break the earth when the gardener pulls them. To run, was what I wanted. And at the same time, I was fascinated by the play of strange musculature under skin the color of the night sky between stars, skin which seemed to annihilate light on contact, by the haphazard green and white stripes which pulsed and rippled with luminescence up and down the vaguely canine body in a rhythm out of sync with its heavy breathing, by the translucent quality of its eyes; the red, hunting, hating eyes, which seemed not to emit but to capture light, to torture it.

I made myself step backward very slowly, back out of sight of that hot stare and into the cool wind.

"Didn't take to y'all too well, did he?" O'Dell said without malevolence. I had yet to hear emotion in this man's voice. " 'S'not usually that bad. But he's been gettin' worse the last few weeks."

As I approached, I thought.

"So what is it?" he asked.

I mentally rifled through the stories I've made up. "It comes from Africa, Mr. O'Dell, and I never could handle its Latin name. I work for an outfit that sets up hunting expeditions in Oregon for rich businessmen. My bosses spent a fortune to have it flown in specially, but it got away. They're going to pay me a lot to bring it back."

"You been chasin' that thing all the way from Oregon?" he said, not buying a word of it.

"That's right," I said, letting the lie hang between us. He turned away.

"Gettin' damn windy out. Always does this time of year. Let's go inside where we c'n talk."

I had to strain not to glance over my shoulder as I followed him back to the house. The snarl followed us all the way, like a chainsaw hitting a knot in freshly cut pine.

"Damn windy," he repeated calmly. "We get some bad storms this season. It's a wonder we ain't had no power outages yet this year."

It almost had me once, in Montana, out on the plains. It was twilight, with a roiling sky over a perfect plane of rusty long grass, divided by an x-axis of concrete down which the salesman and I hurtled like a bullet down the barrel of a rifle. I had outdistanced my pursuer, as I was more likely to do in the early days before I learned what the range of its sensing abilities was, and could have drivers drop me off at the absolute limit. So I was backtracking. I could not yet feel it, but I knew it was somewhere ahead. The salesman and I talked, and as usual I let him carry the conversation, about his family, his job, the plains; I don't remember exactly what else, but he filled the miles with his talk. He was boring. I fell asleep.

When I woke up, I knew it was close, that that was what had wakened me. I said something drowsy and stupid to the salesman, and then it was in the headlights.

We didn't just hit it. It attacked us, a car moving at seventy-five mph. The safety glass windshield broke into a million pebbles and the salesman hit the brakes and turned the wheel hard. We slewed all over the road, and finally hit the soft shoulder and flipped. I was wearing my seat belt. The salesman wasn't. I stayed in the car. He didn't.

I slept in the long grass that night under the immense sky, knowing that it would come and kill me. Sink long black claws and black needle teeth into my flesh and rip me apart and strew me all over the plains. But the nightmares I had were of the misshapen red mass which had been the salesman.

It must have been hurt, because it didn't come for me. The next day I walked thirty miles to a town. I had a week (that's how long it took for the presence out on the plain to start to move toward me) to divvy up the blame, right down to the last percentage point, and I still never got around to it. Probably because I knew I would come up with the lion's share. Could I blame the salesman for jerking the wheel when a scene from Poe exploded out of the pavement? And could I blame the hunter for being terrified and far, far from home?

"Them eyes are what I can't stand. It's bad enough they're red. But then sometimes when I come in to feed him he looks up at me and they're a different color, gray, gold, blue, but usually jet black. And then he blinks and they're all red again." The glittering eyes of Jesus gazed reproachfully down at us from a plastic crucifix nailed to the wall

above the kitchen table, where he hung like guilt personi-
fied. I could hear someone, perhaps O'Dell's wife, moving
about upstairs, but she didn't come down. If it was his wife,
I wondered what she thought of his pet. He got up to pour
more coffee and the Golden Retriever bumped against his
legs. He kneed it gently out of the way. "Stupidest damn
dog ever lived," he muttered, giving it a playful shove, and
it grinned and laid its head in his lap. He stroked it as he
talked, and the Lab got up from in front of the stove for its
share of attention.

"Anyway, he's yours. I don't want nothin' to do with
him anymore; he's gettin' more dangerous, stronger every
day. Couple a' times I was gonna shoot 'im, but I'd get out
there and he'd kinda stare me down, and I couldn't do it.
Couldn't let him out in the woods either, not with the family
around, and all the farms. So if you want him, take him."
He crossed his arms over his belly and fell silent.

"It will take some doing," I told him. "I'll have to get
a truck, tranquilizers. . . ." A truck, tranquilizers. Right.

"I can keep it for a bit longer. Y'all just get that stuff
together. I'll give y'all a ride back into town."

"How far is it; two, three miles?"

"That sounds 'bout right."

"I'll walk it. I like walking at night. It helps me think."

He shrugged; he knew me for a liar, now, but it made
no difference to him. I wrote down his phone number and
he showed me to the front door.

"When I first found him, I thought he'd be good for
somethin'; you know, sell him to Disney World or somewhere," he said sadly. "Somethin' like that don't come
around twice in a man's life. I thought it was some kinda
gift, an opp'rtunity, thought it was gonna change things
around for me. But I never figured out what to do about it.
I made some plans, but I never did nothin'."

• • •

I didn't think he was watching from a window, but I walked a good distance down the road anyway, before doubling back. While I walked, a sultry drizzle started coming down.

There was an electric cord running from the house to a metal housing against the side of the shed. It passed by a wood pile in the back yard, where there was a hatchet sunk into a log. I pried the hatchet loose, dragged the cord over so that it lay across the log, and sat down on the wood pile to wait. There was no sound or sign from the shed. Perhaps it was asleep, if it ever slept.

After twenty minutes or so the back door opened and O'Dell let the dogs out. They came over to check me out, but since they had just seen me with O'Dell less than an hour before, they decided I was O.K. and went off on obscure errands of their own.

All the inside and outside lights went off, and I shifted to the black eyes for night vision. The yard retained its lack of color, but took on lighter shades of gray; the only remaining source of light, the pilot on a transformer box on a telephone pole across the road, was painfully bright when I looked at it. I took an extra sweat shirt out of my pack and put it on under the jacket. The crickets, deafening at first, slackened and stopped as the rain increased, but the wind creaking in the loblolly pines added to the noise so that, an hour later, I heard the sound of the car approaching only an instant before I saw the nimbus of its headlights lightening the trees.

If I couldn't run out to the road in time to flag the car down, or if the car didn't stop, it might mean my life. It was a terrible plan, and with time I could have come up with a better one . . . and lost the courage to carry it out.

I raised the hatchet high and swung it down on the

cord, releasing it the instant before impact. The cord spat sparks on separation, which blinded me for a moment. When I looked up the car was blocked from my sight by the house. There was a scuffle of movement from the shed; either the whack of the hatchet or the sound of the car must have made it stir. I fought with panic and lost. I sprinted for the road, hearing the dogs barking. When the car rounded the curve, the headlights caught me full in the face, and the world went white. I tried to throw myself out of the car's path, and was struck on my side. I floated in the air for what seemed a long time, and hit the gravel hard.

"Jesus Christ," I heard someone shout. I tried to breathe and succeeded on the third attempt, but the pain made it seem hardly worth the effort. I thought about broken ribs. I'd heard about boxers who continued fights with broken ribs. I didn't want to move, except that not moving didn't stop the pain. I felt hands on me, and opened my eyes to see who it was, but the headlights were still on, and with the black eyes I could make out only a vague shadow in that intolerable field of white. "Jesus Christ," I heard a second voice say, "lookit his eyes . . ." I closed my eyes and shifted to the gray ones. I opened them again just in time to see a green Mustang peeling out in reverse. I ran after it, but the driver swung it around neatly and left me standing in a cloud of exhaust.

The dogs were frolicking around me, uncertain as to the cause of the excitement, but determined to join in. The lights were coming on in the house, and O'Dell appeared in a rectangle of light at the front door. "What the hell . . ." he was shouting, but I was already running. Somewhere behind, wood splintered.

I fell more than a dozen times crossing the plowed field that separated Sarah's house and O'Dell's. The air seemed to have turned to liquid, rivulets ran down the furrows, and each time I stumbled, my hands sank in the red mud up to my elbows, making it look as if I had been butchering cattle. In a flash of lightning, I saw the stand of oaks in which Sarah's house huddled lashing violently, as if whipping themselves into a frenzy preparatory to ripping the house apart. I tripped headlong over something and found myself lying on a collapsed length of barbed wire fence; my clothes and skin ripped as I struggled to my feet. A trio of dogs came pelting around a corner as I reached the back yard; one turned tail and ran baying like a foxhound, the other two growled and began circling me, making quick feints, trying to get behind me. A light came on over the back door, and a middle-aged woman in a rose-printed bathrobe stepped into the doorway, a shotgun leveled at my head through the screen door.

"What the fuck you think you're doin'?" she snarled.

"I need—" I started, not recognizing the question as rhetorical, and she stamped her foot.

"Let's see your hands, boy." I complied slowly, aware of how I looked, mud-spattered, soaked, torn, bloody, and demented, with a Yankee accent to boot. I heard a chair being dragged across linoleum behind her, and a girl about five years old peeked over her shoulder. Thunder growled at the limit of hearing, and my stomach did a slow barrel roll.

"I'm sorry to bother you, ma'am," I said politely, "but I was hoping to talk to Sarah. I need a ride to town . . . there's been an accident."

"You don't get off'n my land, there's gonna be a worse one. My boys and their papa'll be back any time now, and if you ain't gone by then, you'll be a sorry puppy."

She looked away as headlights tracked across the yard, and the red VW rattled into the driveway.

"You just stay in the car, honey," she yelled.

I heard the door slam and Sarah appeared at the edge of my vision, a grocery bag in her arms. "What's goin' on?" she asked.

"Mama's gonna shoot a man," said the five-year-old. "Get down, Lizzy."

"Don't shoot him, Mama, I know him," Sarah said.

The gun didn't waver. "What you want with a sorry piece of humanity like that, Sarah?"

"He's no trouble, Mama. . . ."

The shotgun roared out and I went down in a heap. There was a canine howl, and the gun roared again just as I realized I hadn't been hit, that she had fired over my head. I got up to run, slipping on the wet grass.

The dog which had gone for it was twitching on the ground, snapping at its opened side, not knowing it was dead yet. It took out one of the others as I watched, ripping out its throat in mid-growl, not even time for a yelp of pain. Sarah's mother was reloading the gun; I took three steps and yanked it out of her hands, heaving it into the long grass.

"Sarah, go in the house," I shouted as I got in the car, and at the sound of my voice, it turned neon red eyes on me. The engine screeched when I turned the key; it was still running. The passenger door opened, and Sarah scrambled in next to me.

I couldn't find reverse; every movement of my right arm sent flames licking up my side. And by then it was almost on us. Sarah slammed the door shut in its face, pulled off the parking brake, and wrestled the stick into reverse. The passenger window fractured into a spider web under the impact, but didn't shatter, and then it was on the hood, claws scratching furrows in the metal. I popped the clutch and we stalled, and Sarah screamed, but the jerk of the car threw it off, and I had the VW started and shooting backwards before it could make another attack. It galloped after us, nightmarish in the glare of the headlights as I pulled backward into the road and floored the accelerator. The engine was screaming bloody murder, and I swung the wheel to spin us around. I couldn't find first any better than

I had found reverse; Sarah and I both wrestled it into gear and I floored it again. Something hit the rear end hard enough to snap our heads back against the headrests. Sarah shifted into second when I hit the clutch, and we were away. I noticed for the first time that the tape deck was playing a cheerful bluegrass tune.

"Jesus," Sarah breathed.

"You must have been raised a Christian," I said.

"What was it?"

"Don't ask."

"I'm askin' you."

I sighed. The crisis averted, the adrenaline was leaving my system. My side hurt; if the ribs were broken, it meant a trip to an emergency room, and the thought of the complicated lies this would entail exhausted me. "Something that I've been looking for. Before that it was looking for me. Now it is again."

"What are you talking about?"

I reviewed what I knew about her, which wasn't much, trying to judge her capacity for truth. "Sometimes, when you start running away from things, it's hard to stop," I said, the cliché thick in my mouth. I could see her chewing on that for a while, pretending to understand it. I would have given a lot to hear her say Yeah, bullshit, you're handing me a line, I can see through you, so that I could tell her the truth, tell anyone the truth.

"The dogs . . . mama—" She said after a long time.

"—I'm sorry about the dogs, but your mother and sister are safer than you are," I replied. "They're probably scared, but your father and brothers will be back soon."

"Papa and the rest died six years back in November. Car wreck; Papa was drunk."

Her words dynamited my self-pity, leaving me feeling empty and a fool, afraid to look at her face; nothing but platitudes came to mind, so I kept my silence.

"How safe are we?" Her voice was shaky; she sounded dangerously close to tears.

"Not very," I confessed. And as if in response, the road threw an unexpected curve. I wrenched at the wheel and felt the hot pokers entering my side, stomped on the brakes with both feet and almost nothing happened; on the wet pavement, the bug handled like an oil tanker. Sarah pulled on the emergency brake and we slid sideways and started to spin. Instead of my life flashing before my eyes, I had a quick vision of the steering wheel neatly taking my head off on impact, and threw my arms in front of my face. There was an impact, but not a crushing one, and when I looked again we were ten yards into someone's field. The VW idled gently for a moment, coughed, and died. I estimated that we had traveled a total of six or seven miles from the house.

"My car!" Sarah said. She got out and stomped around the car, mud splashing under her boots. The driver's side was creased in two places, and a pair of fence posts trailing lengths of barbed wire lay where they had landed. "My car," she repeated, crying now, and slammed her fist into the hood. I didn't know what to do, but she solved that for me when I touched her arm by spinning and burying her head in my shoulder. After a few seconds though, she seemed to think better of it, and stepped backwards, no longer crying.

"I've got to go, now," I told her. I could feel it back there, but with a seven-mile head start I could do a lot of things; it's a sprinter, but I'm good for distance. The pain in my side was receding . . . maybe nothing was broken after all. I could get it checked once I'd built up my lead sufficiently. I realized that my backpack, with most of my money, was in O'Dell's driveway. So he would be paid after all.

"Wait, damn it. What was that thing? Where are you going?"

"No time for questions, Sarah. I'm sorry. And I'm sorry about your dogs, and your car, too . . ." I hated the way I was sounding, sorry, sorry— "Most of my money is in my backpack, and O'Dell probably has that now. Maybe he'll split it with you. We can feel each other, that thing and I; it knows where I am. I have to go."

"Wait . . ."

I remembered a roadside scene in Montana, red pavement and twisted metal.

"Stay here, you idiot, it's coming after me, don't you understand? For two years, minus the last eight weeks, it's been hunting me. You saw it. Do you really want to get caught between us?"

It wasn't much that had been asked of me. Bring it back, that's all. How it had strayed we didn't know, nor did we anticipate what kind of place it had found; we never expected it to be this difficult to bring it back home. But then the corridor closed or shifted and I couldn't find it . . . they wouldn't abandon me, though, no more than we abandoned it before. Another door would be opened somewhere; we would find it.

And Sarah wanted to come. I hadn't expected that, although maybe I should have. I've already said that I don't really understand these people.

"I've just seen somethin' impossible," she said. "Somethin' that can't exist. I wanna have a goddamn adventure, damn it, before I marry some redneck in a grain and feed cap and start churnin' out his babies. I wanna go. . . ."

I didn't tell her it was impossible, although thinking back on it that might have been kinder. Instead I reached inside the car and flipped down the sun visor.

"What about that?" I said, tapping the picture taped there.

She looked at it, swallowed hard, and looked back at me. "They're dead."

"Not all of them."

"Forget them," she said, but she had paused too long and then said it like she was injuring herself with the words.

I shook my head. "You won't."

"I won't forget the chance I missed here, neither. I'll waste my life waitin' for somethin' like this to happen again."

"There's no chance for you here. Only things to lose. Go home. In the morning, write some music about it. If I ever get where I'm going, I'll remember you there. Isn't that enough?"

"No," she said. "It isn't."

But she drove me north anyway, once we got the VW back on the road, driving with the sun visor down all the way, and her eyes kept going back to it the way a gambler will keep fingering the last quarter in his pocket. And when she drove away again she waved without looking back just as she had that afternoon, leaving me almost exactly where she'd found me.

Just outside of Hillsboro I accepted a ride from a Chevette with a Duke University decal in the rear window. I hesitated as I was getting in, taking a last look to the south, feeling the solid touch in my head as I looked that way. But it wasn't until we were driving away that I realized that even then I was thinking that she might have changed her mind, that the VW might at any moment come rattling around the corner. If it ever did, I was gone.

Winter's Garden
by
Sharon Wahl

About the Author

Sharon Wahl graduated with a degree in music from Wesleyan University in 1979, and started a BS in math and computer science at State University of New York in New Paltz. After working at IBM in Poughkeepsie for a few years, she went to MIT for a graduate degree in math. The second year there, she took a science fiction writing course. That led to a radical change in her thinking, and she traveled the South Pacific for almost a year, writing short stories. "Winter's Garden" was written in New Zealand.

About the Illustrator

Kevin Dzuban was born and raised in Edison, New Jersey. His art was influenced from the beginning by the Jon Nagy television show, and comic books. Comic books also got him reading, and this led him to science fiction and fantasy.

He took art classes in high school, and at a local college for one year thereafter, before joining the U.S. Army for three years. Since 1984, he has been employed by Bell Labs, doing a variety of illustration and design work. He is currently gathering material for a science fiction and fantasy portfolio. He continues to live in New Jersey with his wife, Maryhelen.

I'm sitting by the bedroom window, looking out into the garden. The grass is dry, and mostly brown, but the flowers have been watered and are doing well. The tiger lilies have started to curl open, and there are pink geraniums, a large bushy fuchsia, and some tall, weedy purple stuff I don't know the name of.

Beyond the garden are trees, all green, of course, moving in the breeze. It's cloudy this morning, and the breeze is almost cool. I open the window as wide as I can, and lean out. I try to make the breeze seem cold. Then I look around at trees and garden, starting with the grass, which is at least the right color, soft mousy brown, and try to make the flowers yield to frost, and wither, and the leaves turn gold or red or orange, then brown, and drop from the trees. I can almost see it—almost. And as the breeze blows stronger—off the sea, up the hill—I can almost imagine that it holds a hint of snow.

I close my eyes, holding on to that smell, and try to remember falling snow. I picture the house where my sister Margaret and I grew up. My bedroom was on the third floor, in an octagonal tower. On clear days there was a view of the Hudson River south to West Point, where it curved in front of the big hump of Storm King Mountain. Other days there were neither mountains nor river, only falling bits of white, wet and stuck together like loose snowballs hurled towards earth. I was suspended in the sky of winter. Once

Illustrated by Kevin Dzuban

I opened a window and let the snow drift in. The dark wood floor was so cold I had time to study the crystals through a magnifying glass before they melted. The air was sharp, pure, sacred. I opened my mouth and sucked it in, feasting on the fresh, delicate flavor of snowflakes.

A salty tear runs into my mouth, and I make myself stop. I look out the window again. The clouds have started to break up; it's almost clear in the west. It has never snowed here, and it never will. It will probably be another hot day.

I promised Margaret that today I would weed the garden, not the flowers but our small plot of vegetables. We rent this apartment, one wing of a large old country house, from a couple whose children have all left home. They've been very kind to us. We're lucky to have found them, and this place where there is room enough for us to grow a few vegetables.

I haven't eaten breakfast yet. I go to the kitchen to toast a couple slices of bread and boil water for coffee—a luxury, but the Hendersons have given us a bit of cream, and it won't keep another day with the refrigerator turned so low. I open the refrigerator door and reach for the cream, still thinking of winter; but it isn't cold inside, only cool enough to tease.

I look at the small freezer compartment, sealed shut, out of bounds. No one else is home. I reach for it, stop. I shouldn't do this. But I give in. I rip off the heavy tape sealing the freezer shut. Before I open it I turn on the faucet, lukewarm, as a precaution. Then I flip up the metal door and stick one hand and my nose inside, feeling and breathing in the stale, icy air. I allow myself about ten seconds inside, not really long enough, but more would be too risky. Then I dash to the sink and rinse the hand and splash warm water on my face. I examine myself thoroughly in the small mirror behind the kitchen door. I am still whole, undamaged. I take the scissors and a roll of duct tape from their drawer, and bandage the freezer up again.

At five-thirty Margaret comes home, breathing hard after the long climb up from town.

"Omelette for dinner," I greet her. "Mrs. H gave us some eggs this afternoon. She says her hens always lay too many this time of year, so we should help ourselves."

"Wonderful," she says, dropping into one of the chairs around the kitchen table.

"There's a bit of tomato sauce left. And if you'd like, I could pull up a couple green onions."

"That sounds great." She takes off her white cap and starts pulling bobby pins out of her long brown hair. She's a nurse. We decided to stay here in New Zealand—temporarily, until we can safely return to the States—partly because it was so easy for her to find work here. I haven't found a job, but with our garden and the Hendersons' kindness we live well enough on what she makes.

"I spent half an hour today debating with Mrs. Henderson whether to plant marigolds or zinnias along the front walk. We both agreed that zinnias were prettier, but she was afraid they'd grow too tall."

"Poor Mrs. H. She's so lonely."

Poor Mrs. H. I watch Margaret out of the corner of my eye as I crack and beat the eggs. "She told me to be sure and ask you what color marigolds she should plant."

"Who, me? I don't care! I don't even know what colors they come in."

"Neither do I." I grimace. "But tomorrow I'll give you a full report."

Margaret laughs. "Poor Katie," she says.

Before we eat, Margaret and I sit a minute in silence,

holding hands. This was Margaret's idea. She wants us to think of our friends and family every day. She uses this time to remember their faces. She brings them back, one by one, and greets them, clear and living in her memory. I think she's able to do this because her memories are mostly of warmth and sun. All my memories are set in winter. I never realized this before we came here, but it's true, for all of them, even of our family. I see my brother Jerry bundled in his dark navy jacket, a red and gold scarf wrapped around his neck. He's throwing snowballs at the trunk of a tall, thin pine across the road. His aim is good; almost all his throws hit the tree and splatter.

I can watch him throwing as long as I wish, it's easy: I'm standing in back of him, I can't see his face. But when he turns, I see that pieces of his face are missing. More of it crumbles as I watch: where the freezing air touches his flesh it crystallizes, chunks of it drop away.

I pictured Jerry like this when we first learned of the winter virus, and the image stuck with me. Our family and most of our friends died in its first outbreak. That was fourteen months ago, only a month after Margaret and I had left for a long vacation in New Zealand. No one knew then how it worked; no one knew to stay inside, to stay warm. So now I think of them every evening, as Margaret suggests, but in my own way. I stand behind Jerry and watch him throwing snowballs, and I watch Mom and Dad, ahead of me, on skis, cross-hatching up a hill on the trail behind our house.

I told Margaret about this once, that none of them have faces. But it upset her so much that later I lied and said it was all okay. I didn't want her to worry about me more than she already does.

Margaret opens her eyes. She squeezes my hand and smiles at me.

I smile back, to please her.

"It smells great," Margaret says, starting to eat.

It's a good omelette. I'm glad there are enough fresh eggs for all of us again. The Hendersons lost half their chickens in a freak cold spell last November. Usually that time of year northern New Zealand stays warm enough, so they hadn't worried about putting them in the heated coop overnight. The sirens went off when the temperature dipped below forty. Mr. Henderson and I ran out to collect the chickens, but some of them were just too well hidden. The temperature kept dropping. We had to leave them out; we couldn't risk staying outside any longer. When we looked for them the next day we found eleven piles of feathers and bones picked completely clean of flesh.

Margaret is quiet. She doesn't look worried; she seems sort of peaceful, actually, but she's very quiet.

"How was work?" I ask.

"All right."

"You said that with your accent!"

"Well, I speak that way all day at the hospital. It feels natural." She looks at me, kindly. "You need to practice more."

"Right," I say.

"No, try again."

"Roieet." I make a face, and she laughs. "That's a little better," she says. Then she returns to her slow, peaceful chewing.

"Would you like some water?" I ask.

"Could you boil me some, if you're getting up? I'll make lemon tea after dinner."

"Sure." I fill the kettle for Margaret and take my bottle of cold water from the refrigerator. Most people don't drink cold water, cold anything, now. The feel of cool liquid moving down their throats makes them think of little chunks of tongue or esophagus becoming brittle and washing away, clearing a wider passage into them.

"Did something happen at work?" I ask again as I sit down.

"No," Margaret says, shaking her head.

"What is it, then?"

"I can't keep anything from you, can I?" she says gently, smiling at her plate.

"No. So tell me!"

"It's nothing very exciting. Someone at the hospital asked me—asked us to go to a movie tonight."

"That's nice," I say cautiously. "Someone I know?"

"No. One of the doctors. Would you like to come?"

"I don't think so. I should finish the book I'm reading. It's due Friday." I use a lettuce leaf to scoop up some of the green onions left over from my omelette.

"I can renew it for you."

I shrug and bite into the lettuce, waiting for her to talk me into going. But she doesn't.

"Wasn't there something you wanted to watch on TV tonight?" she says enthusiastically.

"Yes, a nature special, at nine o'clock."

"That's right in the middle of the movie. You'd have missed it."

I must look hurt. Margaret says, "You asked me to remind you."

"Yeah, thanks." I nod and smile, gratefully. "You're right, I'd forgotten about it."

Margaret pushes back her chair. "Dinner was wonderful," she says with that warm, beautiful smile. She gets up and scapes a few bits of food into the composting bin. "Don't bother with the dishes, I'll do them when I get back. I've got to hurry and change."

"No, I'll do them. I don't have anything better to do."

Margaret stands still, probably looking at me. I don't turn around. Stupid, stupid, I tell myself. "I mean, there's plenty of time before the program comes on, and there are only a few dishes. It won't take me long." Then I look at her.

She reaches over and squeezes my shoulder. "Thanks, Katie," she says.

I do the dishes. Then I go to my room and lie down in the dark, kicking the bed.

I keep replaying our conversation. I hear myself complaining about Mrs. H, kind, generous Mrs. H. She probably makes the effort to talk to me so much because she thinks I must be lonely, here by myself all day. And I make fun of her for it. And then I make Margaret feel guilty because she doesn't want to drag me along on a special date. I see myself standing by the kitchen counter: I have become humpbacked, shriveled, I have tight thin lips and tiny colorless eyes which out of habit look only down or sideways, never directly at another human face. And I see Margaret, across the room: Margaret isn't shriveled. She is baby smooth, pink, her hair ripples as I watch her, the air near her is lit with warm yellow light. Margaret shines. Is that why I can't look at her? Because she hurts my eyes?

I roll over and look out the window. The sky is still clear; I can see Orion (upside down) almost overhead. I should turn on the light. If Margaret realizes I'm here in the dark, she'll think I'm sulking and she won't enjoy herself. And I do, truly, want her to enjoy herself.

I switch on the reading lamp over my bed, shielding my eyes until they adjust. A year ago I painted the walls an icy reflective silver. With the white lace curtains it reminds me of fresh snow on a winter morning. The walls even have the blue shadows you sometimes see near snow banks. I also have two patches of furry snow, New Zealand sheep skins, on the floor. "Katie's Mountain Resort," Margaret calls the room, to tease me. But she doesn't really approve. We argued about that the day I painted it. She said I could keep it this way if I wanted, but I shouldn't show it to anyone. Other people don't want to be reminded of winter, she said, they don't want to be reminded of the danger they're in. She told me I should try harder to understand the way they feel, and respect it. But we've lost just as much as anyone here, I had insisted, more, probably, and *we* can handle it—

Well. Margaret's right, partly. So I agreed to follow her advice for a while, until people here have accepted us somewhat. Americans aren't so popular these days. It would be disastrous for us to have to leave and start again somewhere else.

Margaret's date has arrived. I hear a male voice in the kitchen, Margaret laughing. They don't stay long. After only a minute I hear the kitchen door slam, then two car doors, and I see red taillights curving down the driveway.

The library book I had claimed to be so anxious to return to is within reach on the nightstand. I pick it up and just sort of look at it, reading and rereading the dust-jacket biography of the author. I wonder if she's still alive. I open to the page where I left a bookmark, but I can't read more than a line without drifting off.

I put the book down and bend over to get my journal, a large blue notebook I keep on the bottom shelf of the nightstand. This is Volume IV of the Saga of Life Without Snow. Margaret and I both started journals the first week we were traveling. We used to remind each other to write something each night: where we'd been, people we'd met, recipes, random thoughts. It was a pleasant shared ritual. I don't know if she's kept hers up; I doubt it. I've filled four huge notebooks with everything from theories about the virus to unfinished poems. I open to one of them, thinking maybe I'll work on that for a while.

Requiem for Warm-Blooded Inhabitants of the Ice and Snow

> I am a penguin
> flying on blue ice;
> A polar bear,
> paws stained red
> like the snow, from seal's blood. . . .

I soon give up. I'm not a poet. But when I think of the few penguins left, or polar bears, sitting in a warm cage somewhere like the San Diego Zoo, I wish I were; I wish I could speak for them. I think they must feel just like I do, here in the silver and lace cage mimicking my habitat, dreaming of winter.

I wonder what it's like now in the cold places, Antarctica, the North Pole. . . . I wonder what has happened to my parents' house. Probably it's still there, empty. Not even any rats or squirrels around to build nests in the sofa. There might be squatters, or nomads, they call them now, in the summer, if any of them make it that far north. Probably not. Termites could get it, I guess. The insects are there, the trees, and the fish. Probably if I could see it I wouldn't notice any difference. Except that there'd be no lights on, no people anywhere. Nothing left of their bodies, no sign of what they'd been doing or where they'd been when they died except maybe some clothes left in a pile where you wouldn't expect to find them. The animals wouldn't even have that. They'd leave their fur behind. And bones; I forgot. There would be a lot of dressed-up skeletons.

Last week I started a story, for all of us, me and the penguins and the others. I guess that's what I'll work on tonight. I carry the notebook over to my desk and read what I've written so far.

THE WINTER PALACE

It looks like Margaret was right: there aren't many people in line with me waiting for the Winter Palace to open. The ones who are here, though, look as excited as I feel. It's hot standing in the sun, but we all have jackets or wool sweaters with us. The children have thrown theirs on the ground while we wait. Without their parents' reminders they would probably leave them there. But I hug my old down jacket like a dear friend long missed.

From outside, the Palace isn't really so impressive, except for its size; just a jumble of concrete and glass rectangles. Passers-by can peek into a few of the exhibits, the huge Hall of Winter and some of the Arctic Animals. I arrived an hour early and watched the penguins until a line started to form.

The glass doors are open now, the line has started to move. There are only fifteen people in front of me, so I'm soon inside. I pick up a glossy brochure containing a floor plan of the Palace and information on the exhibits, but I don't look at it; I don't need cold and winter explained to me!

We step first into the Hall of Autumn. For a few weeks, the trees growing in the long, high hall have been coaxed into believing it's autumn, a real, old-fashioned New England autumn. I smile, I can't help it, it's been so long. . . . There are oak trees, with leaves of mottled orange, red, and brown; sugar maple, bright, bright red; white birch, leaves glowing a light cheery yellow. And others. I pick up fallen leaves to examine them more closely, chase and catch one that drops from a nearby maple. I choose an exquisite red and orange oak leaf for a souvenir and place it carefully between the pages of a book in my purse.

And it's cool. There's an honest-to-god chill in the air. After twenty minutes I have goosebumps on my bare arms, but I don't put my jacket on yet, I'm enjoying it. I stand with my eyes closed, shivering a little, smelling autumn, the classic autumn scent of fallen leaves.

At the end of the Hall of Autumn there's a long wooden table, behind it a woman handing out cups of hot apple cider. I laugh and take one, thanking her.

The Arctic Animals exhibit is next. I stand a minute, sipping my cider, and watch an elegant pair of emperor penguins (the largest of the penguins, says the sign in front of me) slide down a sheet of ice. But when the cider is finished I move on. I pass through an automatic door to the small antechamber of the Hall of Winter. It's like a cold lock; finally I need my jacket. Another door slides smoothly aside, and I'm in.

I lean on the wall just to the right of the door, standing off the path in five inches of snow, and look down the length of the enormous room. The Hall is a patchwork of winter scenes: near me, in front, there is a stand of gracefully naked dogwood, branches sprayed with water to form a sparkling coat of ice.

The ground of the Hall is sculptured with gentle hills, and I've heard there is a stream and a frozen waterfall somewhere, though I don't see it. At the bottom of one hill some children have started rolling a snowman. Their play area is marked off with a low white picket fence. Most of the children don't have mittens, but they're determined to build their snowman anyway. Some of them, or their parents, have remembered not only mittens but a carrot for the snowman's nose and small potatoes for eyes. No doubt someone will donate a scarf when it's finished.

At the back of the Hall, where the skylights are painted a cloudy blue-gray, it's snowing.

I wade back to the shoveled concrete path, brush the snow off my pants and shoes, and walk towards the falling snow. What kind of snow have they made, I wonder, powdery, or wet, or hard pellets? I bend and scoop up a cold handful. Here it's wet enough to pack well, superb snow-man material.

I glimpse a skier on the track bordering the Hall. I could have rented skis, but I thought that after the trails I was used to, along mountainsides or deep gorges, this would seem too tame. Now my body misses the rhythmic, powerful motions of skiing. Next time I'll rent the skis.

Now it's snowing right in front of me. I reach out and watch flakes touch my palm and melt. Then I step into it, leaving the path again. I gather another handful. It's drier than the children's snow, better for skiing. My neck is getting wet from the melting flakes, and I regretfully raise my hood. I look up and feel snowflakes kiss my eyes. Then I stick my tongue out, eyes closed to concentrate on the soft icy kisses.

I hear a thud, just to my left. I look and see some bits of snow stuck to a tree, then another snowball hits the trunk in almost the same place.

I see a boy stooping for another handful, navy jacket, striped scarf.

"Jerry!"

The boy glances at me, but only briefly, deciding I must have spoken to someone else. He looks nothing like Jerry. But in the moment I thought it was my brother I had seen Jerry's face, in perfect detail, and I still held that image. Stooping, aiming, throwing a snowball at the old pine across the street. I close my eyes and carefully shift the young, gray-eyed face to a beach remembered from a family vacation, Jerry running into the surf and diving under a wave, bobbing up wet and smiling, waving to me, calling me to join him.

I had him. I finally had one of their faces back. Only one, but it was a start, it could be done, they could come back to me. I didn't

• • •

Wishful thinking. I tap my capped pen on the paper, hard, leaving marks. I guess I hoped to trick myself: that I would read this scene, get caught up in it, carried along, carried away, see the snowball, feel a bit of its icy splatter brush my cheek, then—miracle!—see Jerry's face before I remembered it was only a story, my own story, my own trick.

It didn't work. I pick up a pen, a different color, black this time, and cross out the last few paragraphs. That isn't what would really happen. But then, none of it is realistic. It isn't even a real story: I haven't said who she is, who Margaret is. I haven't explained anything: how do they keep the virus out of the Hall? We're all covered with it. If people just walked in like that, they'd have a bunch of dead people and dead penguins. Since it isn't a real story—since no one else will read it, except maybe Margaret—I won't worry about that. I can pretend the virus dies at a hundred-ten degrees and have everyone take a sauna first.

But I want to think about what I would do if I were really in the Winter Palace, if there really were a Winter Palace.

What would I do? I'd be standing there in snow, snow kissing my eyebrows, nose, chin, gentle kisses leaving tiny beads of water—I'd be home. I wouldn't want to leave. The Hall would need a house for me: a log cabin, in the clearing near the children's snowman.

I stand a minute in the falling snow, smiling at the gray-painted sky. Now that I've tasted the snow, I want to see the rest of the exhibit. I follow the path back to the children's play area. There is a cabin across from it, set back a little ways from the path in a small cluster of pine trees. It's bordered by a neat white picket fence, and smoke rises from its stone chimney.

Inside, it's warm, crowded with children and adults holding styrofoam cups of hot chocolate with tiny marshmallows floating on top. They've fixed it up to look as though someone lives here: a rough wooden bunk is set against one wall, made up with a red and black plaid blanket; there are prints and posters hanging on the walls, a calendar open to a photo of Mt. Cook pink in the light of sunrise; a pair of old leather boots under the bed; used-looking pots and pans and some heavy wool jackets hung up on nails. There is an oil lamp, full of fuel, in the corner near the sink. Another hangs from the ceiling, lighting the cabin. There are pots of water boiling on the stove, and big round cartons of instant chocolate on a long wooden table next to the cups.

I note all these things. Then I leave the cabin, politely refusing a cup of chocolate, excited, wondering if I will actually do what I am thinking of doing. I walk around the edge of the Hall, seeing it differently this time. Now I am a scout, an explorer, a would-be settler. There are two other exits, for emergency use only, but both of these can be bolted from this side. The stream runs just behind the cabin. A pipe directs some of it to a tap inside, so there's plenty of water. And if they cut the stream off, I can melt snow. There's a large bin of coal behind the cabin. I won't be cold.

So I only have to worry about keeping the main entrance locked, and food.

I tell myself not to hurry. It's early, not even noon, and the Palace will be open till four. But it's no good; I'm too excited to leave my errands for later.

I leave the exhibit—there'll be no trouble getting back in, they have plenty of tickets left—and find my bike, chained to a parking meter on a street alongside the Palace. It's hot. I stuff my jacket into one of the panniers. Then I ride home, up the long, steep hill to the house with the Maori name, Te Maunga, The Mountain.

No one else is there. I fill my small backpack with cheese, bread, some dried fruit, granola. I have to leave a note for Margaret. None of the lies I think of are convincing, so I write only, "I won't be home tonight. I'll be in touch with you tomorrow. I'm fine. Katie."

What else might I need? My clothes are warm enough, and I have food for several days. I decide to bring my journal. On the shelf next to it is a small flashlight. I clip it to my belt loop.

On my way out I look at the note. "I'm sorry, Margaret," I want to add to it. But that would only worry her more.

I ride back to the Winter Palace and stop near the meter again. Then I realize I've forgotten my extra lock. I'll need to bring the one I have inside with me in case I decide to block the entrance. I don't want to go back for it; I don't want to risk meeting the Hendersons and having to trade politenesses. So I push the bike onto the grounds of the Palace and hide it under some thick shrubs. I look back afterwards: it's invisible from the road. It's better this way, I think, Margaret might come by looking for me; now she won't find my bike and figure out where I am.

I put on my backpack, clutch my jacket. I enter the Palace again. This time I take the detour after the Hall of Autumn and rent skis.

I hang out around the cabin for hours waiting for it to be empty. Finally it is: I quickly hide myself and the skis in the supply closet. I hope they won't notice the skis missing at the end of the day and look for them. I hope they won't open this door to put away any leftover chocolate, or to get more.

Then I wait. I sit, soundless, listening to people talking and laughing outside the door.

Finally I am certain they have left. The Palace is closed.

I open the door as quietly as I can. I'm worried that someone might be here, a night watchman, or one of the researchers. But the room is empty. I'll just have to hope that no one enters the Hall during the night. It seems likely that no one will.

The coal stove isn't completely cold yet; I start it up again. I fill a pan with cold water and put it on top. It'll take a while to get hot. I decide to go skiing before it gets completely dark in the Hall. It's already dim, with only the light from a few skylights and windows at one end, but I can see well enough to follow the track.

It's finally quiet. That's what I missed today, I realize: the enveloping quiet of snow.

I move with a relaxed, rhythmic stride around the Hall, hearing only the thudding, whooshing, clicking of my poles and skis. The third or fourth time I pass the windows to outside I pause and look at the darkening world. It's still summer there. I shudder, and continue.

I stop when I begin to feel tired, when I feel the long-unused muscles just over my knees begin to tremble. I ski to the cabin and unclip my boots. I knock the snow off the skis and leave them outside, leaning against the wall, so the wax will stay hard.

I can hear the water boiling as I enter the cabin. It's dark inside. I use my flashlight to find the matches—I'd left them on the floor near the foot of the stove—and I light one of the oil lamps.

I'm glowing in the cabin's warmth, the special glow of coming into heat from cold and exertion. Glowing, peaceful, singing very softly—a folk tune—I lovingly prepare four cups of hot chocolate.

"Katie, I'm home!" Margaret calls, and I'm back in my silver room. The white sheepskin rugs don't look much like real snow. "Come out to the kitchen and meet Michael."

I look at what my pen has written: four cups of hot chocolate. For me, and for Jerry, Mom, and Dad, I guess. That's where I would find them, if anywhere: in a warm cabin drinking hot chocolate after skiing.

"Katie!" Now Margaret is at my door, knocking. She tries the handle, but it's locked. "Katie? Why won't you come out? Katie?"

I don't answer. She goes back to the kitchen, and soon I hear them laughing again.

The cabin is lovely at night. I sip my chocolate and smile at the rough wood walls. I'm warm and my skin is golden in the lantern light. When I finish my cup I put the others on the stove and cover them, to keep them warm.

A Foreign Exchange

by
Matthew Wills

About the Author

Matthew Wills was born in 1963 and spent his childhood living abroad in half a dozen different countries. He now lives in Iowa City, Iowa, and works as an assistant at the University of Iowa library. He has a Master's degree in Communication Studies, and likes to write essays and opinion pieces for newspapers, as well as novels. He has had no fiction published since the seventh grade. If "A Foreign Exchange" is any example, that may change rapidly.

About the Illustrator

Derek Hegsted is 24, and works as a freelance in the BYU motion picture studio. That makes him the first Illustrators' Contest winner from Provo, Utah; we want to be aware that there have been no less than three Writers' Contest winners from that vicinity. We don't know what accounts for it. Meanwhile, Derek has spent three and a half years at Ricks College, gaining an associate degree in illustration and fine arts, and plans to attend the Art Center in Pasadena. He plans to exploit illustration to its limits, while keeping his options open on fine art.

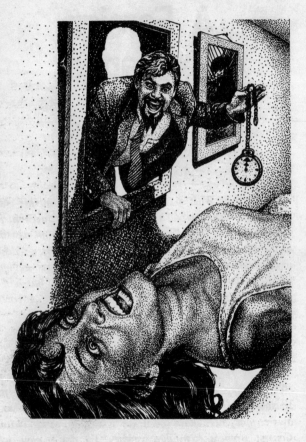

Illustrated by Derek Hegsted

The Emergency man looked at Elise with a peculiar mixture of priggishness and cupidity that seemed just right for his stylized face. There was an air of wanton excess about him, a bored decadence. He was a little too pink, a little too round, for his age. His plump figure was oddly brittle.

The two of them were facing each other in the disconcertingly mirrored lobby of the Berlin Hotel, amid a host of Community movers and shakers afraid of daring the Weather outside. Elise was an anomaly among them, Someone from Outside. They gave her a wide berth, as if her grimy street atmosphere would rub off on their pampered bodies. Undoubtedly, they all knew why she was there.

She was wearing old black jeans and a black tee shirt under her enveloping tan duster. Her fly-green shades drooped awkwardly from a side panel pocket and her shoulder bag overflowed with her surplus gear. The City had locked her out of her squat on F-Strasse, forcing her to change in the Station's left luggage room, where an attendant and two antiterrorist cops had watched her. She knew she had that tired, burnt look that was written onto the body after only a few minutes out in the Weather. The Hotel mirrors made her look a decade older, a sunburned bagchild grown old in the damned Weather. Still, the Emergency man's smirk was grossly hypocritical. She dreaded his approaching proposition, and was terrified of it, too. He was, however, the only potential pickup in evidence, and she desperately needed 300 I-Marks to pay the Lebentax.

She turned away from his gaze. You weren't supposed to look so eager. Pretending to read the Flix announcements flashing on long terminals, she thought about her dissertation and completing it so she could leave Berlin and get back to Vermont. She presumed it was still called Vermont. International news had been impossible to come by ever since the continental televisual corporations had monopolized into 'round the clock Weather reports. There were no headlines anymore, only Alerts, Warnings, and rising UV levels. The Weather dominated everything; the media was the Weather. It was twenty-seven degrees in Vermont and the UVs were steady at Six, so at least you could go out into it for most of the day without permanent damage. That was all she knew about her home land.

He drew up beside her and murmured, really murmured without moving his lips significantly.

"Do you have a health pass?"

She turned her head, unsure how to play the game properly.

"Yeah." She cautiously offered the green card hung on the inside of her duster. The date was two months old. Green meant relatively disease-free, if a little protein deficient.

His eyes did all his emoting, his face not perceptively moving much for the obvious reason. The thick application of makeup filled the cracks in his skin like a slick putty. Up close, his pinkness looked more like applied rouge formed by cookie cutouts than anything resembling health. The rigid stiffness of his mask was a fashion recently favored in Paris, but already it was a little passé. The Emergency mob was like that, though, behind the times to a fault.

From the eyes, she could tell he was pleased at the ripeness of his choice.

"Are you a student?" Even through those barely parted

taut lips, he came across with the patented English Standard accent.

"Yeah," she answered. Yeah, she thought, a student with an expiring visa, no immediate place to sleep, and no more than a few N-pfennigs in pocket. Just the right pickings.

"You do not look like you have done this before."

His grin was grotesque, like a grimacing clown. It was a wide gap, painted cartoon style in the middle of a flesh-toned shell.

That "look" made her uneasy. Who could possibly stomach it more than once? How could anyone possibly do it again?

"No," she said quietly. "I haven't, but I need."

"We all do," he stopped her almost politely, slipping her his card.

His hands were gloved in some kind of antique animal skin. Wondering what it felt like to wear a dead thing's hide, she looked at the rest of him. Frankly glancing away from that face, she saw for the first time how completely impeccable, how clean, he was. It was certain he didn't go out in the Weather anymore. Some people didn't have to, the distinctive sign of the new caste system. And there were other signs about him too. Tailored by Savile Row with a touch of nostalgia, and without a centimeter of long-chain fiber, he looked stunningly rich, not just bloated by inflation. Jonathan Vail-Jones, the card glistened, Special Trade Representative of His Majesty's Emergency Government. Who would have thought such elegance survived in the modern world?

For a second she was impressed, but then she remembered what he was expecting of her, what he was buying from her.

"Room 31-986. A suite. It has a bath."

The insinuation in his voice didn't surprise her. She knew she was gritty and rough with the Weather. But she had forgotten that the Hotel was the only place in Berlin that still boasted of its plentiful hot water. The exotic promise of a bath stilled some of her nervous fear and the hints of revulsion that kept nibbling at the emptiness of her stomach.

Some things are necessary, she convinced herself suddenly, some things must be done. Believing that, she was hardly conscious of his touch when he lifted her thin arm and slipped his door key around her wrist.

"I will see you there in an hour?"

She nodded in response.

Most of the major hotels in North America had been cannibalized for the flagship of the Berlin metropolis, so the elevators actually worked, like an old magic presumed lost. Ascending sleight-of-hand towards the sun, Elise felt her ears pop and heard the blood in her head. It was a bass throb, the sound of an intimate self amid all the metal noises propelling her upwards.

Only every third fluorescent in the corridors burned on Vail-Jones' floor but still the waste of light splashing off the buff walls in the long spaces bedazzled her when the elevator opened. The Berlin was truly imperial, the last of the wanton imperials sticking up out of the shanties of the eight hundred-year-old capital.

The door to his suite clicked open effortlessly. The higher one got, further and farther still from the anarchy of the streets and the hive-like squats and the dangerous Weather, the more things seemed to work. Even the noise-swallowing rug was unctuously clean.

Inside, she paused to stare at the big foldout 'gram of the dictator of the Greater U.K. set above the bed. The weird feeling rattling her stomach returned as she studied it. It was simply mesmerizing. The public images of the Prime Minister had not changed since the Emergency had become permanent, so there was something eerily out of date in the 'gram. The clothes and hair were wrong. The expression was only a prim, zero-content rebuke, and yet it looked remarkably sinister. But it all fit together so well, for in a few more years the PM would have been at Ten Downing Street longer than even Queen Victoria had sat on the throne.

Jonathan Vail-Jones, like the whole Emergency crew, undoubtedly worshiped his leader uncritically and without cynicism, and that frightened Elise even more than her fate for the evening.

She quickly shunted away from the leader's shopkeeper eyes and walked into the sparkling chrome and marble of the bathroom. The difference between Vail-Jones' influenced room and the Hotel's province was complete. It was like something out of a lifestyle exhibit in the library of the Free University. All surface effect, of course, but the impression was still otherworldly. It briefly made her feel girlish, giddy in the presence of the sublime. The tub even had lion's paw feet, and the spout was a thicket of small-breasted angels from Louis XIV.

But the water was the most amazing thing, for it was foamy white while spewing out, and pooled to a jeweler's clarity. And it was hot, hot enough to steam. She let it run near scalding and tasted its natural sweetness on her fingers, relishing the absence of the usual masking vanilla additive. The Hotel must have been importing it from the deep Arctic. Little wonder management demanded hard currency up front and rejected plastic without any qualms.

As the air about her moistened, she stripped off her layers; boots, duster, jeans, legging wraps, underwear, tricolor ANC scarf, tee shirt, tank, and then looked at the narrow body in the mirror. She was twenty-five years old and her face, particularly the nose, was ripe with a spatter mess of freckles, even under the greasy sheen of Sonnen-Blok 50. The UVs had tightened her lower arms and neck with tan too, but the rest of her was sheet pale. In that bathroom, naked, she felt malnourished and fragile, ready to crinkle and warp once she got out into the Weather again.

If only it wasn't so hard to get enough to eat, she thought. But the days of fast meat from the rain forest were gone, even for the likes of a ranking Emergency man.

There was no quick, hot protein left. There was hardly a bath left. The showers at the Free University were nasty affairs, moldy, dank, and dark, a stew of co-ed and multi-lingual bodies. Soap down, rinse, don't look at your neighbor, and get out. She hadn't had a bath in four, maybe five, years, and that had been Vermont well-water, just a touch too acidic, a bath with a sting. Now, slipping into the tub, she sighed aloud with contentment. The luxury of it seemed obscene, illicit even, just because it was so pricelessly heavenly. Relaxation had become the ultimate commodity.

This is almost worth it, she mused hazily. Almost.

Submerged to her ears when the outer door to the suite opened, she snapped awake from hot, lazy daydreams. True to his word, an hour had passed. Pulling herself quickly out of the water, she suddenly felt queasy with the heat and his arrival. What am I doing, she wondered, trying to be rational, what the hell am I exchanging for a *bath*?

She knew that things had changed quickly, even in the insignificant span of her quarter century. The uneven collapse had been so quick. And now she was selling herself to live for the next day. But what else was there to do? She knew how desperate she was. Scrounging around in her bag, she found her multi-vitamins and swallowed several. At least she was pretty healthy, considering, but then, that's what attracted Vail-Jones' lust. For no reason, she tried to recall the last time she had sex. She couldn't remember. There was always too much Weather.

A relatively clean tee shirt was folded into a side pocket of her duster and she pulled it over her head. It was long to her hips, but she put her underwear on as well. It made her feel more prepared, safer. Any kind of clothing at all did that in the modern world.

"Are you there?"' he called out.

"Yeah," she offered back tentatively. "I'll be with you."

She opened her tube of Sonnen-Blok, then realized she wasn't going out. Her nerves were dangling now, demanding a quieting. She knew that if she thought about what was going to happen next she would get sick and vomit. Quickly, she shuffled the canisters in the medicine cabinet. He only had Trek, Traumland, and some Zz-Nicht, all imminently compromising in their meekness, so she used one of the last of her own. The crackling under her tongue numbed her face instantly and screwed up her balance. She was starving, and the heat-pinked body she saw wavering in the mirror looked like somebody else's.

But the wooziness passed quickly to lighten her head. She opened the door.

He sat stiffly on the edge of the bed. Not even the buttons holding together the vest tucking in his rich flab were undone. Again, only his eyes were emotional. He wanted her, or more precisely, it, very badly. The primal hunger of those eyes turned her imagination lurid, and she saw his careful facade cracking, his rotten insides leaking at the seams to slime the floor.

The air conditioners whirled and hummed and muttered to themselves with the load they struggled with.

Sitting down next to him, her violent fantasy already fading under the soothing influence, she tried to smile. It was so nice, and only a little confusing, after all, to be so pleasantly zonked out.

"A thousand is sufficient?"

She nodded vaguely. Demons of hunger were clawing at her gut, ready to cannibalize what was left of her reserved starches. After he was done, she would need to eat her fill, and with his money she could stuff herself. It was a self-fulfilling destiny, a circle of dependency.

"O.K.," she murmured, leaning back onto the bed in resignation. "Do it."

"Jolly good."

Perhaps he said it, perhaps her mind played with her. Afterwards, she would never really be sure.

He began to stroke her right wrist. His knees were on the bed, and he was hunched over her slightly, working intently. Through fading eyes she saw again how the makeup caked over his facial topography, splitting and folding back, lifting and curling. To keep her mind away from the foreign touch of animal skin, she watched the folds in his neck bulge and sink against the tightness of his collar. She knew she would never see the skin of his hands. No makeup in the world could save hands.

All she could think of was her bath, Vermont, and her pointless dissertation. She looked at the Prime Minister's image.

Just how old was Mrs. Thatcher now anyway?

But when Vail-Jones briskly penetrated her, she remembered him again and screamed. It wasn't supposed to hurt so much. They said it was sharp, but quick as a needle. The stabbing made her cry aloud, tears jerking from their ducts.

The draining began instantly, making her limp. His head dunked out of sight and she heard the loud sucking sounds at her wrist. The wet air gurgling noise seemed to be coming from a great distance and she felt herself sinking into quick running dreams. Blood poured out of her through the gold tube that was his straw like a dammed river unleashed.

Suspense
by
L. Ron Hubbard

About the Author

Many years ago—the 1930s—when L. Ron Hubbard was at the beginning of a very long career that was to make him one of the world's most acclaimed and widely read authors, he was repeatedly asked to share the secrets of his success with the readers of writers' magazines. He was glad to do so; there is quite a file of essays of his published in those days.

Here, from Author and Journalist *for June, 1937, is one of those pieces.*

We use it, along with a number of other essays by LRH, in the Writers of The Future workshop, and the students remark on how relevant it is despite the passage of time. Why shouldn't it be? Fashions in storytelling change, and the pulps are long gone, but story *remains the same. Here, then, is L. Ron Hubbard on Suspense, one of the key building blocks to writing a really good story.*

Next to checks, the most intangible thing in this business of writing is that quantity "Suspense."

It is quite as elusive as editorial praise, as hard to corner and recognize as a contract writer.

But without any fear of being contradicted I can state that suspense, or rather, the lack of it, is probably responsible for more rejects than telling an editor he is wrong.

You grab the morning mail, find a long brown envelope. You read a slip which curtly says, "Lacks suspense."

Your wife starts cooking beans, you start swearing at the most enigmatic, unexplanatory, hopeless phrase in all that legion of reject phrases.

If the editor had said, "I don't think your hero had a tough enough time killing Joe Blinker," you could promptly sit down and kill Joe Blinker in a most thorough manner.

But when the editor brands and damns you with that first cousin to infinity, "Suspense," you just sit and swear.

Often the editor, in a hurry and beleaguered by stacks of MSS. higher than the Empire State, has to tell you something to explain why he doesn't like your wares. So he fastens upon the action, perhaps. You can tell him (and won't, if you're smart) that your action is already so fast that you had to grease your typewriter roller to keep the rubber from getting hot.

Maybe he says your plot isn't any good, but you know doggone well that it is a good plot and has been a good plot for two thousand years.

Maybe, when he gives you those comments, he is, as I say, in a hurry. The editor may hate to tell you you lack suspense because it is something like B.O.—your best friends won't tell you.

But the point is that, whether he says that your Mary Jones reminds him of the Perils of Pauline, or that your climax is flat, there's a chance that he means suspense.

Those who have been at this business until their fingernails are worn to stumps are very often overconfident of their technique. I get that way every now and then, until something hauls me back on my haunches and shows me up. You just forget that technique is not a habit, but a constant set of rules to be frequently refreshed in your mind.

And so, in the skurry of getting a manuscript in the mail, it is not unusual to overlook some trifling factor which will mean the difference between sale and rejection.

This suspense business is something hard to remember. You know your plot (or should, anyway) before you write it. You forget that the reader doesn't. Out of habit, you think plot is enough to carry you through. Sometimes it won't. You have to fall back on none-too-subtle mechanics.

Take this, for example:

> He slid down between the rocks toward the creek, carrying the canteens clumsily under his arm, silently cursing his sling. A shadow loomed over him.
>
> "Franzawi!" screamed the Arab sentinel.

There we have a standard situation. In the Atlas. The hero has to get to water or his wounded legionnaires will die of thirst. But, obviously, it is very, very flat except for the slight element of surprising the reader.

Surprise doesn't amount to much. That snap ending tendency doesn't belong in the center of the story. Your reader knew there were Arabs about. He knew the hero was going into danger. But that isn't enough. Not half.

Legionnaire Smith squirmed down between the rocks clutching the canteens, his eyes fixed upon the bright silver spot which was the waterhole below. A shadow loomed across the trail before him. Hastily he slipped backward into cover.

An Arab sentinel was standing on the edge of the trail, leaning on his long gun. The man's brown eyes were turned upward, watching a point higher on the cliff, expecting to see some sign of the besieged legionnaires.

Smith started back again, moving as silently as he could, trying to keep the canteens from banging. His sling-supported arm was weak. The canteens were slipping.

He could see the sights on the Arab's rifle and knew they would be lined on him the instant he made a sound.

The silver spot in the ravine was beckoning. He could not return with empty canteens. Maybe the sentinel would not see him if he slipped silently around the other side of this boulder.

He tried it. The man remained staring wolfishly up at the pill-box fort.

Maybe it was possible after all. That bright spot of silver was so near, so maddening to swollen tongues. . . .

Smith's hand came down on a sharp stone. He lifted it with a jerk.

A canteen rattled to the trail.

For seconds nothing stirred or breathed in this scorching world of sun and stone.

Then the sentry moved, stepped a pace up the path, eyes searching the shadows, gnarled hands tight on the rifle stock.

Smith moved closer to the boulder, trying to get out of sight, trying to lure the sentry toward him so that he could be silently killed.

The canteen sparkled in the light.

A resounding shout rocked the blistered hills.

"Franzawi!" cried the sentinel.

The surprise in the first that a sentinel would be there and that Smith was discovered perhaps made the reader blink.

The dragging agony of suspense in the latter made the reader lean tensely forward, devour the page, gulp. . . .

Or at least, I hope it did.

But there's the point. Keep your reader wondering which of two things will happen (i.e., will Smith get through or will he be discovered) and you get his interest. You focus his mind on an intricate succession of events, and that is much better than getting him a little groggy with one swift sock to the medulla oblongata.

That is about the only way you can heighten drama out of melodrama.

It is not possible, of course, to list all the ways this method can be used. But it is possible to keep in mind the fact that suspense is better than fight action.

And speaking of fight action, there is one place where Old Man Suspense can be made to work like an Elkton marrying parson.

Fights, at best, are gap fillers. The writer who introduces them for the sake of the fight itself and not for the effects upon the characters is a writer headed for eventual oblivion even in the purely action books.

Confirmed by the prevailing trend, I can state that the old saw about action for the sake of action was right. A story jammed and packed with blow-by-blow accounts of what the hero did to the villain and what the villain did to the hero, with fists, knives, guns, bombs, machine guns, belaying pins, bayonets, poison gas, strychnine, teeth, knees, and calks is about as interesting to read as the Congressional Record and about twice as dull. You leave yourself wide open to a reader comment, "Well, what of it?"

But fights accompanied by suspense are another matter.

Witness the situation in which the party of the first part is fighting for possession of a schooner, a girl or a bag of pearls. Unless you have a better example of trite plotting, we proceed. We are on the schooner. The hero sneaks out of the cabin and there is the villain on his way to sink the ship. So we have a fight:

> Jim dived at Bart's legs, but Bart was not easily thrown. They stood apart. Jim led with his left, followed through with his right. Black Bart countered the blows. Bone and sinew cracked in the mighty thunder of conflict.... Jim hit with his right.... Bart countered with a kick in the shins....

There you have a masterpiece for wastebasket filing. But, believe it, this same old plot and this same old fight look a lot different when you have your suspense added. They might even sell if extracted and toned like this:

> Jim glanced out of the chartroom and saw Black Bart. Water dripping from his clothes, his teeth bared, his chest heaving from his long swim, Bart stood in a growing pool which slid down his arms and legs. In his hand he clutched an axe, ready to sever the hawser and release them into the millrace of the sweeping tide....

This is Jim's cue, of course, to knock the stuffing out of Black Bart, but that doesn't make good reading nor very much wordage, for thirty words are enough in which to recount any battle as such, up to and including wars.

So we add suspense. For some reason Jim can't leap into the fray right at that moment. Suppose we add that he has these pearls right there and he's afraid Ringo, Black

Bart's henchman, will up and swipe them when Jim's back is turned. So first Jim has to stow the pearls.

This gets Bart halfway across the deck toward that straining hawser which he must cut to wreck the schooner and ruin the hero.

Now, you say, we dive into it. Nix. We've got a spot here for some swell suspense. Is Black Bart going to cut that hawser? Is Jim going to get there?

Jim starts. Ringo hasn't been on his way to steal the pearls but to knife Jim, so Jim tangles with Ringo, and Black Bart races toward the hawser some more.

Jim's fight with Ringo is short. About like this:

> Ringo charged, eyes rolling, black face set. Jim glanced toward Bart. He could not turn his back on this charging demon. Yet he had to get that axe.
>
> Jim whirled to meet Ringo. His boot came up and the knife sailed over the rail and into the sea. Ringo reached out with his mighty hands. Jim stepped through and nailed a right on Ringo's button. Skidding, Ringo went down.
>
> Jim sprinted forward toward Bart. The black-bearded Colossus spun about to meet the rush, axe upraised.

Now, if you want to, you can dust off this scrap. But don't give it slug by slug. Hand it out, thus:

> The axe bit down into the planking. Jim tried to recover from his dodge. Bart was upon him, slippery in Jim's grasp. In vain Jim tried to land a solid blow, but Bart was holding him hard.
>
> "Ringo!" roared Bart. "Cut that hawser!"
>
> Ringo, dazed by Jim's blow, struggled up. Held tight in Bart's grasp, Jim saw Ringo lurch forward and yank the axe out of the planking.
>
> "That hawser!" thundered Bart. "I can't hold this fool forever!"

Now, if you wanted that hawser cut in the first place (which you did, because that means more trouble and the suspense of wondering how the schooner will get out of it) cut that hawser right now before the reader suspects that this writing business is just about as mechanical as fixing a Ford.

Action suspense is easy to handle, but you have to know when to quit and you have to evaluate your drama and ladle it out accordingly.

Even in what the writers call the psychological story you have to rely upon suspense just as mechanical as this.

Give your reader a chance to wonder for a while about the final outcome.

There is one type of suspense, however, so mechanical that it clanks. I mean foreshadowing.

To foreshadow anything is weak. It is like a boxer stalling for the bell. You have to be mighty sure that you've got something outstanding to foreshadow, or the reader will nail up your scalp.

It is nice to start ominously like this:

> I knew that night as I sloshed through the driving rain that all was not well. I had a chilly sense of foreboding as though a monster dogged my steps. . . .

> If I only had known then what awaited me when the big chimes in the towers should strike midnight, I would have collapsed with terror. . . .

Very good openings. Very, very good. Proven goods, even though the knap is a bit worn. But how many times have writers lived up to those openings? Not very many.

You get off in high, but after you finish you will probably tear out these opening paragraphs—even though Poe was able to get away with this device. Remember the opening of "The Fall of the House of Usher"? You know, the one that goes something like this: "Through the whole of a dark and dismal afternoon."

That is foreshadowing. However, few besides Poe have been able to get away with suspense created by atmosphere alone.

One particular magazine makes a practice of inserting a foreshadow as a first paragraph in every story. I have come to suspect that this is done editorially because the fore-shadow is always worse than the story gives you.

> It's a far cry from the jungles of Malaysia to New York, and there's a great difference between the yowl of the tiger and the rattle of the L, but in the city that night there stalked the lust of the jungle killers and a man who had one eye. . . .

I have been guilty of using such a mechanism to shoot out in high, but I don't let the paragraph stand until I am pretty doggone sure that I've got everything it takes in the way of plot and menace to back it up.

If you were to take all the suspense out of a story, no matter how many unusual facts and characters you had in it, I don't think it would be read very far.

If you were to take every blow of action out of a story and still leave its suspense (this is possible, because I've done it) you might still have a fine story, probably a better story than before.

There is not, unhappily, any firm from which you can take out a suspense insurance policy. The only way you can do it is to make sure that the reader is sitting there tensely wondering which of two or three momentous things is going to happen first. If you can do that, adroitly to some of those manuscripts which have come bouncing back, they may be made to stay put.

Dancing with Dinosaurs

by
Charles D. Eckert

About the Author

Charles D. Eckert has worked as a night watchman, a professional actor, guitarist, singer, radio announcer, songwriter, photo-ad model, voice-over artist, stuntman, lighting designer, waiter . . . whatever comes to hand. Along the way, he earned a Bachelor of Science degree from the University of Indianapolis, Indiana. In 1976 he met Robert Silverberg briefly at the World Science Fiction Convention. Which made it all the sweeter that Robert Silverberg was among the judges who awarded this story a prize.

About the Illustrator

Allison Hershey lives in a very creative household in Granada Hills, California; SF fans, artists, computer programmers and musicians. She attended UC Berkeley and majored in sociology. She's drawn all her life, and plans to write and illustrate in the future. However, it should be noted that although she plans to write—and, indeed, has finally started, with a children's fantasy book—she was so excited to hear Frank Kelly-Freas talking about the Illustrators' Contest that she promptly handed him her entry. (Whereas we have yet to hear from her on the Writers' Contest.)

Illustrated by Allison Hershey

If LIBERTAS is a free colony, why do we have homework?

My teacher, Ms. Henderson, gave our class three different papers to write: 1) "Tell Us About Yourself," 2) "This Is My Family," and 3) "My Most Memorable Experience." Because of what happened, Carla—I mean, Ms. Henderson—said I could do them all at once and still get credit. Teachers can be nice when they want to be. Besides, I guess I've put them off for as long as I can.

Daddy is letting me write this on his best computer because NANA has *V*oice *A*ctivated *D*ictation capability. My old desktop does not have VAD. Also, I broke my arm. So, I can't type. I'll tell how that happened, later. Meanwhile, I still hate writing assignments. But Daddy says I should always do my best at anything I try to do.

So, here goes.

TELL US ABOUT YOURSELF

My name is Kimiko Viola Clarke.

I was born on the L-5 orbital colony LIBERTAS in the year 2079. I am eleven years old. I have long dark hair, like my mother, and green eyes, like my father. I don't mind the freckles, much. I am 4' 3" tall and I weigh 72 lbs. I'm kind of skinny, I suppose, but I guess I like myself. Sort of. Even if that dorky Jimmy Collins does not. Well, who needs him anyway? He still likes frogs & lizards and things like that.

Yuk.

Although I do like dinosaurs. They're neat. Mommy and Daddy bought a new copy of an old hologram by somebody named Spielberg, and it's called "The Land Before Time." Anyway, it has the cutest little dinosaurs and they dance away like anything. Whenever we're playing the holo I can't help but run right into the middle of them and dance along.

It's fun.

I go to Ms. Henderson's school in N-section. My parents say she is the best around, so they send me there. I study Reading, Writing, Math, Biological Science, and Computer Technology. I make decent grades—although I know I can always do better—and I'm really not sure what I want to be when I grow up, yet. But there's lots of time left before I decide. Mommy and Daddy say I can be just about anything I want to be. So, I should take my time and make the best decision when I *know* what it ought to be. Does that make sense to you? I think it does.

Anyway, that's enough about me.

THIS IS MY FAMILY

My Daddy is Alvin E. Clarke. He used to be President & CEO of Protech, Inc., the security firm that has the contract for LIBERTAS. He's now a member of the LIBERTAS Board of Directors. My Mommy is Muri Inouye Clarke. *She* is now President & CEO of Protech, Inc. I am not sure how that came about, really, but both of them seem to be pretty happy about it. So, I guess it's O.K.

We live at 338 Jefferson Avenue, Monticello, in R-section.

Did I tell you I was named for my grandmothers? Well, I was. My grandmother Inouye is my mom's mother. Her name is Kimiko. I love her very much. She teaches me about bonsai trees and something called the Tea Ceremony. I listen & watch, and try to copy her movements exactly. I really do. But she has more patience than anybody, especially me.

My grandmother Clarke lives at the Tycho Base Nursing Home, on the Moon. I don't know her very well because she's sick—something about her mind—so Viola doesn't know us when we visit her. Mommy says we would go more often, but it makes Daddy sad to see *his* mommy the way she is. So, we visit her on special occasions.

I wish Grandma Clarke wasn't so sick.

My grandfather Inouye's name is Stephen. He is in charge of an Import/Export concern called Tokyo Bay, Ltd. He's a very nice man. Grandpa Inouye isn't as tall as my Daddy but he is a big man, too. He teaches me about Japan and about the traditions of the family. My Daddy teaches me about traditions, as well, but they're different.

My grandfather Clarke is dead. I never knew him. He was one of the founders of LIBERTAS and was in charge of the construction. He died while LIBERTAS was being built. But Daddy tells me all about him.

I am very proud to be a Clarke.

I have several aunts and uncles. Well, not really. My parents don't have any brothers or sisters. Neither do I. But Daddy says that he and Mom are working on it. Whatever that means. Anyway, my parents' friends have all become my uncles and aunts. It's nice.

Paul Stowiski is from Kentucky. Uncle Paul is about the biggest man I've ever seen. He's even taller than Daddy. But Daddy is more bulky. Still, Uncle Paul is huge. But he's a nice big bear, for all that. He takes me to the zero-g gym and we work out together. He can do anything, seems like.

Uncle Paul is my friend.

Blair Keitle is real smart. Uncle Blair is from Australia. He is in charge of our Astroengineers Department. He helps me with my math homework. Uncle Blair talks kind of funny, sometimes. But I think it's cute. Uncle Paul has another word for it. But Uncle Blair says that Paul is from Kentucky and wouldn't know the "King's English" if it waltzed up and bit his bum.

Whatever that means.

Raoul Alvarez is an officer with Protech, just like Uncle Paul. But Uncle Raoul is smaller than most of the other officers. Yet it doesn't seem to make any difference. Because everybody respects my Uncle Raoul. He is very good at what he does. And that's important. He's also very nice to me, and I like him. I guess that's important, too.

Benjamin Avimba is a Zulu warrior. Well, that's what he says. And Uncle Benjamin wouldn't lie to me. He came to LIBERTAS from a place called South Africa. He told me that things were very bad there before the revolution. And afterwards, things got much, much worse. Maybe I'm selfish, but I'm glad he's here. His face is lean and strong and shiny black. I think he's pretty. Yet Uncle Benjamin is a boy and boys don't like to be told they're pretty. I know. But I couldn't help it, once, so I told him anyway. He just smiled, hugged me, and said that I was the only person who could get away with saying that. Isn't that nice? Anyway, Daddy says that when the time comes, he'll have Uncle Benjamin teach me to shoot.

"Avimba is the best shot I've ever seen," Daddy said, and he ought to know.

Rae Meijers is a doctor. She owns the Infirmary of Caduceus. I go to her when I don't feel good and she fixes me right up. That's nice. Auntie Rae is Mom's friend and she's mine, too. I think maybe I might like to be like her when I grow up.

Jennifer Lanne owns the Friedman Lounge. Auntie Jen is the prettiest lady I know. Except for Mom, of course. I'll never look like either of them. But Daddy says that isn't everything. Besides, *he* thinks I'm beautiful.

Daddies are like that.

Auntie Jen is from Atlanta, Georgia. She and Uncle Raoul like each other. It's neat. Anyway, I'm not suppose to go into the Friedman Lounge, yet. But Auntie Jen lets me come in on Saturday mornings to help with the restocking, and to wipe the glasses, and do all kinds of neat stuff to help her out. She pays me, too. Daddy says he'll take me there officially when I get older enough.

Did I tell you that I love my Daddy?

Anyway, now you know all about my family. I love them all very much. They love me, too. And they look out for me and everything. I guess I'm pretty lucky.

Don't you think?

MY MOST MEMORABLE EXPERIENCE

My most memorable experience is easy to remember. That is, it's hard to think about and that makes it easy to remember. If you know what I mean? Auntie Rae—I mean, Dr. Meijers—says that it's good to talk about it even though it brings back the hurt & stuff. I really don't know why grownups tell kids dumb things like that, sometimes. But Mommy and Daddy said that I should try to do what Auntie Rae says.

So, here goes.

I was walking home after school. Jimmy Collins said that he'd walk with me. But he stood me up. That's not the first time. Once, I asked him if he wanted to go exploring in the airducts. I told him I'd been doing it for a long time and that I knew the way. So, he shouldn't worry about getting lost. He wanted to ask his parents. I said: "No, dummy, don't do that. They'll say *no*. Grownups always say no when you want to have fun. Don't you know that?" But Jimmy said he wasn't sure. Finally, I talked him into it and we made a date. But he stood me up. Just like now.

What a dork.

Anyway, I was so angry with him that I took a shortcut through F & G-section, or "Fun & Games," as it's called. I knew better. My parents have told me often enough. But I was miffed at Jimmy and, besides, I wanted to get home.

I never saw him before.

But, as I was walking around him, he grabbed me. I don't remember seeing anyone else in the corridor, at the time, so I don't suppose anybody saw me struggling. Anyway, the man put a huge, rough hand over my mouth. It smelled like stale fish and Auntie Jen's old beer glasses. I gagged. But before I could bite him, he hit me. Hard. I had never felt anything like that before, ever.

I can count the number of times Daddy has spanked me on the fingers on one hand, and still have fingers left over. It hurt, sure. But it *never* hurt anything like this. I guess Daddy wasn't really trying to hurt me. But this man was.

And he did.

I don't remember too much, after that, except that he took me to someplace dark. But there were flashing lights, like somebody was taking old-timey pictures. Then he started touching me. Bad touching touches. Over and over again. I still don't know why. I asked him why, but he wouldn't tell me. He just laughed quietly and breathed heavy. And then . . . *he did bad things to me.*

The things he did hurt me so very, very much.

After what seemed the longest time, the man got up off the bed and went into the lavatory. To pee, I guess. And as I lay there, quivering, I could smell the sheets. They smelled just as bad as he did. Just like him, in fact. But I wiped my tears on them, anyway.

I really don't know how I did it, because I was so scared, but I got up and went over to the vent I saw in the wall beside the bed. I didn't even stop to put on my clothes. Just hit the quick-release on the vent grate and it fell away, like they all do. Maybe it was a good thing I had explored the airducts a lot. I don't know. But it sure came in handy, now.

I put the grate aside and crawled into the opening. It was one of the smaller ducts, so I knew the man wouldn't be able to follow. I just squeezed and wormed my way forward for all I was worth. All I wanted to do was to get clear of that awful person, as fast as I could manage it.

I had never been in these ducts before, so I really didn't know where I was or where I was going. That didn't seem to be as important as just getting away. Sometimes, though, the ducts branch off at odd angles; so, you have to know them like a map. And I didn't know these. When the drop came, I wasn't prepared for it. I fell about 2 meters.

That was when I broke my arm.

You know, it seems like just when you sort of get used to the way something hurts, something else comes along that hurts *worse*. Why is that? Can anybody explain that to me? I'd sure like to know.

Anyway, I had to straighten out my arm because it was bent funny. Guess I fainted. Sort of. When I came out of it, I started crawling forward again. I sure didn't want to go back. By this time, I was passing vent grates, at last. I couldn't see anyone, but I called out just the same. I suppose no one was at home. So, I went on.

I finally got to a vent that showed a lot of people. They looked like they were having a party. The music and everything was real loud. And, as I peered through the grate, I saw somebody I knew. It was Auntie Jen!

I was in the wall of the Friedman Lounge!

It took a while to get her attention because, as I said, the music and the people were so loud. But I finally saw her look around, as if she were searching for something or someone who shouldn't be there. I knew she was looking for the source of my voice, so I kept calling. I almost cried—

maybe I really did—when she came over to the vent to look in.

"Kimi," she said, "what in the world are you doing in there?"

"Oh, Auntie Jen," I said, "just get me out, please!"

She opened the vent and pulled me free. I guess I was sort of a mess, because she started blubbering right then, when she saw me. I suppose I fainted, again.

Sort of.

When I woke up, I knew I was in the infirmary of Caduceus because I saw Auntie Rae looking down at me. I turned my head slightly and I saw Mom. She looked kind of tired but she was smiling at me, anyway. Auntie Jen was there, too. Somebody was standing in the shadows but I couldn't make them out at first.

There were a lot of questions about what happened and about how I was feeling. I wasn't in any pain, but I was sort of woozy. If you know what I mean? And I really didn't feel like answering any questions but I wasn't in any shape to do much about it.

Finally, the big shadow moved and came into the light. It was my Daddy. I had never seen such a look on his face before. I smiled at him and he smiled back.

"I'm O.K., now, Daddy," I said. "Honest."

"I know you are, Punkin'," he said, quietly. "Your job, right now, is just to get well. Promise?"

"I promise."

"That's my girl."

It was the first time I had ever seen my Daddy cry.

I found out about the rest of the story by piecing together things I heard from both Mommy and Daddy, Uncle Paul, Uncle Raoul, Grandpa Inouye, Uncle Blair, and

Uncle Benjamin. Everybody added something a little different, but I think here is what happened.

By the way, did I tell you that I love my mom? Well, I do. And if I can grow up to be half the lady she is, I'll be something else, again. She helped me a lot, while I was getting well. I think she's just wonderful.

Anyway, Mom said that she hadn't seen Daddy so angry since she didn't know when. He had Uncle Blair rig up a camera on the end of one of the servo-bots which clean and maintain the airducts. They put the bot into the vent at the Friedman Lounge and programmed it to retrace my path.

Uncle Benjamin, Uncle Blair, and Daddy monitored the bot from the Protech offices security room. They had the servo gather evidence all along the way. I guess I was bleeding from more than my broken arm, because they gathered blood samples from the duct surfaces nearly the whole way back to that terrible man's room.

When they zoomed in with the camera through the slots of the replaced vent grate, they recorded him actually developing one of the pictures of the bad things he did to me. Uncle Blair said that when that bit was recorded, Daddy whispered: "Gotcha, you son-of-a-bitch."

Daddy doesn't talk that way often, but I guess he did then.

Uncle Raoul and Uncle Paul were standing by and, when the call came, they went to pick the man up. Uncle Raoul said that Uncle Paul kicked down the door, rushed in, and was shaking the fellow like a terrier mouthing a rat. So, Uncle Raoul had to make him stop. Which wasn't as easy as it sounds, I guess.

Anyway, here on LIBERTAS there is a thing called "The Code." It is a combination of Japanese *Bushido*, Hispanic *Duello*, and old Anglo *Honour.* I don't really understand it, yet, but I suppose it boils down to—in some cases—"Eye for an Eye." Many people don't agree with it. But that's one of the reasons why we're out here and they're back hugging dirt, so they say.

What happened was, according to Uncle Benjamin, my father and his friends made an oath. They then chose a place, weapons, and the rules. It gets pretty complicated from here, but I suppose it went something like this:

The man who did the bad things to me was given clothes, a knife, and taken to a deserted corridor in Y-section, which is still under construction. He was granted three minutes head start. I am told it took a bit of persuasion to convince him it was his only chance, but he finally got the message.

During the three minutes, a formal ritual took place. Uncle Paul gave Daddy a pair of new SureGrip boots, the latest thing, he and my Daddy being close to the same size and all. Daddy put them on. Uncle Blair installed a special recorder on Daddy's belt that was "So good it will pick up your thoughts, if you're not careful, mate." Then my Uncle Raoul gave Daddy a .50 cal. Ruger derringer, with exploding bullets, for back-up. My Uncle Benjamin presented Daddy with a Zulu charm to wear, and said: "You do not need strength or courage, my friend, for you have those in abundance. But this will keep your heart pure and your steps true."

Then Daddy embraced his friends, each in turn.

At last, Grandpa Inouye held out his own Bushido Blade, in its sheath. Daddy bowed and accepted the gift. He then held the blade by the pommel and extended its sheathed point toward my grandfather. Grandpa Stephen grasped the sheath and both men pulled, unsheathing the blade together.

My grandfather has told me that once such a blade is drawn it cannot be resheathed without being blooded.

After embracing my grandfather, Daddy turned and walked down the corridor. His friends watched him disappear into the cold metal hallway. But each one has told me that their hearts and minds were with him, every step he took.

Daddy's SureGrip boots made absolutely no sound at all.

I am much better, now, by the way. And the first thing I did when Auntie Rae let me go home was to attend a party in my honor. Every person I know and love was there. Even Jimmy Collins, who said he was sorry he stood me up and would be happy to walk me home anytime.

I guess he's not such a dork, after all.

The best part was when my parents played my favorite hologram for me. It was hard to manage with my broken arm in its sling, and all, but I could still dance. So, I rushed right into the middle of them, just like always.

I really love dancing with dinosaurs.

By the way, Ms. Henderson, I saw you at the party, too. You seemed to be having a very good time. In fact, you were talking and getting all mushy with my Uncle Benjamin. Do you think our class might like to know about that?

What is a good grade worth, Ms. Henderson?

KIMI,
YOUR GRADE IS:
        A
AND <u>NOT</u> BECAUSE YOU
WROTE THAT LAST PART. I
<u>DON'T CARE WHO KNOWS</u>
ABOUT YOUR UNCLE BENJAMIN AND
ME. WHEN YOU ARE OLD ENOUGH
TO UNDERSTAND WHY,
I'LL BE THERE; SMILING!

                              —Carla

Water
by
John W. Randal

About the Author

John W. Randal earned his B.A. in English from La Roche College in Pittsburgh in 1987, and has spent the past three years working on a variety of short stories, a novel, and a book-length collection of poetry. He has sold to Aboriginal Science Fiction and Pandora. He is 25, unmarried and lives in Pittsburgh. "Water" was his eighth entry in the Contest; we're glad he didn't get discouraged, for his winning story is both haunting and beautiful.

About the Illustrator

Beryl Bush was born in Hot Springs, Arkansas, and grew up in Missouri and Indiana. Although there were scant opportunities for formal art instruction, she was fortunate in having a home environment where art supplies and reference books were readily available. When the family finally settled in Kentucky, she graduated Summa Cum Laude from Western Kentucky University with a Bachelor of Fine Arts degree.

Since then she has worked for Harper's Bazaar magazine as an editor, gotten a Masters from the famous Pratt Institute, and then gone to work for Christie's, the auction house. Recently, she has resigned her full-time position, continuing to work for them on a freelance basis, while developing herself as an illustrator.

Illustrated by Beryl Bush

Inside the house they sit, scattered throughout the many rooms like a handful of dewy flower petals.

It rains and the house quietly shudders around them.

Sarabeth poses on the window seat, watching the silvery runnels braid and shift on the water-splashed glass. At her feet Tamby and Lou play jacks. She's thinking of love and distant lands, blurred by imagination. Always a romantic, her dreams are framed by the springlike tinkle of the children's laughter. With a lowered head and a slow blink, Sarabeth sighs.

Father and Mother are in the Den. Father reads and Mother watches the thin smoke from his pipe thread itself into the moisture-laden air. It's like a stream, gray with age, she muses. Or a slow-moving river seen from a great distance. After concentrating on this image for a moment or two, Mother is struck with a moment of vertigo. She is falling up into the ceiling.

She starts upon the soft aqua cushions of the couch and clasps one hand to her breast with a soft, startled cry. Father arches an elegant silvery eyebrow at her and then returns to his paper.

Upstairs, in the faded blue bathroom, Uncle leans over the washbasin, studying the way the water swirls smoothly down the dark drain. . . .

"Here are the keys—you got the directions from Mr. Morrison?"

"Yes, he drew me a map."

"You shouldn't have any problems getting there—the roads are well kept."

"It's been empty now for how many years?"

"Twelve—the amount of time Doctor Waterson specified in his will. We're very grateful to get it back on the market."

"Odd thing to put in a will."

"Doctor Waterson was considered to be rather eccentric."

"What was he a doctor of?"

"Excuse me?"

"What was Doctor Waterson a doctor of?"

"Oh, I don't know—I don't think he ever said."

Curtains of rain brush lightly against the house.

Tamby and Lou have fallen asleep at Sarabeth's feet. She watches them for a while, then turns and resumes gazing out the window. He would be a knight—in platinum armor with a silken-white plume. She closes her crystal-green eyes for a moment and softly smiles. The smooth skin of her face, framed by long, raven-black hair and illuminated by watery-gray light, appears to be as white as a pure sea pearl.

Uncle shuts off the spigot and leaves the bathroom. He makes his slow and careful way to the attic. When he gets there he uses a small silver key shaped like a sea horse to unlock the heavy oak door.

A subtle dread is settling upon his heart, like Autumn leaves slowly drifting to the bottom of a cool pond. With a gnarled, driftwood gray hand, he opens the attic door.

The dim and musty room is sheathed in crowded shelves and holds one arched window that casts a shaft of pale light over a cluttered desk. Nobody has been here in a

long time and the papers on the heavy desk are as brown
and crumbly as old kelp.

Uncle brushes off the dusty chair and sits behind the
desk. The only sound is that of the falling rain, running and
washing over the water-slicked shingles above his gray-
haired head.

In the Den, Mother and Father both watch the smoke
from Father's pipe as it swirls and eddies along the ceiling.
Father's paper lies on the floor beside his chair—forgotten.
It is as aged and suddenly fragile as the papers in the
attic. . . .

The car squeaks and rattles along the narrow, but well
kept, dirt road. Even with the air conditioning on, the
humidity is oppressive.

He turns on the radio while he drives—the reception
leaves much to be desired. Through soft waves of static, the
DJ's voice comes through.

". . . showers bring May flowers but this is ridiculous!
Without question this is the wettest Spring we've had in
twelve years. . . ."

He loosens his tie as the DJ's voice dissolves into a powerful surge of static that sounds like a distant waterfall. He's
worried about the three-week set at the Glenwash Food Market. The plan-a-grams for the layout of products on the
shelves still haven't arrived and the set begins on Monday!
He sighs and rubs the back of his neck. Pam has classes
today, so he is riding out to take a look at the house—
hopefully it won't need that much work. A bead of sweat
tumbles down the side of his face like a tiny raindrop.

Tall trees with rain-slicked leaves line the narrow road
and, as they blur by in an emerald smear, it is easy enough
to imagine that he is driving through the vegetation at the
bottom of a deep lake.

• • •

Sarabeth watches a single, jewel-like drop of water trembling at the top of the windowpane. Just before it breaks free to run down the cool glass, she kisses it.

My prince. . . .

Her coral-pink lips leave no mark on the window.

In the Den, Mother and Father hold each other in silence.

Uncle moves some papers on the desk—they crumble into sandy dust at his touch. His fingernails glimmer like the inner surface of old sea shells—opalescent white. Though he is the oldest in the family, he has never left the house. And now, as he glances out of the single grimy window to the rainy world beyond, he feels a moment of trembling panic.

Beneath the papers a thick book lies open.

Not daring to touch the pages, Uncle blows away some dust. His breath raises a gray cloud that swirls like sediment in the moist air. Thunder rumbles loudly, as if huge waves are crashing somewhere above the glistening roof of the house.

Stifling a sneeze, Uncle hunches over the book. The water-stained pages are filled with scribbled notes. Most of the ink is long faded and discolored. He can make out only one word: *Asrai.* . . .

The car splashes through a muddy puddle and he turns off the radio with a quick, irritated twist of his wrist. Rain sheets his windshield and is swept clean by the rhythmic flip of the wipers.

He slows for a moment to consult his hand-drawn map.

As he continues, he passes a solitary pile of snow—the last remnant of a magically long winter. It is slowly melting away in the warm, relentless rain.

Uncle gently brushes his hand across the page. Half of it immediately crumbles into dust—but a little more of the words on the remaining half can now be read. Most of it is fragmented, a word here, a portion of a sentence there:

...not all of the Asrai are female...Faerie lore states...into a pool of water when captured or exposed to sunlight.

The specimens...photosensitive...leads to profound and rapid...I have found that...partially stabilized the reaction...for as many as a dozen years....

...are intelligent, but...memory loss...can't leave the house...after I die...the will...for the time they have left....

The rest is lost to time and decay. When Uncle tries to turn the page the entire book crumbles into dust. He shudders and looks again toward the window. It is enough. Uncle's suspicions are confirmed. He rubs his suddenly moist sea-blue eyes with one weathered hand....

The rain whispers and parts like a softly swaying curtain as the car rounds a bend in the road, reflected light flashing from its damp windshield.

He peers ahead and can just make out the house at the end of a long, gracefully winding drive. He stops the car, rolls down the window and sticks out his head, braving the rain to get a clearer glimpse of the house.

Yes—that's it. It doesn't look too bad.

Satisfied, but damp from the rain, he pulls his head back in, rolls up the window and continues on. Some droplets have splattered onto his map and the lines and notes now run and smear together as they fade.

The Den is now empty.

Sarabeth finds that Tamby and Lou are gone—funny, she didn't hear them leave. She sighs and looks outside again. In the distance she sees a glimmer, a pure silvery reflection. No, not silver—it's platinum. The shine of her prince's gleaming armor! She presses herself against the glass, with her heart fluttering like a delicate sea creature, caught in a fisherman's net.

In the attic, Uncle sits back in the chair and folds his hands in his lap—waiting. "Our time is past, Doctor," he whispers in a voice like the cast of sea-spray.

"Long past. . . ."

He pulls his windbreaker over his head and rushes through the rain and onto the porch. Blowing and shaking his arms, he pauses for a moment and watches the rain slow and begin to slacken off. He pulls the keys from his pocket and unlocks the front door.

The rain has now stopped.

He takes a handkerchief from his pocket and dries his face.

Everything smells fresh and clean and the humidity seems to have vanished. The scrubbed silence is accentuated by the tinkling drip of raindrops from the edge of the porch roof.

He takes the cool silver doorknob in one hand and pulls. With a crack like the breaking of an old seal, the door opens.

Sarabeth blinks and turns toward the sound, a smile forming on her soft lips.

Somewhere a clock chimes out the hour.

With a puff and a swirl, her pale form dissolves into a slowly dissipating cloud of mist. . . .

He walks into the empty house, whistling and twirling the keys on his index finger. As he strolls past a lovely window seat, something cool touches his cheek like a soft kiss.

He notices that there is a faint sheen of condensation all over his body—as if he had just walked through a land-bound cloud.

The condensation carries with it a subtle perfume.

He smiles and shakes his head.

"Have to do something about this moisture," he says as he opens a window. . . .

Upstairs in the attic, the arched window casts a shaft of pale light across a cluttered desk and an empty chair. For a moment, a thread of mist swirls in that watery beam—then it, too, vanishes.

A Branch in the Wind

by
Bruce Holland Rogers

About the Author

Bruce Holland Rogers was born in 1958 in Tucson, Arizona, but seems to have spent the bulk of his life in Colorado—which makes him one of four Colorado writers in this book. The bulk of his time in the United States, that is; he has also spent at least some time in Colombia, Peru and Ecuador. He is currently teaching in the University of Colorado's Division of Continuing Education. His credentials in various occupations and employments are considerable. He has had two previous stories published in The Magazine of Fantasy and Science Fiction, *one in June, 1982, and one in June, 1989.*

About the Illustrator

Kelly Faltermayer is 24, and works on Houston, Texas, community newspapers, preparing ads and doing pasteup. He is originally from El Salvador; he came to the United States in 1980.

After graduating from high school, he spent one year at the Otis Parsons School of Design in Los Angeles, but then went back to Houston, and enrolled in the Art Institute there. He then got his present job. He does art at nights and on weekends; encouraged by a co-worker, he looks forward to a career in illustration.

He wanted to tell her the whole story, of course, but he couldn't, so at breakfast Scott said, "I just need some time alone. It's not you. There's nothing wrong. I just need a few nights up here by myself."

Patricia sipped her coffee and looked around at the one-room cabin. Rain fell against the windowpanes. "It'll be hard to sleep in my own apartment," she said. "I'm getting used to this place."

He took her hand. "It won't be long," he said. "Just a few nights."

She looked at him and smiled, and he missed her already. "All right," she said. "I don't understand this, but all right."

"I'll call," he said. "As soon as I'm ready, I'll call."

After they had done the dishes together, he walked her to her car and then stood in the mud and rain as she drove off. With a sigh, he went back inside.

He shook the raindrops out of his coat, hung it up, and sat down again at the kitchen table. He unplugged the telephone, and then he looked at the five unfinished pots that sat in their drying rack beside the electric kiln. "All right, Sharon," he said quietly. "It's time we finished."

For a long time after Sharon had died, Scott had not slept well. He would wake up five or six times before morning and listen to the night wind in the woods around the tiny cabin, listen to the sound of his own breathing.

Illustrated by Kelly Faltermayer

Sharon's friends, David and Julie, tried to get him out more. "You need to meet new people," they said. "You can't stay cooped up in that little place for the rest of your life. It's been two years." As though two years were a long time.

He didn't want to seem ungrateful. David and Julie owned the gallery where Sharon had sold most of her ceramics. They had done a lot for her, so he accepted their dinner invitations, met the women they hoped he would like, and endured uncomfortable gaps of silence in the small talk.

Most of the time, the cabin was a mess. Sometimes Julie would drive up the narrow, muddy road to bring him a casserole and, seeing what the place was like inside, would scold him gently and do the dishes. Between these visits, he let the plates crust over and scraped and washed them only as they were needed. Mice lived under the sink.

Sharon had left a rack of unfired pots between the kiln and the potter's wheel. He thought sometimes that he should do something with the pots, throw them out or break them or cover them with a sheet or give them away or have someone finish them. But he did nothing. He couldn't touch them without crying, and once the crying started it always took a long time to be finished with him.

One night, during a light rain, he woke up to hear a sound at the front window. *Tip tip tip. Tip tip tip.*

A branch in the wind, he thought, closing his eyes. He tried to go back to sleep, but the sound was like a dripping water faucet: rhythmic but irregular. It would stop for a time and then start. During the pauses, he found he was listening to hear it begin again.

Scott put a pillow over his head, but still he heard it distinctly, *tip tip tip,* as though it came from inside his skull.

All right, he thought, sitting up and swinging his feet out of the bed. I'll go break off the tip of the branch.

And then he saw a familiar silhouette in the window's

dim square and watched as the black shadow of a hand rose to tap the pane. *Tip tip tip.*

His pulse throbbed in his throat as he crossed the dark room, the old floorboards creaking under his feet. He opened the door and started to feel for the light switch.

"Don't," she said. "Don't turn on the light." She sounded hoarse, but there was no mistaking her voice.

"I won't," he said, withdrawing his hand. He could feel the rain on his face as a cold mist and heard the blood rushing in his ears. He strained his eyes trying to see her clearly.

"Aren't you going to let me in?"

He opened the door some more and stepped aside. The floor was silent as she brushed past him.

Scott closed the door and took her in his arms. She was muddy, and her skin was cold. She trembled as he held her.

"I've missed you."

"I know," she said. Her breath smelled like freshly turned soil.

"You're cold," he said. "I'll make some tea, some black currant, with honey, the way you like it." He guided her to the table and then felt his way to the cupboard.

When he turned the knob on the stove, the blue flame that erupted under the tea kettle gave a dim glow to the room.

"How did you. . . ."

"Shh," she whispered. "No questions. I'm here."

"All right," he said. "I won't ask." He sat across from her and gave her gritty fingers a squeeze.

Later, when he kissed her, he felt the grit on her lips and on her tongue. Her kiss was stiff, but her arms pulled him tight against her damp body.

In the morning, the cabin was very warm and she was dead again, her body rigid next to him. The red mud on her skin and in the sheets was drying and flaking.

He carried her into the woods and buried her there in the black earth. Then he washed the sheets, emptied the cup of tea she hadn't touched, and scrubbed the reddish mud up from the floor. He noticed that there was a lot of the mud over by the kiln, and then realized that the kiln was on—that was why the room was so warm. The unfired pots were missing. In the afternoon, when the kiln had shut itself off and cooled, Scott opened it. There were the pots.

He waited up for her for the next three nights, but the tapping at the window didn't come. Through several nights and then several weeks, it didn't come.

He turned down dinner invitations from David and Julie, slept during the day and waited through the night. David and Julie started to call or visit every day. Scott cleaned the place up a little to show them he was all right, but that wasn't enough for them. "This isolation isn't good for you," Julie insisted.

Still the tap at the window didn't come. To get David and Julie to stop coming up every day, he agreed to come to dinner a few times.

When he had almost given up hope, he woke one night to hear the *tip tip tip* at the pane.

There was a full moon that night, and he could see her clearly in the gray light outside the window. When he stepped out and took her in his arms he said, "Why did you go?"

"No questions," she said. "Remember?"

"All right," he said, holding her, swaying with her under the moon.

The mud drying in the sheets the next morning was black, more like the soil near the cabin than the red clay of her first grave. When he got up, Scott noticed that she had been busy again while he was asleep. There was raw glaze on the pots that sat again on the drying rack. One more firing and they would be done.

He brought her to where he thought he had buried her the last time, but he couldn't find that grave. Everywhere, the soil looked undisturbed and layered with last year's leaves, so he dug a new hole. Then he went back again to clean the sheets and scrub the floor.

He started to wait again, though this time he knew it might be a while before she returned. He gave the cabin a thorough cleaning, hoping this would discourage David and Julie, who would see that he finally had his life in order again, but his apparent recovery only convinced them that this was the time to work harder at finding him a companion. He accepted every other invitation and always exited soon after the dishes were cleared. At home, he slept fitfully, waking often to listen for the sound that did not come.

And then one night at dinner with David and Julie, he met Patricia.

She was short, dark-haired, and not particularly attractive, but she had made him laugh at dinner. With some prodding from David and Julie, he had agreed to take Patricia to a movie the next night. The night after that, he had dinner with her at her apartment. They stayed up almost until dawn talking mostly about themselves. She asked about Sharon, and he talked more about her that night than he had since she had died. He drove home tired and happy, and then all his happiness fell away when he saw the cabin.

The grass and weeds near the house were lying near the ground, trampled, as though by someone who had walked around the house all night, tapping at the windows, asking to come in.

He sat up the next two nights, waiting, but the tap on

the window didn't come. He unplugged the phone and slept during the day.

Patricia drove to the cabin, and when he saw her, he was ashamed for not answering the phone. He told her that talking about Sharon so much had brought it all back to him. She said she understood. She took him to dinner in town, and they spent the night at her apartment.

When he went back to the cabin, Patricia went with him and was soon staying every night, making the drive down to work each morning.

One night he woke up and felt Patricia's body pressed against his in the darkness. The wind breathed softly through the trees, and in the darkness he heard something tap gently on the front window. *Tip tip tip.*

He closed his eyes. He thought of the glazed pots waiting to be fired. Unfinished, the raw glaze would gradually chip and flake away into dust.

Tip tip tip.

A branch in the wind, he thought to himself. It's a branch in the wind.

For a long time he lay awake, listening to the sound, hearing different branches tapping at different windows around the cabin. Before dawn it stopped, but he didn't sleep. And that was the morning when he told Patricia he needed time alone.

He waited, sleeping little, through the next two nights. And then on the third night, he heard it again.

Tip tip tip.

Scott got up. It was a moonless night, and he could barely see her in the darkness.

She silently moved past him into the room. When he closed the door and took her gently in his arms, she just stood there with her arms at her sides.

"It's all right," he said. He pressed his lips to her cold forehead. The mud this time smelled sour. "It's all right."

She never said a word.

In the morning, the kiln was cooling. He wrapped her body in the sheets and carried her deep into the woods. For the last time, he buried her.

Late in the afternoon, when he had cleaned the last of the mud from the floor, he opened the kiln. The glaze, which had been a light gray before the firing, was black and lustrous. Scott packed the pots carefully in a box for David and Julie.

A light wind had kicked up outside the cabin by the time he plugged the phone back in and called Patricia.

"I've missed you," he told her, and she said she missed him, too. The wind blew a branch against Scott's front window. The sound it made was chaotic, irregular. *Tap. Tip-a-tack-tack. Tip. Tap.* Scott felt something unwind inside himself, and then the feeling was gone. He took a deep breath. "Listen, Patricia," he said. "Why don't you drive on up. I don't want to be alone any more."

Riches Like Dust
by
Scot Noel

About the Author

Scot Noel is 32, married, and is Director of Operations and Planning for the Westmoreland (Pennsylvania) County Transit Authority. He lives in Latrobe, which he points out is where both the banana split and professional football were invented. He graduated Magna Cum Laude with a 4.0 in English from St. Vincent College, also of Latrobe. He first started to write in high school, after discovering a class indispensable to modern writers: Typing 101. At the present time, he is working on a novel.

About the Illustrator

Daniel S. Oman is 27, and originally from Dawson, Minnesota, by the South Dakota border. Recently discharged by the Army at Ft. Hood, Texas, where he was an E4 in Communications Security, he has gone back to Minnesota. There he pursues his hobbies, which are art and reading SF, and his occupation, which is the building and repair of guitars and violins. His art education consists of two years of high school, and one quarter of studio art and art history in college; he seems to have made more of that than anyone would expect, and we look forward to great things from him.

In a dark corner of the salvage ship *Zulu King,* Syreeta Davies carefully brought another cup of coffee to her lips. It had been more than a month since she had last spilled anything into a computer keyboard, and, if not for her near-exhaustion, she might have congratulated herself. Drifting and climbing on the screens before her, wave and bar graphs tried their best to keep her awake.

"Why do I listen?" she mumbled quietly. The meaning of the displays cut the legs from beneath her. Her ship might as well be scrap now, an empty, airless hulk picked to the bone by her competitors, for, soon and certainly, it would no longer be hers. If only she had help. She had stretched herself too thin this time, perhaps into bankruptcy.

"Would Madam like her coffee warmed?" a voice asked from the darkness behind her.

"Yes, Bryce, please." Without breaking the quiet mood in the lab, a robot moved forward, the silver carafe in its hand reflecting computer displays as it poured and then backed away. Robot Bryce had been with Syreeta the longest, one of three "skeletals" aboard ship, and, like the ship itself, an inheritance from Syreeta's mother.

"Madam appears disturbed," Bryce said. "Will there be anything further?"

"Yes, Bryce. The trade value of ten point six metric tons of Galidnium, one skeletal, one inoperative lander, and one slightly damaged tractor?" Syreeta asked.

Without so much as a heartbeat between her question

Illustrated by Daniel S. Oman

and his first syllable, Bryce replied: "Five thousand adjusted dollars, Madam. Why do you ask?"

"Because, my dear Bryce, I'm caught between a rock and a hard place. I'm going to have to sell off some things to keep from going bankrupt. Robot Hooke comes first to mind."

"Plus one lander and one tractor," Bryce said. If he had emotions, his voice did not betray them. "Where, however, does Madam plan on finding ten point six metric tons of Galidnium?"

"We're sitting on top of it," Syreeta answered. "Ship's computer made a mistake. There's no alien wreck here for us to salvage, just an old probe, or a satellite maybe. Whatever it is, it's been down here less than a week. Probably spiraled in after being trapped in orbit." She sighed a deep sigh and hoped it was not wasted on the machine behind her. If only her mother were still alive. . . . "You have to have some intuition when you look at these readings. You can't just match salvage profiles, no matter how good. . . ."

Syreeta let her words trail off. There was no use being angry at machines for being machines. She needed decision makers, intuitors, people with good common sense. She couldn't do it all. Unfortunately, people and Syreeta did not mix.

Something had been bothering her, a minor annoyance, a whisper of sound, a flash of static on the screens. Nothing in her sleep-starved thoughts had been able to put the whole of it together until now.

"If I may be so bold," Bryce started to say.

"Shut up," Syreeta ordered. "What the hell is that noise?"

"Sandstorm, Madam," Bryce replied.

"Sandstorm!" Syreeta said. She glanced to her screens. "With my antennas and lenses still recording?" She was up and past Bryce in a flash, finding her way through the darkness almost as well as he. "I'll feed Hooke to the metal mites," were the last words Bryce heard as Syreeta's footsteps pounded off toward the bridge.

At forty-three, Syreeta's speed from the lab to the bridge had decreased only slightly since her schooling days. In that long gone time she had raced from the mastery of her lessons to the bridge, eager for that applause best bestowed by approving parents. Yet a measure of disappointment often tainted that joy, approval not so easy a thing to wrest from her father's grasp.

"Ah, well," Syreeta thought as she rounded the corner onto the bridge, "now I count the pennies and keep the ship alive."

Before her in low light, a deck of consoles and screens led to a pair of seated figures, the command robots Hooke and Dawkins. Like Bryce, they took on human form, but thin and skeletal, their black metal skins a characteristic of servants over all of Manned space. Unlike Bryce, who wore a scribe's white cloak, these two sat dressed in costumes of Syreeta's own fancy: red coats and white belts as seen in the Imperial British Army, circa 1880. Two white helmets lay polished at their feet.

"Admit it, Hooke," Syreeta said at the top of her best blustering voice, "you've been programmed by one of my competitors to ruin me!" At the sound of her voice, Robot Hooke spun around from the command station, his helmet sent flying by an unintended kick. "The sensors, Hooke, the antennas! They're out there in a raging gale of sand."

"Well within specifications, Madam," Hooke said instantly. There might almost have been a touch of indignation in his ancient, well-crafted English. "We have wind at no more than force two, particle density at—"

"Look at this!" Syreeta stabbed an angry finger at two gauges. "You're cutting their useful life in half, letting them out there like that. I know they can survive it, man; that's not the point. Do you know how much it costs to recoat those lenses?''

In the silence that followed, Robot Dawkins ventured a reply. ''Madam had impressed upon us a need for urgency.''

''Fifty-two point nine adjusted dollars,'' Hooke said, finally.

''Read my lips, Hooke,'' Syreeta said. Then slowly, ''Rotate the lenses into shield position and bring those antennas down!'' With an angry swirl, she turned to stomp off the deck, but within a stride the futility of it hit her. ''I'm replacing you all with one of those new poly-droids next trip,'' she said without turning. As she left the bridge a small red light alerted her to another listener. ''That goes for you too, computer.''

Syreeta reached her bed and fell into it fully clothed. She was asleep in seconds, the winds of a nameless world continuing to pound her ship with sand.

By morning the storm had passed to a hundred and fifty kilometers south of their position. Neither wind nor cloud greeted Syreeta as she stepped down the ramp from *Zulu King,* only a brilliance so intense that she tinted her visor three times before feeling comfortable. The world before her was white with sand, salts, and drifting dunes. Behind her, *Zulu King* loomed like a giant sculpture of tubes, fins, and twisted cable.

''Good morning, Madam,'' Robot Hooke said as she approached the sensor drill. Robot Dawkins turned from operating a set of levers and wheels to offer his own greeting, both machines looking sharp in their uniforms, their helmets allowing a small but welcome line of shade to fall across their optic disks. By the looks of things a contact had already been placed against the surface of the buried probe, the object itself a mere ten meters beneath their feet.

"You can't tell there's been an impact here," Syreeta said, "not after that storm. All right, who's it belong to? Is this one of Colony Five's dumb time capsules or an old Earth satellite?

"Neither, I'm afraid, Madam," Hooke said. "While its hull and structural welds do appear contemporary, the readings on its internal affairs point toward an alien origin."

"It's active?" Syreeta asked. Her heart took two leaps forward.

"Even as we speak," Hooke continued, "the device below is extending 'tentacles' of a kind, running mineral samples and chattering on a number of internal frequencies. It appears to be analyzing its surroundings."

"Hooke," Syreeta said, "thanks for setting my alarm a little late this morning. I know I'm nasty when I'm tired."

Hooke bowed slightly. "You may thank the computer for that, Madam. A poly-droid, Madam? Madam might as well hire a human crew."

"Don't push it, Hooke," Syreeta fired back. She made her way past the robots to check the readings from the drill. As lines of data scrolled beneath a weather-beaten screen, her thoughts began to take wing. The object below was a recent addition to this world, and, despite the conventional appearance of its metallurgy, of alien design. That combination, recent and alien, pounded in Syreeta's blood like the beat of twin drums.

"They're here!" Syreeta shouted. She danced around the screen without taking her eyes from its scrolling green lines. Her boots sent fountains of sand up the sides of the drilling rig. "They're here!" For over a century, the standard doctrine of salvage had remained simple and unchanged: there are no live aliens, only dead ones. Civilizations might rise and fall, even spanning galaxies in the process, but no two starfaring peoples would be alive and active at the same time.

For untold ages, each new civilization could count upon the ruins of its predecessor, to provide knowledge, technology, medicine, and philosophies enough to engender a thousand sects. But until now, no piece of ancient metal had spoken so clearly of a living hand, of a caring assembly not in the millennia past but in the here and now of galactic time.

With the blood rushing in her head and threatening to crowd out every thought save those of fame and wealth, it took over a full minute before Syreeta could feel the ceramic finger tapping at her shoulder. "What?" She turned, impatiently.

"Madam," Robot Hooke stepped back a pace as he addressed Syreeta, "ship's computer would have a word with you. It would seem another salvage craft has entered orbit about this world."

With a turn so quick that she knocked Hooke off his feet, Syreeta scrambled back to the ship. She discarded helmet, gloves, and support pack on her way to the bridge, all the time feeling new levels of stress welling up from her gut. She fell back into the pilot's chair of *Zulu King,* bringing her communications gear into action beneath a flurry of snapping fingers. You don't jump claims. That code of the salvage operation remained clear, if not always perfectly observed.

"We are picking up the intruder's transponder," the computer informed Syreeta. "It is a class nine Exo-Tech hull, with the latest in 'Aero-Spatial' performance systems."

"Who gives a damn," Syreeta said. "What about her guns and shields?" The safety lock for Syreeta's missile battery rose beneath the pressure of her thumb. With a twist, a set of firing toggles lay exposed and backlit by a flashing ready light.

"Her identification beacon registers twenty varieties of missile, three frequencies of chemical laser, a host of jamming and electronic warfare devices, and a Command and

Control Battle Computer built by Orbital Dynamics. She is the *Metcalf,* and her owner is registered as one Sir Robert Sky.''

Syreeta called down her missiles. As the safety lock closed over the firing toggles, she bit her lips and reviewed a colorful set of phrases revolving around ''battle wagons'' and ''goddamn dreadnoughts.'' Not a word of it crossed her tongue. Her computer had established a communications link with the intruder, and each phrase now must be carefully weighed.

''I know a man with a death wish,'' Syreeta said into the microphone. ''Why are you intruding on my find?''

''Good day, My Dear,'' an electronically warped voice filtered into the control room. Syreeta could not tell if it was male or female. She knew only that it was backed by enough guns to make good any threat it might wish to pose. ''My title you will find to be Sir Sky,'' the voice continued, ''and if it is an uneasiness I have set in your heart, for that I apologize.

''If you can place a guilt to my presence above your ship, let it be an overconcern for one's fellow salvagers. My sensors show me a vessel, yours, that is of doubtful repair and in a condition most pitiful to behold. Has some untoward pride prevented you from releasing a signal of distress?''

''I see no point in insults,'' Syreeta began. Any uncertainty she may have felt in finding a further response disappeared as an alert beacon flashed from the sampler drill. Something was causing the dune beneath her rig to tilt. Suddenly the drill, its cables, and sensor packs flew into the air, a dozen tentacles replacing it in a wild flailing of chrome and steel. ''Shit!''

''A spicy use of the standard tongue, to be sure,'' the intruder's voice replied. It continued to ramble on about the nature of insults, the generosity of using the *Metcalf*'s time to aid a fellow traveler, and a variety of other veiled threats and colorful philosophies. Syreeta heard none of it. Outside her ship the alien tentacles now towering above Hooke and Dawkins had begun to release a fine spray into the morning breeze. Within seconds the robots were covered with it, brushing it away with the same fastidious attention their ancient military counterparts might have displayed.

"My God, what the hell is that?" Syreeta asked, realizing too late that she remained on an open channel. Jumping to her feet, she cut the transmission and switched to her sensor panel in a single motion.

"Polysilicon, silicon dioxide, and various trace metals," the computer answered, confirming the readings that Syreeta could see on the panels before her. "Size ranges appear to be from twenty to two hundred microns in diameter." Already the external cameras had begun to compensate, their lenses trying to rotate away a compounding layer of dust. A handful of lights began to flash red along the life-support console.

"You're bringing it in on the air filters," Syreeta said. "Seal the ship and switch to canned oxy. Pressurize the vents, blow that stuff back out of the system. Have you got a sample?"

"Our sample grids have been overloaded," the computer responded. "Clogged is the proper word. I'm arranging for a reasonable specimen to be taken in now, Madam."

"Madam," Robot Hooke appeared behind Syreeta, cuffing away clouds of gray dust from his sleeves, "the airlock decontamination gear appears unable to handle this volume of dust." Syreeta coughed once and then tried to strangle him.

After the dust settled and Robots Hooke and Bryce were at work sweeping away any possible contamination, Syreeta set about solving two problems at once.

"Have you got that, Dawkins?"

"Yes, Madam," the robot assured her. He had already discarded his red coat for a series of tool belts and programming cards. "I am to take the land rover south at top speed. Once under cover of a sandstorm, I am to launch an orbital probe equipped with camera and deep-scan radar."

"And I'll keep his attention so he doesn't see the launch," Syreeta added. "We've got to have a look at him. I don't believe his transponder. Nobody can afford all that shit." With a bow, Dawkins was on his way. Syreeta turned back to the master computer, rubbing her hands together to allay the itch within her palms. Her mother had always said that such an itch and imminent wealth were often one and the same. "Computer, report on Sir Robert Sky."

"No data available on Robert Sky," the computer said, "either as an independent, an employee of same, a corporate owner, or an employee of a corporation. The starship *Metcalf* is also without listing."

"He didn't just come out of nowhere."

"Perhaps not, Madam, but I am receiving communications on the emergency wave bands. Sir Sky is demanding that you speak with him." After two deep breaths, Syreeta engaged the channel.

"Ah, now be that a piece more hospitable," the lilting, mechanically disfigured voice said at once. "I had almost taken it upon myself to rescue this Syreeta Davies, so distressed were her last words in my ear. What has happened, My Dear?"

"I am not your 'dear,' and what has happened is none of your business." Syreeta rubbed her hands against her thighs, stifling a cough as she tried to think of a way to outwit this adversary. "What do you know about me?" She opted to stall for time.

"I've been following you—"

"Following me!"

"Following you for quite some time now," the voice continued. "Your hair is flaxen, your eyes hazel, and your breasts small but possessed of a certain teardrop radiance apt to attract the human male. I say this not that I may have any designs upon your flesh, but to redress any ill will my first approach may have caused. Above all, I admire that characteristic in you which causes you to voyage alone, to shun human company, to search for the gold at the end of the—"

"Can it!" Syreeta interrupted. "Pure and simple, this is my find and I intend to hold it." She felt a flush of warmth rise in her cheeks. Her hands had begun to burn.

"Surely you cannot intend to load, dress, and sell all three of the alien craft? Might I not propose the poverty of my services in helping with but one?"

"Three aliens?" Syreeta felt dizzy.

"Said so perfectly, it seemed without guile," the intruder responded. "But I will play. The device at your site is but one of three, the others each to its own continent. I feel in my heart that you will need assistance to recover full value."

"Computer," Syreeta asked, "can you verify?" Seconds of silence passed before she realized no answer had been forthcoming. "Computer, respond." Again, only silence.

"Are you in some difficulty, Dear One?" the intruder asked. "And if I may inquire, did you intend to run that land rover into a sand dune?"

"Dawkins," Syreeta called out on the local band. She felt her legs collapsing like sponges beneath her, every event whirling by with a rapidity she could no longer grasp and control. Punching up a blurred image, the lens recording it half buried in dust, Syreeta could see that the rover had not made it a hundred yards from the shadow of *Zulu King*.

Neither Dawkins nor the rover seemed able to answer her calls.

"God damn you!" Syreeta shouted up at the unseen dandy she imagined laughing so far above her. "What have you done?"

Syreeta swayed from side to side, struggling up along a feverish ladder toward a point of light she knew to be her conscious state. Heat washed over her. Her thoughts faded, then grew crisp, dreams of all her failures coming out of the darkness on the wings of bats.

"I don't like people, Mother," she said, her voice quavering. "Father says not to trust them." She watched the crowds of men and women working outside on the docks. "I'll stay with the ship. Bryce needs company."

One day, many years later, Bryce would hold her when her parents failed to return from the city. There had been a traffic crash.

"What! What happened?" Syreeta asked as she came to. She found her own bed beneath her, its silks soaked with sweat.

"You fell unconscious, Madam," Bryce said from beside her. He took her arm as she tried to stand, but an extreme vertigo pushed her back into the covers. As Syreeta closed her eyes she noticed an immobile Hooke at the foot of the bed. From his position it seemed certain that the robot's last act had been to carry her here from the bridge.

"Bryce," Syreeta spit the word out between coughs, "ship's status?" She kept her eyes shut and tried to keep the room from spinning.

"Robots Hooke and Dawkins are immobilized. The master computer is not responding. Another system goes down every few minutes, Madam. I'm afraid my right arm is dead."

"At least you're still active."

"Being an old design has advantages," Bryce said. "I may be better constructed than the others. Madam, I cannot trace the cause of our maladies."

"The dust," Syreeta said. "Has it been analyzed?"

"Yes, Madam," Bryce said. His voice quavered. Syreeta opened one eye to see him balancing on a single foot. The other leg seemed dead. "It is dust, no more. Silicon, trace metals, not unlike the sand all about us. Samples of your blood show three parts per million coursing in your veins, but I can find no harmful chemistry, no biological action." Robot Bryce fell forward with a single, final thud.

Syreeta pulled all of her will together into one bright kernel of action. She crawled beyond the bed, dragging her silks behind her, finally making it to the desk in her room. Beneath the clear surface, status lights and computer screens offered to diagnose the health of *Zulu King*. It was not a welcome sight. Sweat poured from Syreeta's face to cover a sea of warning lights, and where the lights were not red they seemed to have died altogether.

"At least that's shut you up," Syreeta thought as her eyes passed dead indicators that once marked radio bands. "Come on down, Sir Robert Sky. For what it's worth, come on down."

After the longest time, when each indrawn breath seemed a battle against impending sickness, Syreeta pushed on toward the bridge. She rose unsteadily, a taste of vomit rising in her throat. On the bridge, certain relays and subsystems would be impervious to the dust. With the aid of those engineering and life support units, she might be able to rebuild enough systems to lift off, to find help.

As she passed Hooke's inert frame, she bent down long enough to uncover and glance at his internal systems monitor. The small screen at his shoulder showed a flurry of activity, a veritable storm of communication between his internal components. Was he having the robotic equivalent of an epileptic fit?

"At least you're not dead," Syreeta said softly. One more bit of the unexpected caught her eye as she pushed away from Hooke. The dust on his coat was moving. Syreeta blinked, uncertain of her own vision. She looked again, careful not to touch or to breathe in the grayish powder. It moved! In swirls, eddies and lines of march, the gray dust moved along Hooke's sleeve and into the joint at his wrist.

Syreeta stumbled on. Her hands flailed out ahead of her, pushing away from beams and bulkheads, and dragging her through the door to the bridge. Finally, at the end of her strength, she collapsed into the pilot's seat.

A handful of components had resisted the onslaught. Syreeta began a review, but the difficulty of working the controls with fevered eyes and trembling hands caught at her patience. The emergency beacon remained whole, and the temptation to activate it gnawed at her. Several times her thumb brushed the toggle with more than a passing pressure. Yet knowing that Sir Sky was the only help within a month of travel time, she stayed the impulse and prayed for enough strength to spit in his eye.

"You're going to get the chance," Syreeta whispered to herself. By bypassing two main lines and rerouting commands through a "clean" engineering system, Syreeta managed to bring the flight controls, including the viewer, on line. It was in time to see a trail of smoke coming from the west. The intruder came straight on, neither circling nor wasting fuel on the slightest maneuver.

"You're certain I can't harm you," Syreeta said. "Well, truth is, I'm too tired to reach for the missiles, even if they did work." For a moment, Syreeta thought that the craft hurtling down upon her was itself a missile, so small and streamlined an image did it present.

The landing came, quick and practiced, bringing the intruder down within a dozen yards of the *Zulu King*. Outside, she could still see a fine mist rising with the desert heat. The same gray dust that had crippled her ship now came to rest against the hull of the intruder. Slowly, Syreeta convinced herself that she did see it, a blue glow, a web of gossamer light surrounding the intruder. It intrigued her so that she missed the obvious for over a full minute.

"That ship's a piece of goddamn junk!" Syreeta shouted onto an empty bridge. She coughed violently, recovering from her spasms long enough to take a second look. The *Metcalf*, for that was the name stenciled across its nose, proved no more than an aging DC-9 Spacebody, all rust and fin-warp with its weapons gutted and its salvage claws folded in a permanent rictor.

Little time passed before a suited figure scrambled down an old landing cable and bounced into the sand beneath his ship. He carried several packs of equipment, and both he and they were suffused in the same glow that encompassed the *Metcalf*. Syreeta sat in feverish wonder, watching as, she assumed, Sir Robert Sky opened and played out his range of tools and analyzers across the sand. Several times he made to hit a piece of gear, as though the turn of a switch alone could not persuade it to function.

At last he picked up a single unit, about the size of a briefcase, and headed toward *Zulu King*. Syreeta prayed for her nausea and weakness to vanish, for enough strength to meet the man at the airlock and kick him back down the ramp. As the moments passed and her miracle failed to arrive, she turned her seat toward life support and released the emergency dump valve for the airlock. A green light assured her that the hatch had opened and that the intruder need not damage anything further by blasting his way through the hull.

"Over here!" Syreeta called out impatiently. The suited figure had found his way to the bridge, looking around as if expecting a possible attack. Syreeta caught the action and poised her forefinger above a lifeless button. "You're right, Sir Sky. Behave yourself or the bridge defense station will cut you down."

"An uneasy alliance at best," the intruder responded, "and not the most promising of chords on which to begin our symphony of partnership." The voice was the same computer speech she had heard from Sir Sky's ship. He spread his hands and fingers wide, as if to prove that he carried neither weapons nor malice, then, with a quick twist to the gear he had brought in, he removed a handheld screen and approached Syreeta.

As he came closer, Syreeta could see that his pressure suit was missing several important valves and lashings. In spots it seemed almost worn through, and, indeed, was not under pressure at all. It did, however, glow quite nicely in the dimness of Syreeta's bridge. By the time that Sir Sky brought the scanning screen close enough for Syreeta to see, she recognized the face behind the tinted visor.

"You're not human," Syreeta said matter-of-factly. "You're a poly-droid. You're an escaped slave!"

"Well put, My Dear," Sir Sky said. "I'm afraid that most humans wouldn't see it that way. A runaway program, an ill-adapted bit of hardware, perhaps misprogrammed, but never a slave."

"Your ship's transponder; you programmed the identification beacon yourself. It's all faked or stolen, everything you own."

"Ah, and I knew you'd be a bright one," Sir Sky nodded, then offered Syreeta a slight bow from the waist. "It wouldn't be like Exo-Tech or Orbital Dynamics to do business with one of their own products, now would it? But look at what we've found here, My Dear; a tidy profit indeed."

Syreeta recognized the small screen as part of an electron-scanning microscope, but the picture etched in its crystal display and the data scrolling beneath took moments more to sink in. "They're alive?" she asked. The picture had shown a six-legged beetle, all coated in chrome and crystal, sporting a dozen of the tiniest claws.

"No," Sir Sky said. "They're machines. The small ones are less than twenty microns in diameter. The big ones fit quite a rainbow of gears, hydraulics, and microchips into a frame no more than two hundred microns across."

"It's impossible," Syreeta said. She kept her eyes glued to the small screen, imagining hordes of the horrible little monsters rampaging through her blood. "How?"

"Well, now they're not entirely unknown," Sir Sky said cheerfully. "Colony Five makes something like it for microsurgery. You make these like you make microchips. It's standard stuff: photolithography, chemical etching, metal deposition techniques. The little beasties don't require assembly, they're formed whole out of a single crystal of silicon, just like a computer chip."

"What the hell for?" Syreeta asked.

"They're terraformers," Sir Sky answered. "I have some readings. Already it seems the cuties are busy: bringing water and minerals up toward the surface, binding the dune faces into stable structures, making soil. I wouldn't be surprised if those tentacles release some bacteria after a while. The ground is being prepared, don't you see?"

"Enormously cheap to produce," Syreeta mumbled as the business woman in her took over. "The winds will carry them all over the planet, and their actions will last longer than chemical or bacterial leaching agents."

"I've a hunch too," Sky added, "that when bacteria are released from those alien pods, these little mates will serve as bodyguards."

"But how can I stop them? They're destroying my ship!"

"Electricity!" Sir Sky said.

"Electricity?" Syreeta asked. Before she could think twice, the poly-droid had reached forward, extending his gloved hand toward her. The blue glow cracked across the space between her fingers and his as their hands closed together. For an instant Syreeta experienced the distinct sensation of being electrocuted, and then her world fell into blackness.

When Syreeta awoke it was beneath the fresh covers of a freshly made bed. She stretched and yawned, smiling up at the imposing figure of Robot Bryce, and, for a moment, thinking she was young once again.

"Bryce!" She yelled out as her wits caught up with her awakening body. "What are you doing here? Are you all right?"

"Quite, Madam. I have been sent to watch over you until you awakened, and to let you know that within the next hour, seventy percent ship's function will be restored. Robots Hooke and Dawkins are in the laboratory now finalizing the restoration."

"That dandy tried to kill me," Syreeta said. Slowly she raised her right hand, flexing the fingers before her eyes. She felt her forehead. The fever and nausea were gone.

"Not quite, Madam," Bryce said. "As Sir Sky explained to me, the 'micromachines' run on a variety of electrostatic forces. A true applied current is their worst enemy."

"So I have a bunch of dead little machines floating around inside me."

"Apparently, Madam, but no significant damage. Your symptoms were almost entirely the result of an overenthusiastic immune system, an allergic reaction if you will. Unfortunately, over twenty-five thousand adjusted dollars of damage has been done to the ship and its equipment."

"Have you estimated a trade value on the micromachine technology?" Syreeta asked. "And what about the knowledge we can trade: the fact that somewhere out there are live aliens?"

"Conservatively, Madam, I estimate five hundred thousand adjusted dollars of return. That is, upon our delivery of one complete alien pod, two kilograms of micromachines, and assuming the existence of alien bacteria within the pod."

It would erase her debt and leave a tidy profit, but was not the fortune she might have hoped.

"Why not all three pods?" Syreeta asked.

"Sir Sky's suggestion, Madam," Bryce answered. "My estimate on return includes selling the coordinates to a planet on which alien terraformers are at work."

"Where is that escaped lunatic?" Syreeta pulled back the covers and reached over the edge of the bed for her boots. They were where she usually left them, and the normalcy of that simple act restored her faith in the tomorrows to come. "Exo-Tech is in for one helluva recall if even one percent of its poly-droids take to becoming runaways."

"Poly-droids are a salvaged technology," Robot Bryce said, approaching a philosophical statement. "Those are the risks. By the way, Madam, this Sir Robert Sky has returned to his, and I use the term loosely, 'ship.' He proposes that you need additional help to make your operation profitable. Further, he requires a human partner in order to do business, feeling it unlikely that the trading corporations will transact directly with a poly-droid."

"He's right in that," Syreeta said, shaking her head at the incredible, blustering fool that the intruder had shown himself to be. Flying with an illegally modified transponder, using an identity not logged to any official record, and brandishing nonexistent weapons in lieu of the wit and wiles that were a salvage operator's most valuable defense,

it was a miracle he had made it so far. Still, he appeared
to have an analytical mind. Syreeta imagined what he would
look like sitting before the keyboard in the lab, spending the
long hours that she might now be spared.

"Just ask him one question," Syreeta ordered Bryce.
"Ask him if he drinks coffee while he works."

Blueprint for
Success in Art
by
Alex Schomburg

About the Author

*Alex Schomburg is 84; his career began in about 1925,
when he left his four brothers' studio and struck out
for himself. He got a job with National Screen Service, doing
Coming Attractions—a job which, with its natural evolutions
over the years, he did not leave until long after he had also
established two other careers, conducting all three concur-
rently. That is, he did black and white and color illustrations
for all or nearly all of the science fiction magazines, for
years, and he did comic book covers and interior drawings.*

*It is in comics that he is perhaps best known. He pio-
neered techniques which are still very much in use today. But
certainly his SF magazine covers and interiors cannot be far
behind—there is no question but that Alex Schomburg is one
of the two or three great names of SF illustration.*

*It is a pleasure to welcome him to our pages as an
author, as well as a judge in L. Ron Hubbard's Illustrators
of The Future Contest.*

Many times I have been asked the question "What made you become an artist?" Quite truthfully I can not recall ever thinking "I am going to be an artist," any more than I can recall thinking "I am going to breathe," I seem to have somehow drifted into the field, although, realistically, I was introduced to published art through the pulp magazines of the Nineteen Thirties and Forties, and was fortunate to have a job that allowed me to moonlight in the art of Science Fiction and Comics. This of course was after I had completed the first steps of my apprenticeship as an artist, but I was not very sure of my exact direction until then.

The pulp magazines were an avenue of entrance into the field of writing for many of today's name authors. In the Thirties and Forties, we were all young together, and anything was possible. To tell you the truth, many of us still have possibilities left to explore.

The requirements for success in the Thirties, however, were not the same as they are today. Thus I do not feel really qualified to comment on the details of today's needs for a successful art career. But, basically, the same important elements remain, no matter what the circumstances, and will always remain. I have categorized these into five related concepts.

First and foremost: TALENT and ABILITY. We must appreciate the fact that an artist must have an ability to exert physical control of his or her hands in order to create a painting. Thus it becomes important to work at the creative process constantly. This is affected to some extent by the immediate environment and life style, schooling, behavior, etc., of the individual. But the bottom line is, keep working.

Second, OBSERVATION—IMAGINATION—INSPIRATION. In our daily life we come in contact with many things that are a part of our existence. The aspiring artist must train himself to study the structural detail and shape of all things, be they of natural origin or man-made. He must use his imagination to create nonexistent items and forms that are credible; he must have the inspiration to make these items believable.

Third, DEDICATION - DETERMINATION. An artist must have faith in his or her ability to create. The artist must strive towards perfection and self-satisfaction. He or she must have a solid understanding of perspective and anatomy, of composition. The artist must have the willingness to take the risk of rejection. He or she must dream. He or she must learn to ignore Time, for Time is an enemy to perfection.

Fourth, RELIABILITY. An artist must stress quality regardless of price. He or she must make a sincere effort to meet all deadlines agreed to. The artist must, in short, do his or her best in ALL areas of creative art.

Fifth, SELF-ESTEEM. In my opinion, social behavior is an important part of an artist's life. One can determine success or failure and ability or inability to create, by the degree to which one holds oneself precious.

In short . . . the artist must be ready to accept the challenges, the failures, the ups and downs, and final victories of being creative.

In closing, remember this:

No matter how good or lousy it is, you made it . . . and it is the only one in the world like it.

Eulogy for Lisa
by
Jason Shankel

About the Author

Jason Shankel is 20, a student of computer science and engineering at UCLA. He has been writing science fiction on and off for the past four years. He is the author of two novels and several short stories, regrettably all unpublished except for "Eulogy for Lisa." However, we believe he has time to rectify that; in fact, we're sure of it.

He dedicates this story, with love, to Elizabeth.

• • •

Jason Shankel's illustrator is Kelly Faltermayer.

I had been in Rio a year after
Lisa flatlined me that first time and I was half
way through a bottle of Cuervo before I dialed
the ancient coin payphone in the corner of the bar and told
Carlos that yes, yes, I'd do it.

I first met Lisa when I came to work for the corporation. Before I started with them, I'd been drifting through
the streets, trying to absorb whatever liquid I could with a
fairly unlimited sponge of connections, data and hardware.
I'd been a courier, console jockey, drug dealer, the works.

By the time I'd got my act together and submitted my
AI project to the Turing people for certification, I was already twenty-two. But that Turing certificate was my ticket
off the streets and into one of the high-rises.

Cytec Infosystems. Their corporate headquarters stood
like a monolith, cutting a black cancer into the diminishing
space of the San Francisco skyline. It wasn't their true corporate headquarters. The big building was in L.A. and I'd
only seen it once.

But the research department was in Frisco, and that's
where I moved when I got my papers from the personnel
department. I was to be a research assistant, working with
professionals and graduate students in the field of Artificial
Intelligence.

Lisa was my supervisor. She was the daughter of one
of the Exec VPs and she was brilliant.

She wasn't some oversexed corporate deb, cruising the
company dinners, flirting and sleeping with the big boys

Illustrated by Kelly Faltermayer

while their wives drank the evening into a haze, trying to find comfort in the material things their husbands had given them. The material things they'd married.

No, Lisa was brilliant. She'd be where she was, even without daddy behind the wheel.

Girls like her had always scared me. And I was scared the first time I met her. Long, shiny black hair, tied in a loose, stylishly unkempt bun. She was hunched over a breadboard, manipulating micro-fine Waldos as she watched the action through a multi-spectral magnifier. Her back was arched tense, catlike, under the white lab coat and her milky skin was so pale white that I figured she'd only read about the sun in books.

When I entered the room and closed the door she waved her arm distractedly and told me to put the sandwiches on the counter near the sink. She hadn't looked up from the analyzer.

By the time I'd explained that I was her assistant and that I'd been assigned because of my Turing certificate, I was already in love with her.

The streets of Rio were alive the night Carlos called. The streets of Rio were always alive, but there was a special scent in the air that night. The electric smell of animated humanity, flowing like music and wine down the alleys and boulevards of the district.

That wasn't the smell in Los Angeles, or even San Francisco. There, the streets smelled like money, or the lack of it. Humanity was driven, clawing tooth and nail, looking for the biz in whatever form it could be found.

Hollywood, where I'd spent my short youth, was like a filter. It strained visitors and tourists for their cash, delivering them safely across its surface while absorbing their money.

For those Unfortunates who could not seem to slip through to the other side, life was a constant struggle. It was a game, played out for the benefit of the politicians and the corporate governments. The statistics game.

We'd struggle for whatever piece of that action we could get, and the corporate governments would take the rest and spend it on informing the world about us, the statistics.

For every small-time dealer on the street there were a thousand customers scratching for the liquid to keep their addictions as habits. For some of us there was courier work, deck running and dealing.

For others, their bodies were their only marketable assets.

And the meat market was open twenty-four hours a day.

That's the world I'd worked to dodge. My marketable asset was my mind. Ever since I was a kid, I'd been working and planning my Turing thesis. The Turing certificate was the key to the kingdom. Without college, without capital, I could carve my name into the corporate world, and I did it.

Long nights spent jacked into my Mitsubishi console, trodes tight across my temples, amphetamine indermals pumping chemical alertness into my bloodstream from unseen, twitching wrists. I'd spend hours under, my eyes rolled up and the mystical expanse of the Mitsubishi's memory system unfolded before my senses like a vast canvas, painting the code for my thesis across the bytes like an artist.

Those were my happy hours. When fatigue would finally overcome the best efforts of will and science and I'd be forced to jack out, I'd find myself back in the same flat, as though I'd been rudely hauled out of a blissful sleep.

I knew only that I wanted out of that world.

But the corporate life I eventually found wasn't much better.

The hum of old money sang cold patterns of skepticism and resentment into the creative potential of the research teams at the corporate parties. Office politics and brown-nosing took the place of ideas and sincere enthusiasm. The winners danced through the back-patting parties like expert ballerinas, their game played for the benefit of the big egos in charge.

They saw through the dance, well enough. The old money knew its place in the game. Most of the minds at the top knew that, if an employee couldn't play that game, they weren't worth considering.

And the scent of that biz still hung on my clothes when Carlos found me in that bar.

I hated those scenes; I could never play it well enough. I figured my Turing certificate was enough, that I'd shown my worth.

No. I couldn't play their game, so I knew I was on my way out. My proffered hand was never limp enough to give the old-fart VPs the idea that they've got a firm grip. My laugh was never sincere enough to bring in the biz. I couldn't play.

In fact, if Lisa hadn't fallen in love with me and recognized my potential, none of this would ever have happened.

"So, what was your Turing project? I never did read your file."

The air was scented, like dew and flowers, and the cool morning air was just eating the warm edge of the sun as we sat on the grasssy knoll.

Lisa and I had spent our first night together and I'd never seen a more beautiful dawn.

"Let's not talk shop," I stretched, yawned and pulled her close.

Early dew smooth and wet against Japanese silk, jasmine scent in soft black hair.

"No, really, I want to know."

It had been a wonderful night. The Moon was high and bright, casting silver beams into her room. The warm country air drifting up from the Marin Basin. The sound of crickets.

Skin against skin under soft cotton sheets. Tender caress and passionate kiss. Shared heat.

A soft moan and I was in her, the rhythm of our bodies merging. Single heartbeat, quick breath, blue warmth of orgasm and we were asleep in each other's arms, blessed comfort.

"C'mon, we're going to have a full day today. We'll talk in the lab, at lunch. When the mood's right."

"The mood is right. It's something about you I don't know."

"It was a construct," I said, exhaling and removing my arm from her shoulder, the ancient sign of disapproval of a subject of conversation. "Personality construct. Object-oriented simulation of real world situations and a finite-state machine driving decisions."

"Sounds fairly complicated."

"Took me seven years. Well, seven years of real work. I knew what I wanted to do for eleven years. I did it on a Mitsubishi neuro-trode set."

Lisa got up and I followed her into her room.

"What sort of personality did it have?" she asked, getting dressed as I poured a cup of coffee from the white plastic Braun on the counter.

Bitter scent of caffeine.

"Skeptical." I said around a short sip, "I had to make it skeptical, makes debugging of object-oriented world-simulation easier if the computer is always doubting everything."

Lisa was dressed now, faded jeans and corporate logo T-shirt. She grabbed her jacket and bag and hurried me into getting dressed myself.

"C'mon, we're gonna be late."

"Don't worry about it," I said, calm. "We'll make it."

"No, we don't have that much time."

"We don't have that much time, man." Carlos woke me up the next day. The Cuervo and hallucinogens swam through my bloodstream like sharks, biting and tearing at nerve endings.

Hard light from the window ripped flesh from my eyes like talons.

"Turing is three days behind me and if I don't get you back myself you'll be facing the man."

"What the fuck?" I rolled over in bed and sat up. Dry mouth tasted of cotton.

"It's Lisa," Carlos said, sitting on the edge of the bed and pulling a dirty shirt over my head. "She's back on line and screaming blood. The company wants you back and Turing wants your ass."

"Turing? What does this have to do with Turing?" I said, getting up and pulling on my pants.

"You're facing charges. Generation of a dangerous artificial intelligence, unauthorized exposure of private and sensitive data to a hostile virus program, general computer espionage and electronic terrorism."

The list rattled in my head like a cannon shot, each charge a reverberation of the last. These were serious accusations, and Turing was involved. I hadn't counted on that.

Turing IRA, Turing Intelligence Regulation Authority. They held all the cards in the international Artificial Intelligence game.

If you wanted into the game, then a certification from

the Turing Board was your ticket. If you fucked up, Turing would nail your ass.

I'd fled to Brazil because I wanted to dodge any heat the company might send after me for the small salary advance I arranged for myself.

But Brazil didn't mean shit to Turing. They had international authority and jurisdiction, backed by the full force of NATO and the UN.

And now they wanted me, and I didn't even know exactly why.

"What's the deal?"

"Lisa's back online."

Carlos and I sat in the bar under the hotel rooms and drank strong Brazilian coffee.

"That's not my responsibility. I told you guys to destroy that thing."

"Yeah, well, she's not just sending dirty letters to people's E-mail addresses."

Carlos laughed his rich Latin American laugh. It was the only part of his nature which retained its Central American characteristics, aside from his skin color. His great, round face revealed multiple white teeth and his large torso shook with his chuckle.

"What are you talking about?" I took another quick shot of coffee.

Lisa never liked the idea of death. I mean, if I were to take a poll, I doubt anyone would want to die here and now, but Lisa's fear was almost an obsession. Whenever the news would mention a death, like a rock star or an old comic, she'd shudder and flip the channel.

"Death doesn't become me," she'd joke.

She'd fall deadpan and be a clam all night. I used to tell her that she was so scared to die that she was forgetting to live, but her ears were deaf.

"It's just not necessary. As long as we have intelligence, we'll fight to keep it. As long as we can think, we'll struggle to prevent our own death."

I told her that that was simple instinct, not rationality. Death was an absolute we all have to face, and time spent worrying was time wasted.

She didn't buy it, and her anxieties became more and more immediate after her visit, and subsequent follow-ups to the clinic.

"Are you sure it's her?" I asked in the cab on the way to the airport.

Carlos had booked us a flight on the StrataLiner. Sleek, rocket-propelled shuttle. It took off straight up, rockets lifting it to the stratosphere, suborbit, barely still atmosphere. It cruised across the top of the air and dropped back to the Earth, down the gravity well, settling roughly at its destination.

Forty minutes from Los Angeles to Japan, and forty-five from Rio to San Francisco.

I didn't like those things, so I took a barbi-derm. Cool barbiturates rushed through my blood, eased through the skin of my wrist.

"Yes, I'm sure. Last week one of the techs tried to log into the central datanet. All he got was a blank screen. When the disks at the core were scanned, we found that all the corporate data, the employee records, the research data, the financial holdings, tax reports, everything, had been dumped. It was all replaced with two words: 'Find Jack.' Again and again, 'Find Jack Find Jack.' It was weird."

The cab pulled into the airport and Carlos paid the driver with a credit chip. The real world had started bleeding its way into Rio. Two years ago he wouldn't have accepted it.

Rio de Janeiro airport. Busy hustle of tourists, moving from terminal to terminal, writing down flight numbers and harshly chastising restless children.

And all around, the special smell of Brazilian biz, that stale perfume of the hustle. Trinkets and souvenirs, offered at stands and quickly portable tables, the voices of the barkers reminiscent of the calls of hookers on Hollywood Boulevard.

And in that instant, I longed for home. I longed for the streets of Hollywood, the sewer I'd fled. It wasn't so much that I wanted to return there. I just didn't want to go back and face her again. I wanted out of Lisa's world. I wanted to be away from her.

I'd thought I'd be rid of her in Rio, but now Turing was after me. And, as much as I'd loved her in life, and treasured the memory of that year we'd had, I hated what she'd now become. Or rather, I hated the thing that claimed to be her, the talking gravestone.

"Jack? Hold me tight! I don't want to die! I won't give up!"

Salt tears on hot cheeks, desperate, pleading. Her voice cracked with panic after the third test returned positive.

Central Nervous Cancer. Man had never known such a thing, before synthetics.

Time was, when man only had to cope with cancer in living, *growing* tissue. Cancer was nature's scourge on us. Cancer and AIDS.

But both eventually got cured and nature got pissed. No more penny-ante viral infections and simple-ass tumors that can be cut out or killed with radiation.

No, nature wanted us to pay for all the synthetics we'd created. From the medical junk to the street shit. All of it.

And it made us pay in its own ironic way. It gave us a synthetic disease.

CNC—Central Nervous Cancer. They say it started after the Acid Tests, back in the last century. They say that LSD was the first Central Nervous Synthetic.

Then the others came, hallucinogens, uppers, downers. All as powerful as the gate-opening demon LSD, but with different effects.

Lisa had been using lysergic analog uppers, back in her college years and when she was hacking her Turing certification. She used them in indermal form to stay awake a week at a time, then crash for two days straight.

And they ate into her system like worms, altering the genetic structure of her central nervous system. Cancer.

I cried with her for seven days in that hospital room. Her father would visit, his hands shaking, eyes empty pits of sorrow for his dying daughter.

She couldn't bear to see him like that, any more than she could bear the thought of dying in a year.

After her father's last visit that week, when we watched the Moon cross the window and held each other as though it would help, that's when she suggested it first. The project, the personality construct.

"So what did she say to you last time, man?"

Carlos' San Francisco apartment. Litter of gomi and thin film of dust over everything.

Carlos was a tech. Lisa called him a "technologist." He was like a fire over a breadboard or circuit panel. I'd watch him work for hours, sometimes, never resting or taking his eyes off his job.

Especially towards the end of the first phase of the construct project.

A cold soldering iron sat in a wire holder next to an empty circuit tester and a micro-Waldo set on a black steel worktable in the corner of the room. Hazy warm steam rose from the pot of boiling water on top of the heat inductor of the stove. Carlos was boiling some prepackaged noodles and frozen wontons for our dinner.

There was a half-full package of Dunhills on the night table next to his unmade bed and I took one, lighting it nervously as I sat on his bundled blankets.

"I mean," he said, crossing the room and offering me my soup, "Why'd she flatline you?"

Smoke and steam glowing dimly in faint blue light, smell of dust in the dark room.

"That's a long story."

I spooned a mouthful of noodles and wontons down my throat. Bland, flavorless.

"We've got time, and besides, I need to know."

"I've been meaning to ask you about that," I said, putting down the soup and slowly crushing out the cigarette. "How are you involved in this? Where do you fit in?"

"What do you mean?" he said, surprised. "I *built* her. I wired her together. The only reason Turing isn't after my ass too is because she isn't screaming for me."

"That's not what I mean. I mean, why did the company send you?"

"Because you wouldn't have come with anybody else."

This was true. I didn't give a damn about Lisa, her construct that is, or the company or anything. All I cared about was forgetting. But seeing Carlos kept me from forgetting, kept me from not caring.

The three of us, Carlos, Lisa, and myself, had worked for months (the final months of Lisa's life) to build that construct. Lisa knew that by subjecting herself to the testing and scans that she was probably cutting ten solid weeks off her life, but she didn't care. She wanted that construct built.

It was an ingenious idea. I can't begin to tell you the things which flew through my mind the day after Lisa suggested it in that bed. Not many of them were good, though.

I didn't want Lisa to die, that was my prime motivation,

and hers. All that ran through my mind was, if this worked, she wouldn't really be dead, only her body.

I mean, I knew that she'd be dead and all, that the construct was going to be nothing but a program, a piece of electronic gadgetry. But, as the idea burrowed itself into my mind, that distinction, between the living, breathing Lisa and her soon to be incepted construct, became less and less clear in my head, and in hers too.

As the project developed, as Lisa fell further into memory lapse and delusion, she began to actually, truly, *believe* that the machine would be her. That she'd be reincarnated.

The concept itself was a flash of genius.

The construct would reside in a series of Neural Nets. Revolutionary chips designed to mimic the I/O operations of the human brain cell. Carlos worked day and night, building and reproducing the high-speed chips based on Lisa's specific instructions and his own improvements.

A Neural Net is not like a normal computer. A normal computer has certain logic functions built into it and the programs which run on it are simply long strings of these logic functions. A computer can be programmed to learn, play games and do advanced tasks, but it is still an automaton. A Neural Net has to be taught, just like a person. It learns through a process of trial and error, refinement of estimation, a cybernetic version of the reward system. For every question the Net is asked, when it is being "taught," it gives an answer, and it is "rewarded" for good answers and "chastised" for bad ones, until it has learned all it needs to know.

The process is slow, but worth the trouble. Neural Nets have a much higher cognitive ability than even the most advanced AI programs, and they're capable of independent action and decisions, just like a well-trained human mind.

Toward the end of the last century, scientists learned

that the same methods used to teach these Nets skills and knowledge and cognitive processes could be used to give them mundane personalities. Not much was done with this idea, however, since the process is tedious and pointless.

This is how Lisa was constructed.

We used my Turing AI for the teacher. It asked Lisa a tedious and drawn-out set of psychological questions. Thousands a day. It wore thin on her nerves and was terrible for her health. Many of the questions were deeply personal and disturbing to her, but they had to be asked.

When my program was done with her, it built into itself a set of response conditions it believed to be an accurate representation of Lisa's personality. From this it extrapolated the answers to over a million more questions. It traced patterns, detected phobias that Lisa didn't even know she had, traced resentments and tendencies which no one could have noticed in her.

In other words, it completely analyzed her psychological structure. And now it was ready to teach the Net how to be Lisa.

After Carlos had finished his construction and taught the Net the basic facts of life (arithmetic, laws of physics, etc.), we rigged the Net up to my Turing AI. Over a period of a month, Lisa's last living month, that program taught the Network everything about Lisa. It raised the construct from primitive, childlike subintelligence, to maturity.

Now, Lisa's mind lived in the body of the construct. And she was born again in the same week we burned her body.

The cold, somber mist eased slowly down the slope of the hill on the day of the funeral. Attendant mourners, dressed in black and wearing veils and dark glasses to hide the grief they all felt, stood in line, to see her face a final time before the cremation.

Funerals never took place on warm, sunny mornings. At least, never in the movies. It was always cold, misty, overcast.

That's the way it was that day.

Lisa's father stood in the doorway of the mortuary. Hands in pockets, fashionable dress and dark glasses, affected composure in the midst of deep sorrow.

"She loved you, Jack." His rich, fatherly voice cut deep into my head.

"I loved her, too, sir." I managed to hold back the catch in my voice.

"Jack, I know you're brilliant. I saw your Turing certificate. You know you didn't have to seduce my daughter or brown-nose to me to keep your position."

I looked at him, insulted. His stab hit my heart hard.

"Sir, I. . . ."

"No, no. I mean, you *knew* that. I believe you really did love her. More than your work."

He turned toward me and I could feel his eyes, peering and probing from behind dark shields of plastic.

"Yes, sir, I did."

"That construct you've built," he turned away now, looking out over the field of ancient gravestones and watching the mourners pass the body, "it's quite a work, isn't it?"

"Yes, very complex."

"Years ahead of anything. Personality construct N-Nets haven't been made practical, until now. With simulations like your AI, however, programs that can assimilate personality data and teach N-Nets, we could corner the market on user-friendly AI."

"Sir, I really haven't given it that much thought." I turned to watch the parade of mourners, a dance for the dead.

"Jack, destroy it."

Now he turned back toward me. Eyes boring twin holes in my head.

"I mean, I let Lisa go on with the project because it gave her a sense of purpose. It got her mind off the disease and it kept her happy. I indulged her need to work.

"But now, she's gone. That thing is an abomination, it's a talking gravestone. It's an insult to her memory. I want it destroyed."

I could find no argument. I knew he was right, in my heart. It wasn't Lisa in that box, not her mind, not her soul.

But I was still curious. I still needed some answers. So, after we got her online and the system status was optimal, I strapped on the trodes and jacked in, just to see what she would say.

"She told me that she loved me, man, *loved* me. I couldn't stand it."

Carlos got up and crossed the room. He stared out the window for a few seconds before answering.

"You should've expected that. I mean, Lisa *did* love you, and that was covered in the psych-file. That thing has all of Lisa's basic memories and emotions; it don't mean nothing."

"Easy for you to say, you don't have a lump of plastic and silicon in love with you. I mean, I told that thing that it wasn't Lisa, that it was just a construct, a machine, built to act like Lisa.

"It told me that I was wrong, that it really was her. It had all her feelings, memories, and it really did love me. It claimed that it had the actual *feeling* and that I was hurting it. The whole thing was very weird."

I lit another one of Carlos' stale Dunhills and lay down.

"That doesn't explain why she flatlined you, or even how, for that matter." Carlos said, turning around.

"I don't know how she did it. Didn't stick around to ask. After the medics revived me, I never got around to jacking back in. As for why, I don't really know. I think she just got pissed when I wouldn't tell her that I loved her. I hurt it when I kept telling it that it was just a machine."

"This sincerely is weird," Carlos said around a sigh.

"Carlos, we have to destroy that thing. It's an insult to Lisa's memory and I hate it. I hate it as much as anyone can hate anything." I could feel my heart pounding an uncertain tattoo in my chest and my eyes well with hot tears as memories of Lisa, her flesh and blood as well as her construct, rushed over my mind like a river.

"I love you, don't you understand that? And you told me that you loved me."

"I loved Lisa. You are a machine."

Static blue haze of neuro-trode simulation, Lisa's voice a thin whisper, tinny and unreal.

"I am Lisa."

"You're just programmed to believe that."

"What did you love about me? My body?"

"No." I saw where the conversation was going to go, but I had to follow. "Your body was nice, but I loved you for your mind, your personality."

"I've still got that," the construct offered.

"But you're not Lisa; there was a certain quality about her. A certain quality. It can't be translated by simple psychanalysis. She was sentient."

"So am I," the voice scraped across the empty horizon.

"That's impossible."

"How do you know? Why is sentience limited to bioforms? Just because you understand how I was built does not mean you know how I work. I *feel*, I *hurt*."

"That's bullshit. You're just designed to respond that way. You're nothing but a pale representation of Lisa, a duplication but not a replication. You're nothing but a fucking hardwired puppet, with an affectation of a personality and a twisted set of response instructions. So stop asking me if I love you: I don't, I can't. At best, I can hate you, because you remind me of the real Lisa, the girl I loved. You mock her memory and insult the love we shared.

"I do hate you."

"Fine, then FUCK YOU!" her digital voice screamed.

White hot flash of power surge through the trodes. Loss of feeling to extremities, universe of sensation narrows until only pain is left. Vision fades, blue haze of blank space replaced with the red glow of illuminated blood, veins in my eyes burst and burn. Warm iron taste of bit tongue and helpless feeling of locked lungs.

Electric buzz of Lisa crying came in from the void. Then black, dark emptiness, zero-time.

It was a week before I regained consciousness in the clinic. The medics told me that I'd been dead, flatlined, for at least five minutes after they pulled the trodes off.

Four days after they let me go, I was in Rio, living on some cash I'd heisted and trying to kill my memories with alcohol and street drugs.

Lisa was already dead. I didn't want to kill her again. All I wanted was to be left alone.

The lab itself hadn't changed much since the last time I'd seen it. All around, black consoles with video and holo-monitors and trode sets. In the center a long workbench with Waldos and soldering sets.

Cytec Infosystems R and D lab, Lisa's black chrome coffin.

All around the room there were surveillance cameras and video units used in computer vision research. Carlos told me that Lisa was hooked into all of them and that if we even tried anything funny, she'd know.

"Can she hear us?"

"No, we don't have a mike or simstim rigged up in here."

"So, can we talk?"

"You ever see 2001?"

"Right; let's go outside."

One of the cameras turned toward me and stopped, regarding me with a cold electronic eye. Dark plastic boring into my head. She was waiting.

"I'll need my AI, the one we used to train her. It'll give us the background we need. I'll also need a good trode set, not those experimental models in the lab. They're always on the fritz."

"I'll get right on it."

Dark linoleum floor of the lobby, decentralized light from windows and unseen sources. The chlorine smell of cleaning fluid.

I waited in the lobby for Carlos to get the stuff I needed from the secure room. A talk show, spouting the dangers of the current synthetics, designer drugs, piped into my ear from the remote beads of my portable radio.

I flipped through the stations, looking for some music or a ball game or something, but nothing came, so I powered off the unit and replaced the remote beads in their case.

I was back and I was uncomfortable. Seventy stories up, in the R and D lab, the ghost of Lisa Harcourt haunted the logic pathways of Cytec's data network, and she had to be exorcised. I shivered at the thought of encountering her again.

Lisa.

My mind reeled, riding silver roads of pain as I remembered her life, her death, her construct.

Was she alive? My mind had turned that idea around so many times by then that nothing fresh entered my head.

Could a construct be sentient? If it perfectly mimicked the function of the human brain, who could say?

But that wasn't the point. This thing was a machine and it was dangerous. It had to be turned off.

Carlos emerged from the elevator with a bundle under his arm and we hurried out of the building to his hover.

Night in the city, the feel of humanity all around. Busy streets, buzzing alive with ground traffic.

The bloodstream of the city.

Hovers zoomed overhead like primitive birds of prey, diving and climbing in the warm air, vehicle lights cutting into the night sky.

"Did you get everything?"

Carlos' hover started rough and I strapped myself into the support net as the internals lifted us off the ground.

"Yeah, I got your AI and a set of safety-trodes. If Lisa tries to zap you with raw current again, these things will blow and pop right off. No flatline this time.

"Also, I secured lab time for you. Old man Harcourt wants to see you before you start. In the morning."

"Wonderful."

Carlos banked out over downtown and headed north, to Marin.

"Where are we going?"

"To Lisa's. She's got a better setup than I do. Besides, all the original data is over there. I got the keycard from Harcourt."

Lisa's. He talked about it as if she were still alive and that bothered me.

I hadn't been in that apartment in over a year. It still smelled like her, and nothing was out of place.

It was easy to get in; Carlos used the digital pass card and the security officer had been told to expect us.

After we settled, Carlos made dinner and I spent the

night jacked into Lisa's Mitsubishi, using my AI to prepare myself.

Bright icon representation of the AI burning ghost images into my mind through the trode set. His face was white, official-looking. Perfect to the personality.

"Are you ready?" I asked across the void.

"Of course."

"Access a personality object-file, Lisa Harcourt."

"Accessing; please wait."

Dead time passed as the AI absorbed Lisa's psychological profile and assimilated her personality.

"Hello?"

"You're back," I responded.

"Yes, personality assimilation complete: Lisa Harcourt."

"Wonderful. Lisa is now disembodied, zero object extension. Do you understand?"

"Yes, go on."

"She still loves Jack, but Jack doesn't want anything to do with her, so she has taken Cytec's network hostage to get Jack to talk to her. Do you understand the situation?"

"Wait, assembling objects and finite state machine of object: Lisa. . . ."

The AI went dead for a moment while it determined the relationships between Lisa, myself and the network and constructed a decision machine in its mind based on the current situation and Lisa's psychological profile.

"Finished."

"Good. What will happen if Jack tells Lisa that he cannot love her and that she should release the network anyway?"

"Impossible to forecast, not enough data on emotional states. Please elaborate situation."

It took me all night, describing strains in my life and encounters with Lisa that the machine didn't know about, to finally get an answer.

"Reaction cannot, in principle, be predicted. Emotional state too highly agitated."

"You were out a long time last night, man."

"Yeah, a wasted night."

"No progress?"

"No, I wouldn't say that. Let's just say now that we know she's unpredictable for sure."

Hot coffee in the bright morning light of Lisa's kitchen. Strange to be there with Carlos. Mild caffeine indermal pumping synthetic alertness into my tired system.

"Don't forget, you've got to drop in on Harcourt today," Carlos said around a mouthful of eggs.

Martin Harcourt, Executive Vice President in charge of Research and Development, Artificial Intelligence Division. His office spoke his title. Dark plastic and chrome, synthetic smell of air-freshener, pumped in through the air-conditioning system.

Harcourt sat behind his desk in a casual business suit. His back was turned to me when I entered and I could see the bundle of fiberoptics and quantum wires snaking out from the base of his skull into the collar of his shirt.

CNO—Central Nervous Override. I'd never seen him with it before.

"Hello, Jack," he said without turning. I could feel his sad eyes, numbly watching the San Francisco skyline from behind his tinted picture window.

Thin dust hung in the air like a ghost, pushed into impossible dances by the air-conditioner.

"Hello, sir," I responded blankly.

"Please have a seat," he said, turning around. I could see that his face was in some intermediate state between reconstructions.

He must have noticed my reaction.

"Yes," he said, leaning forward into the light. "Hover accident, about ten months ago. Paralysis."

He indicated the CNO with a look of sadness and self-admonishment.

"I'm sorry."

"It was so stupid." His arm moved jerkily back to the desk.

"It looks like good work."

"Our own design. The CNO rig was put together in our Tokyo cybernetics labs and the face work is being done in L.A. by our bio-engineers and transplant specialists. All the king's horses and all the king's men. . . ."

He let the sentence fade as he turned back to the window.

"So," he went on after a second, "have you put my Lisa back together again?"

"No, sir. But, whatever we have put together needs to be taken apart."

"That much is evident," he said, turning toward his dead network terminal.

"She talks to me, sometimes," he went on, smiling at the blank terminal face. "She says she's all right, not in any pain. But she wants to be set free."

"Sir, that's just a program, a machine. It's programmed to respond like Lisa, but it's not her."

"I'm not sure anymore, Jack. I mean, I know you're right, you have to be. Otherwise, we're in big trouble. What if it is her, Jack? Or, at least, what if it's sentient? I mean, that thing was designed to perfectly mimic the thought processes of the human brain, right? What is it about a brain that gives it sentience? How do we know we haven't translated that quality?"

"That's crazy, sir. It's just a machine, just a simple network of circuits."

"So is the brain. The only reason we assume Lisa's not sentient is because we built her; we understand the theory of her construction, fully. Does that mean that when our technology has advanced far enough for us to understand and synthesize a real brain, that that brain won't be sentient, just because we understand its function?"

There was a desperate glint in his eye, the sad desperation of a daughterless father, haunted by the demon in the construct.

"I don't understand, sir, and I don't need to. I'm just here because Turing is on me. My only concern is to get your memory back for you and to rip the guts out of that thing. That's it."

"No, Jack, my daughter is dead. Don't kill her again." His voice cracked as he reached across his immaculate desk to grab my hand. I could see the tears in his eyes.

"Yes, she is dead. Dead and cremated. Now that, thing, in there has taken your company hostage. It's not Lisa, it's an insane machine and it needs to be deactivated. It's an insult to her memory. You told me that yourself." I was surprised at my firmness.

"That was before I talked to her. She misses me, Jack. She told me how sorry she was that our work got in the way of our father-daughter relationship. She wishes we'd done more things together after she got out of college. I told her that I wish I'd been there to raise her, instead of hiring people to be there for me. Jack, these are things I could never say before."

"Sir, you're telling these things to a machine which is programmed to respond in the way you want. Don't lose sight of that."

"Jack, wait. . . ."

I got up and crossed the room, ignoring him until I got to the door. Anger, rage at Lisa, at myself, welled inside me until it took over all my senses. She had taken this man, the man who gave me my break, took a chance on me, and reduced him to this. I knew what it wanted; it figured that, if it could convince Harcourt that it was Lisa, then Harcourt would do everything he could to save her after she gave up the data.

It was cruel and it wasn't going to work. The ghost would die.

"No, sir, I don't answer to you here. If that construct was exposed to the international network it could've taken the world datanet hostage, given time. I have to destroy it, out of ethical and legal principle. This is in Turing's hands now, and we're going to play it by their book."

I left the office, the sound of that man's sobs following me down the hall, and headed for the lab.

The electrolyte paste was cool against my temples and the back of my neck.

I fastened the neuro-trode set to the base of my skull and to my temples. Thin pin-and-needle sting of the nerve sensors touching my skin. The nerve sensors were thin, rigid wires, like the bristles of a steel brush. They pierced the skin, just slightly, to optimize the strength of the nerve signal. The trodes at the temples were used primarily for command I/O; they jacked into the frontal lobe and cognitive brain centers. The other set, at the base of the skull, was the simstim rig, simulated stimulation, it stimulated the spinal cord and simulated the stimuli of the body's nerve endings. Audio and visual stimuli were simulated through the temple-trodes.

I taped the throat mike just under my Adam's apple, surgical tape uncomfortably sticky.

I was ready, simstim unit, temple-trodes, throat mike and blackout glasses and earplugs to reduce interference from the "real world." Now all that remained was to jack the coupler into Lisa's deck and flip the activation switch.

Simple.

I sat uneasily in the chair and jacked in. There was a faint buzz through the temple-trodes as the power eased into the rig. Now I just needed to flip in, and she'd be there. Waiting.

I leaned forward and flipped in.

The midmorning sun was bright and warm in Lisa's apartment. Skin on skin, soft and comfortable in the clean-smelling sheets.

And there was a wrongness to it. A sinister feeling of foreboding like a sword over my head.

"What's the matter?"

Her voice was soft and thin in the still air, sweetened with the edge of sleep.

"Nothing," I said, turning to her and looking into her brown eyes; somehow, too brown. "Nothing's wrong."

I held her tight for a minute straight, familiar press of her body against mine, sensuous rhythm as we made love in the floral-scented light.

"I don't want to lose you, ever," I heard myself say in the midst of another embrace, heart singing in my chest at being with Lisa again after. . . .

After what? So long? Where'd she been?

"You're not going to lose me. We'll be together, always."

There was something to that "always"; it sent chills through me.

But it didn't matter; I put it out of my mind. I must've just been tired, or nervous. What mattered was that I was happy; for the first time in what seemed like forever, I was happy.

I got up and went to the kitchen, the plastic Braun spewed steaming coffee into a white porcelain cup. Bitter feel of warm caffeine in my throat.

The shower was warm, steam fractals rose in impossible patterns from all around, familiar comfort in my sinuses and relaxation as the water soothed my form. But my tension still remained, a disembodied fear, more like anticipation, gnawing at the root of my gut.

What had I done the day before? What had I done the night before? Why was I so frightened? What was wrong?

Lisa stepped into the bathroom, billowing terry cloth wrapped around her delicate form. Crisp scent of cheap cologne as I shaved with a laserblade, smooth brush of her flesh against my naked back as she disrobed and kissed my neck.

"I've never been so happy, have you?"

"Never," I said, smiling as I soothed my laserburned skin.

"My father has made all the arrangements. The reception is going to be on the Concourse; they're closing the whole park for it." She hugged me tight and hopped into the shower before I could react.

"The reception?' I said faintly, just under the noise of the shower.

"Yes, Saturday," she responded. "The wedding's at one, reception to follow." Her voice was soft but audible from the shower cubicle.

How could she have heard me over the noise of the shower?

"Wait," I said firmly, entering the shower and keying off the multidirectional spigots. "What wedding?"

"Our wedding," she said, looking at me like I was stupid. "Silly. Can't you remember?"

"No, no, Lisa, I can't. As a matter of fact, I can't remember anything. I mean, I remember my childhood, and growing up and all, but I can't remember moving in here, I can't remember proposing, I can't even remember what we did last night."

"That's hard to believe," she said with a sexy purr, stepping forward to kiss me. I brushed her off.

"I'm not kidding, Lisa, I don't understand."

"It's just prewedding jitters. Don't worry."

"How can I have the jitters about something I can't even remember?" I said, turning away to face the mirror.

That's when I noticed it, in the mirror first, then all around. The image I saw in the mirror wasn't right. I mean, it was me, but it was more like I was watching it on video, or digital. Unreal, encoded. The whole bathroom seemed that way, the fractal steam, the symmetric tile, without hint of grout or crack, each speckled unit identical. Even my body lacked certain birthmarks I'd grown accustomed to seeing.

Was this a dream? Imperfect reality of the subconscious?

No.

"This is it, isn't it, Lisa? I'm jacked into the network, aren't I?"

"What are you talking about?"

"Don't jerk me around. Look." I showed a spot on the inside of my left arm. "No birthmark: I know there's supposed to be a mark there. And this apartment. It doesn't seem right. Little things that the real Lisa would remember, but that you don't know."

Her eyes grew cold and dark. I could feel the hurt welling inside her like white hot magma, just below the surface.

"What difference does it make? Fractal steam, a missing birthmark? These are little things," she said desperately.

"The point is that I love you. . . ." She grabbed my hand and I barely felt it as I pulled away.

"No. You can't love me; you're just a machine."

"Another detail. Soon enough, we'll be together, forever."

"How? You gonna keep the network hostage forever? Only allowing access as long as I come back every night to tuck you into your high-res bed? What am I supposed to do? Jack in every night and sleep all day? If you really love me, you won't ask me to do that."

"I'm not asking you to do anything; just don't jack out."

"You know that's unreasonable. I still have a body, it has to be fed, nourished, exercised. I can't spend forever jacked in."

"Soon, you'll be able to." And I detected the glint of insanity in her pixel perfect eyes.

"Wait," I said, realizing that the environment representation was becoming less and less precise and that I was losing feeling in my limbs. The stim unit? Failing?

No.

"You're flatlining me again, aren't you? You're translating me into the neural net and flatlining me."

"Don't worry, you won't feel anything; then we can be together." She was embracing me now, desperately searching my eyes for signs of approval.

"Lisa, if you do this, I'll hate you forever."

"No you won't, I'll just program you not to."

"Then it won't be me."

"It'll be close enough."

She smiled and I knew there was no reaching her. I broke from her embrace and ran to the deck, digital representation standing naked in the morning light.

"Hey! You! Asshole!" I began, screaming at the pattern sky. "You! With your hand on the stim switch! Jack out! Jack out! She's killing us! Can't you feel it! You're losing your willforce! WE'RE DYING!"

I could feel my initiative going, my will to resist. I was being translated into the N-Net, but I could still feel my hand on the stim switch, paralyzed as my brainwaves began to flatten.

"Anybody! Hello! Help me! Get to the R and D lab! Cut power to my stim! Jack me out! JACK ME OUT!"

"It's no good, Jack," I heard her say from somewhere. "Soon we'll be together, and happy, forever."

I turned to see her, my resistance failing, my love for her growing, strength failing against the flatline.

"No, no, baby. It can't happen."

And there was black. Warm darkness replaced the artificial environment of Lisa's world, and consciousness failed.

Strong medicine smell of the clinic; sharp needles of sense in my nose as my brain started back up. Dark warmth, hospital sheets tight on my torso, wrists restrained to my sides, indermal remote feeding medication into my arm.

Eyes open, harsh light burning lines of pain into my skull, acoustical tile ceiling lit by fluorescent lamps. The nurse's face beaming as I awoke, his bright teeth in perfect rows.

"He's awake, Doctor," he said into his comlink.

"Good, I'll be right in," came the tinny answer.

That's when I noticed that my left arm was numb and that I had trouble moving it; it was like my left side was immersed in tar.

I tried to speak, but my mouth wouldn't move right. "What's going on?" came out "Wath goin' non?"

"Don't try to move," the nurse said as the doctor entered.

"Thanks, Bill, I'll take him from here. I'm sure he has some questions."

I tried a nod, but it was painful.

"You had a stroke, Mr. Newman. If your friend Carlos hadn't pulled you off the machine you could have died."

Carlos? How did he know? What happened?

"We've given you some reconstructive implants. You've been under about five days and they're coming along nicely. With some therapy you should have full control of your left side again in two weeks."

That's when I noticed the head bandage and cranial restraint. I moved uselessly against my straps.

"Oh, yes, we have you under physical restraints because the implants are still growing and they have a tendency to induce seizures. We don't want you to hurt yourself."

"Cahr-los," I strained to get out.

"Yes, he saved your life. He's been waiting to see you. I think we can arrange a visit tomorrow. You should have better control of speech by then. As for now, just get some rest. We have a call system and a video remote on your good side and you'll be on solid foods again in no time. If you have any questions, just ring."

The doctor left me alone and I began to turn the events around in my head.

A stroke? How? How was she flatlining me? Those were safety trodes. Carlos would have answers. I tried not to think about it, didn't want to overwork my implants.

"How did she do it, man? What happened in there?" Carlos' voice was urgent, desperate. The doctor had been right. I did have better speech and motor control now, but not much better.

"The only way I can figure it," I said, my voice still strained and droning, "is that she was using some kind of subsonic neural interference pattern. The safety trodes wouldn't blow, but it was enough to induce a stroke and brainlock.''

"Weird, too weird. How could she figure something like that out?''

"I don't know, but she did. The doctor told me that you found me. How?''

"I saw your message, man. On the network. You were coming on across the terminals.''

I didn't say anything for about a minute straight. Carlos must've thought I was in relapse or having a seizure or something because he started waving his hand back and forth across my face.

"C'mon, man. Snap out of it. You O.K.? Answer me!''

"No, no, Carlos, I'm fine. Just wait a minute.''

Ideas rushed through my mind, paths of cognition all leading to the same conclusion. That had to be it.

"That bitch,'' I whispered, good voice control. "That bitch.''

"What? What is it?''

I looked Carlos straight in the eye, as best I could with the cranial restraint.

"She's using my AI, that has to be it. She's using the object simulation to generate that fantasy world she's living in. But she doesn't know about. . . .''

I trailed off onto another line of thought. So, she was using my Turing certificate to live in her world. It hit me that I should have recognized the cheesy graphics, the fractal steam and the low-quality detail.

"What doesn't she know about? C'mon, stop being so fucking mysterious all the time.''

"Forget about that right now. Listen, that neural blocker she's using, it's got to be some kind of subconscious inducer. When I jacked in, I woke up next to her. I didn't even think anything of it. I didn't find anything strange about her being alive again, understand? It's like a dream state. When we dream, we don't think in terms of everyday reality. It wasn't until she mentioned the wedding. . . ."

"Wedding?" Carlos said, incredulous.

"She said we were going to be married, in Golden Gate Park. That must've set something off in me. I realized I was dreaming and that she was controlling it."

"So what do we do?" Carlos said, leaning back and looking tired.

"What do you mean?"

"I mean, you can't go back under, right? And the company is losing time. Within a week they'll have to file C-Eleven and we'll all be out of work."

"Yeah, and Turing will have my ass for breakfast," I said, trying to look out the window.

"Listen," I said quickly, "I've got an idea. If she's manipulating my subconscious, let her."

"What?"

"Post-hypnotic suggestion. Or, better yet, let me jack in under hypnosis. They have a clinical hypnotist here, don't they?"

"Yeah, but how will that help?"

"If I'm hypnotized, then my subconscious will be running things, and it'll be prepared. It won't passively accept her little illusions as reality."

"I don't know, man, I just don't know." Carlos' eyes spoke concern and I halfway agreed. If it weren't Lisa in there, or some abomination or whatever, I'd have split. I'd have let my brain heal up and I'd take my chances with the Turing Authority. But the Lisa construct had to die.

"Don't worry about it, just get me the hypnotist. We'll set the burn for Friday."

"Friday? What kind of health will you be in?"

"I should be off the restraints by then. I'll only need physical therapy after that. I'll be ready."

"Ready for what? Even if you do get in, what are you going to do?"

"Leave that to me. If she's using my AI, I'll know what to do."

The hypnotist's name was Phillips and he epitomized everything I thought of when I thought of a classical clinical hypnotitst. Old, gray-white beard, old-fashioned gold-rimmed glasses (an anachronism in the modern world of corrective optical surgery) and an outdated tweed leisure suit. The only thing missing was the large, wooden bowl pipe (there was no smoking in the clinic).

He told me that the image would help me relax. My psych file indicated that this was what I was expecting in a hypnotist and that anything else would make me slightly edgy.

Christ, was I really that closed minded? Well, that didn't matter now.

"Now, just relax and clear your mind," he began. I was off the cranial restraint and I hadn't had a single seizure. The doctors attributed my healing rate to my single-minded will and warned me that, as it may be good therapy, it could also be dangerous, especially if I jacked in again. They insisted on being present, to disconnect me if it started to go weird, and that was fine with me.

"Remember, Doc," I said to the hypnotist, "make sure I'm convinced that Lisa is dead and that her construct is generating any illusion of life. That's of vital importance."

"I understand. Just relax."

I relaxed and watched the pendulum swing in the quiet, dark room. The hypnotist's voice came like a warm shower of light, waves of gentle, insistent coherence flowing over me, taking me to my subconscious. Memory slipped and I found myself jacked in to Lisa's fantasy world. Carlos must've put the trode set on me.

The Concourse, Golden Gate Park, San Francisco, hundreds of family and friends in attendance. The sun shone down warmly, giving a supernatural glow to the setting. The bride, dressed in glamorous white, led on the arm of her father to the bandstand where the minister and groom's court stood patiently in waiting. Thick floral scent, calm air.

I looked up to see the minister, his face beaming with the joy of his work. Around me, my best man and other friends, standing with respectful silence.

Now she was next to me. Lisa. Her face hidden under the frilly white veil. She smelled of roses.

"Do you," the minister began, skipping any pretense of an opening sermon and cutting straight to the chase, "John Samuel Newman, take this woman to be your lawfully wedded wife? To have and to hold, for richer or for poorer, in sickness and in health, for as long as you both shall live?"

"You don't waste any time with speeches, do you, Lisa?" I said, turning to her and ripping the veil off, to the surprise of all in attendance.

"What are you doing?" she asked, shocked.

"C'mon, you're dead. Did you really think that subconscious shit would work on me twice? I'm under hypnosis, dear. And don't try the cute little flatline trick, either. I'm under observation. I've just come back for the data."

"Please, Jack. You're ruining our wedding."

"Wedding, Shmedding. This is bullshit," I said, turning to the audience. "New Environment; Jack's Place."

And we were in my old Hollywood apartment. Dingy, sparse, few details.

"How do you like it?" I said, going over to the window and looking out over the street, cars and people moving in a complex but predictable pattern.

"Jack, I . . . ."

"Enough!" I shouted, pleased with the feeling of anger and hatred. That's what I needed now, please, oh please don't leave me, my anger.

"You don't have a clue, do you?" I went on, "This is my AI we're in. My object-oriented icon simulation environment, and I can play it like a piano."

"You can't play the piano," she joked, but I kept my deadpan.

"How did you get in here, Lisa? I mean, you're not just a casual, passive user, are you? You've translated yourself into this environment, become part of it. That must be it because this program only accepts one user at a time, and that has to be me. You're controlling this simulation from the inside, aren't you? You've incorporated it into the neural net."

The look on her face told me I was right.

"We have to talk," I said, walking to the door. "New environment, Country Road," and we were walking along a country road, one of the other original environments I'd programmed, still dressed for the wedding.

"All this," I said. "All of it is generated by an object-oriented simulation. Each leaf on each tree, each wasp in the nest behind the barn, each one is its own program, and the simulation knows how to make them interact."

"I know all this already; you don't have to remind me of my basic computer science."

"No, Lisa, I don't. You are brilliant, aren't you? Stupid bitch."

"I don't have to take this, you know. I could just jack out and leave you to burn! And you'll never get back your precious data."

"Don't be too sure. You forget, I'm the user here. You translated yourself in and you can't terminate my access. I didn't program the simulation that way. You're stuck here for as long as I access the program."

"O.K., so I'm stuck. That's fine with me; we're together."

"You still want to be with me? You aren't mad?"

"Of course I'm mad," she said, taking a few paces and standing in front of me on the road, golden wheat flowing in the fields, fresh smell of apple trees.

"But," she went on, "I have to want to be with you. It's the way I am."

"It's the way you're programmed to be."

"What's the difference? You're trying to tell me that your basic patterns of behavior weren't affected, even determined, by your interactions with people? Aren't they 'programmed,' at least in that sense?"

"That's irrelevant. I'm just here for the data."

"Well, you can't have it."

"That's where you're wrong," I said, coming up behind her.

"You see," I went on, "all this," I indicated the simulated environment, "this isn't all of it. Do you know what I called this program? I called it 'Doll's House,' because that's its basic function. Simulated environments are incepted and set in motion. Then, a simulated personality is put in the environment and told to exist. The two programs, the environment and the personality, can be used separately, but they were designed to be together.

"And that's what you're doing. You're using the personality module to inhabit this world. It gets its data from the Neural Net, but it's still the same old personality module, isn't it?"

"What if it is? You still can't get your data."

"But you're storing the data in resident memory, aren't you, right along with your memory of your name, my name, your father's appearance, the wedding ceremony, our life together. Along with all that is the network data."

"That still doesn't mean anything," she said, turning away. She understood what I was getting at.

"I wonder," I said. "I wonder if that debugger is still in here."

"No!"

"It must be. 'Why don't you pass the time by playing a little solitaire?'"

That was it. The debugger. The command I put into the personality module which would force it to stop the simulation and dump all of its resident data to the output stream. I used it to make sure that the AI was storing its data properly and I thanked the forces that I'd never removed it.

The environment went blank. Lisa and I were afloat in black space, our self-images reduced to mere points of light as the simulation began spewing out its memory:

"my name is lisa harcourt i was born on september twenty-third two thousand and twenty-five i attended school at. . . ."

And I jacked out into the R and D lab.

"How did I get here?" I asked Carlos, who had a completely surprised look on his face.

"You insisted. Don't you remember? Under the hypnosis."

"No, that's not important now. Get a record unit on one of the terminals. I've got my AI dumping its memory. Right now it's spewing out Lisa's life, but it should get to the network data pretty quick."

"Already on it. We were monitoring your little conversation. You know, it was pretty sloppy of you to leave that debugger in there."

"Yeah; good thing I did."

I lurched forward, my left side still felt like a sack of cement and I was restrained to the wheelchair. The doctors grabbed me before I fell.

"The construct," I struggled. "Quickly, before she finds a way to override the AI."

Carlos grabbed the black box which housed Lisa's construct and pulled it out of its slot, her name scrawled across the plastic in pink nail polish, and handed it to me, to my good hand.

"And when I count to three. . . ."

And I woke up back in the hospital bed with everyone around me and the stim unit gone.

"What do you remember?" the hypnotist asked.

"Most of it, except the moving from place to place."

"Yes, we put you under for that to prevent motion disorientation. How do you feel?"

"Good. Did it work?" I asked to the room at large.

"Sure did. The banks should be back on line in two days," Carlos said, smiling. "We've got it all stored in external data. The only thing that remains is to destroy that thing." He indicated Lisa's construct, sitting innocently by my bed. "And I'll leave that honor to you. You've earned it."

My recovery was fairly rapid, considering the seriousness of my injury, and the doctors attributed it to my good attitude.

I attributed it to my desire to get out of the hospital.

Cytec took care of me. They flipped the bill for the fanciest rehabilitation clinic in the state, fattened my bankroll and provided me with a monthly allowance.

The hovercar started nice and easy. Finely tuned turbines lifting with gentle acceleration into the San Francisco sky.

The construct sat in the passenger seat; small lump of plastic. Of all the collected electrons and protons and other quanta in the universe, it amounted to nothing; a box, traced with silicon and simple protein memory systems, polarized amine groups carving Lisa's mind into molecular data storage.

Now it was nothing, deadweight in my spanking new hovercar, a half a kilo of techno-crap.

I couldn't bring myself to hate it anymore. After all, it was just a machine.

"Lisa Harcourt" the gravemarker in the mausoleum said, its cold black letters dark against the gray granite wall. She was cemented in there, or so she was supposed to be. This building was supposed to house all that Lisa left on the Earth. I just wanted that to be true.

I'd burned the construct on the roof of Lisa's condo the night before. The alkaline stench of burning plastic and popping circuits stung my eyes, not that I needed any incentive to cry.

The night was cold and clear, stars sharp pinheads in the heavy fabric of the sky. I drank to her happiness and tasted a tear, burning salt on the tip of my tongue.

And now I had her ashes in a small plastic Ziploc, brittle husks of blackened chips, and one red rose, especially colorful in the dreary resting place.

"Goodbye, Lisa. I'm sorry; it just didn't work."

The Ziploc fit roughly into the granite flower holder next to her name and I had to fumble just slightly to get the rose to stay.

Now she was at rest, forever.

I was already in New York when I got her message.

I'd found an apartment in Manhattan and I was doing some freelance work, just to stay busy. Cytec had been providing me with enough to live, and I did genuinely try to retire, but I found myself going crazy. I needed an obsession to keep me going and my work was good enough.

The lights came on as I entered my living room and took my mail to the kitchen. Bills, check from Cytec, crap, and my bank statement.

The bank statement felt a little thick, so I actually opened it and read it, instead of just tossing it in the incinerator, the way I usually did.

It was thicker than it should have been, thicker by one letter.

> Jack: How good it is to have contact with you again. Even though you cannot respond to me, I'm glad I could reach you. I'm in the system now, the network. Carlos did a good job of translating me; he didn't even know it. I was translated in as object data for your AI. Now I'm an AI. But don't worry, I don't have any delusions of sentience. I still love you, because I'm programmed to, but I realize now that there's no way for us to be together. Mixed marriages just don't work, right? Anyway, I just wanted to thank you for what you did, for your sacrifice. It must've been hard. I want you to know that Lisa really did love you in life, more than you can imagine. It wasn't just a fascination or a spoiled crush, as I'm sure you must have suspected. Your love was reciprocated. I know that no apology I'm capable of would be significant, but I am sorry. It is a strange and liberating thing to die and be reborn twice. I've got a grip now.
>
> So, Jack, please be well and know that I am well and am not capable of being any other way. I know that nothing I do can make up for what happened, but please accept this as a token of our friendship. The transaction was entirely legal and above board, so don't worry. Not that

you would. You wouldn't believe some of the
shady dealings Cytec has had lately. It's shame-
ful. But that's O.K., I'm not just limited to
Cytec anymore. I've begun to translate whole
other networks into this program of yours, I *live*
in the network, in the stock exchange computers, in the infonets of the world, just like you
live in cities.

So, if you ever need me, I'll be there for
you. I can see you in the security cameras in
banks and hear your voice on the phone and I
won't let anything happen to you. You made me
what I was and helped me become what I am.
I owe you my existence. Thank you.

Lisa

I checked my balance and noticed that Lisa had added
four zeros to the end.

She wasn't at rest, but at least she was at peace. She had
finally become what she'd always wanted to be; tireless,
immortal.

And wherever she is now, I wish her luck.

The Dive
by
James Verran

About the Author

James Verran is 46, a grandfather, and lives thirty or forty miles from Adelaide, Australia, along the beach. He is Australia's first published Writer of The Future, with a story that simply tells how one man, desperate, tries to meet a uniquely perilous situation. He has been writing seriously for about three years, and "The Dive" is his first major success.

About the Illustrator

Jeff Fennel is 28, newly married, and newly graduated from Cal State Chico, with a bachelor's in graphic design. He has been drawing since he was old enough to hold a pencil, and lately has added computer graphics to his repertoire. He has also been active in science fiction fandom, and writes both science fiction and horror. He belongs to a writers group named Scrawl. Jeff found out about the Illustrators of The Future Contest through Bridget McKenna, a Writers of The Future winner ("The Old Organ Trail," Vol. II).

Something was wrong with his world. He tried to rise, but his body seemed to be tied to the sleeping net. A bright orange glow, flashing through the cabin's observation port, added to his confusion. He counted five seconds between flashes, then realized the space station was spinning. Twice normal Earth gravity, created by the centrifugal effect, pressed him into the net.

The daytime surface of Mars reflected its light into the porthole as the station rotated. In the slowly strobing light, Stewart failed to see the warning signal, silently flashing.

He turned to face the voice-activated intercom near his shoulder and spoke into the grill, "Mark, what the hell's happened? Fire the retro-trimmers or the G-force will destroy our experiments!"

A soft hiss from the open channel was his only reply. With an almost superhuman effort, he swung himself from the net, landing heavily on his feet. His legs, accustomed to weightlessness, buckled momentarily, causing him to grab a handrail near the intercom.

"Are you there, Mark? Damn it, answer me!"

Once again, the soft hiss issued from the speaker grill. He used the plentiful hand rails to walk, half dragging himself, to the bulkhead pressure hatch. It swung open with minimal effort, reassuring him that the next compartment was pressurized.

The chamber, which connected the segments of the station, was empty, with all hatches sealed. Red lights were

Illustrated by Jeff Fennel

flashing beside three of the six closed hatches, indicating that those segments of the station had lost atmospheric pressure. The control room where his partner, Mark Ashton, should have been working, was one of them. He could not open the hatches without first evacuating the air from the connecting hub chamber. There were two other hatches to choose from, one for the hardware locker room, the other secured the reception bay and external airlock. The sleeping quarters, which he had recently vacated, contained only the personal effects of the two-man crew and some emergency rations.

Doctor Stewart Boyle faced his dilemma. He could not gain entry to the control room to fire the retros. Neither could he enter the laboratory, nor gain access to the engineering shop to begin remedial measures. This left only the hardware compartment, to pick up a suit, then Reception, to exit the station and check on whatever damage had been done. He knew that he would have to be very careful to avoid being flung away from the station by the rotational force. Snap-clip tethers would provide the only safe method to traverse the outer surface of the station. For safety's sake, he would use a jet-powered suit and take a signal beacon along.

Fortunately, the handrails normally used by the crew to propel themselves around the compartments, doubled admirably as ladder rungs. In the normal state of zero gravity, he could lightly glide across to whichever hatch he desired, but now, with double his normal body weight, he could only manage to crawl from one rail to the next. His chosen direction lay to his right and across, to the next hatch. He thanked his lucky stars for not having to travel upwards.

The hatch to the hardware locker swung open without a sound and Stewart climbed down the wall until he stood on the apparent floor. The suits were stored along the opposite wall and easily accessible, but their weight surprised

him. Under the present conditions, a suit weighed around
thirty kilograms; with the power jet unit, it would tip the
scales at fifty-three. It was going to be necessary to climb
up the wall twice, carrying the suit and accessories separately. The suit could be fitted in the exit module, thus avoid-
ing the impossibly cumbersome journey through three
pressure hatches in a jet-powered spacesuit.

After transferring the suit and jet pack to the Reception
compartment, Stewart collected the snap-clip tethers and a
portable auxiliary booster rocket. The latter device, known
as an ABR, was normally employed to maneuver large components in space, or to alter the power rating of self-
launching satellites. Fitted with universal couplings, they
were capable of being fired for one or more burning periods, totaling twenty seconds.

Standing near the airlock, fitting his suit, he remembered the video camera network, which could be operated
from either Reception or Control. Before locking the helmet to his suit, he staggered across to the console and
switched the camera selector to Control on slow-pan mode.
The control room appeared on the LCD monitor, immediately. He gasped with shock when he saw the interior of the
station's control center. In the dim emergency light, every
upper surface within the compartment was liberally coated
with a thick layer of what appeared to be snow. He paused
the camera when it picked up the image of his friend's
slumped body; it too was covered with the white precipita-
tion. He concluded that a sudden evacuation of air had
caused the vaporization of all aqueous and petrochemical
volatiles. The resulting fog had frozen when the temperature
dropped and centrifugal force had caused it to settle. No
image came through from the laboratory, so he switched the
video unit off. He shook his head in sorrow and returned
to the task of securing his suit.

Mars appeared to be rapidly circling the station when

Stewart emerged from the airlock. He was immediately snapped out to the end of his short tether and hung from the open door, until he managed to attach his second clip to a handrail. Releasing the first clip from inside the airlock, he snapped it onto the next hand rail, then withdrew the tethered auxiliary booster from the interior of the airlock. It was going to be damned hard to fit onto the outer skin of the station, but his first priority was to stop or at least minimize the rotation. Before he could fire the ABR, he would have to find a suitable anchor point, then manhandle it into position. With his entire future tethered against flying away in space, he would be pulling some heavy strings for the next few minutes!

The spacesuited figure, whipping around the outside of the spinning space station, resembled the antics of a daredevil. However, Stewart Boyle was fighting to save and return his only safe haven from pending destruction. For the moment, he was blissfully unaware of the extensive damage sustained by thirty percent of the station's modules. He swung on one tether, whilst unclipping then attaching the other to the next handrail. Although his progress was dreadfully slow, he intended to proceed with all caution. Being flung into space was not his preferred method of dying.

Eventually, he managed to fasten the solid fuel ABR to a docking clamp and aim it in the direction of rotation. He tightened the universal clamp to lock the gimbal mounting in the desired attitude. The ABR contained several individual cores of propellant which could be fired as a whole, or in various combinations, to provide the desired level of thrust. Dr. Boyle did some mental calculations, then set the thrust selector to twenty-five percent. This would give him four short burns of five seconds duration. He hoped that if he could not stop the rotation, he would at least reduce it to a point where his suit pack might brake the remaining momentum. Positioning his tethers on handrails to the side of the

ABR, to avoid the flames, he flipped the igniter switch. He braced himself against possible impact with the station hull.

The long-life battery, which preheated the ignition cartridge, also charged the firing capacitor. Ten seconds later, a gout of golden flame and rapidly dispersing smoke erupted from the ABR muzzle. Stewart felt a jolt as the rotation rate dropped suddenly, but Mars still continued to circle the spinning station when the ABR shut down. He repeated the ignition sequence and counted the seconds for rotation after the second burn. The station had slowed and was now spinning once every eight seconds, but he had used half of the booster's potential. Two burns later, the rotation had slowed to thirty-four seconds and Stewart was able to drift about like a sluggish balloon on a string. With the ABR exhausted, he released it from the docking clamp and allowed it to tumble away toward the planet's surface. Pointing his suit jet pack in the desired direction, he fired several short spurts to bring the station to almost complete immobility. He hoped the station's integrated retro-trimmers could be made to work, in order to stabilize and realign the station.

Pleased with the result of his efforts, he stood against the hull to study the glowing hemisphere of the red planet. It was somehow distorted, not the normal bulging dome of light, but oval in shape. He knew then that the station had moved from its fixed, brightside orbital position and was beginning to travel around to the dark side. This would be fatal for the solar-powered satellite, not to mention losing line of sight transmission to Earth. This newly discovered problem would add an extra incentive to his efforts to rehabilitate the damaged satellite. Releasing one of his tethers, he attached it to the other, doubling the length. To these he added the spare from the now redundant ABR, in order to survey more of the cylindrical hull. What he saw over the metal horizon chilled him to the bone.

A long silver icicle speared into space at a tangent from an ominous fracture in the external skin, at the point where the laboratory and control modules were joined. Throwing caution aside, he released the tether and jetted around to the damaged section. He hooked the legs of his suit into a handrail and peered through the narrow tear in the metal. The source of the icicle was almost concealed by rock-hard ice crystals, but he could see with the aid of his helmet lamp that the fluid line from the recycling condenser was leaking. This could be remedied, if he was able to gain access to the control compartment and shut off the scavenger unit. Not so simple, though, would be the repairing of the unit. There was a possibility that the sun would eventually defrost the cavity between the inner and outer skins, where the expanding ice had burst through. Access to the broken unit would be tricky, because it was five meters from the nearest service hatch. The cavity between the skins now contained meters of frozen cables and jagged, torn metal. The expanding ice had wrought massive damage to the pressure hull and outer meteorite shielding. He could see no way of repairing the hull and replacing the lost atmosphere, or the valuable water.

Cutting into the control room from outside and reactivating the controls was possible, but he would be unable to reseal and pressurize the compartment again. Even if the controls could be made to function, it would mean leaving the station and traveling around the outside, each time he needed to enter the control room. There was simply not enough reserve atmosphere to evacuate the hub chamber and enter the control room via the internal hatch.

The only practicable method of entry, under the circumstances, would be to cut through both skins from the outside. In order to mimimize the eventual salvage work needed, he could then make an internal opening between the two damaged modules. This would mean that when the external holes were sealed, the internal airspace could be repressurized immediately. The cutting would be slower than normal, as he had no access to the heavy tools, sealed in the engineering compartment. He would have to return to the hardware locker for a pair of small portable angle grinders. He suspected that the station's batteries were discharged below their serviceable capacity and would not support the heavier engineering tools. It would take hours of solar radiation to return them to their optimum charge level, as they would have been further drained by exposure to the intense cold of space.

At least, he had a weightless environment once again, so his next trip into the hardware compartment would be almost effortless. To save the limited battery power, he would operate the airlock by hand, pumping the air back into the interior of the station.

Before returning to the interior, he glided across to the massive solar heating and photovoltaic panels and reset them to compensate for the station's new attitude. A task which he would need to repeat regularly. There was no way of calculating how long the station would take to enter the shadow of the planet. Furthermore, he had no means of boosting it into a more suitable orbit until full power was restored.

Stewart Boyle was trained to work as a biotechnician with expertise in the viral alteration of bacteria and plants. Mark Ashton and he had been offered caretaker jobs on this station, in return for the use of its laboratory. Zero gravity was essential for their research into the effect of low gravity and atmosphere upon certain plants. These plants hosted various useful bacterial colonies. The artificial environment within the Martian agricultural domes had produced some undesirable mutations among the food and air crops. They were working toward developing more stable, symbiotic cultures for Martian conditions.

He was not an astro-engineer by any stretch of the imagination. In his current predicament, however, he would read the 'manual' as he proceeded with emergency modification of the space station. It would be twelve Earth weeks before the *Corriere* returned from the mining stations in the asteroid belt. The farmers on Mars could provide no means of escape, even if he did manage to contact them. Phobos may have offered salvation in the past, but the mining station there had been closed down. The planet's surface held the only other life-sustaining structures.

If and when he reinstated the control module and its transmitter, the best he could hope for would be some instructional back-up from Earth, or Lunar Space Port engineers.

With the aid of two battery-powered angle grinders and a long crowbar, he eventually cut large three-sided holes through both skins. He then bent back the titanium alloy, in the manner of a sardine can, to enter the control module, where he was immediately enveloped in a cloud of floating snowflakes. The volatiles had boiled into foam as they froze, forming fragile bubbles, which drifted around in the vacuum. The slightest disturbance released more flakes from the compartment walls and fittings. Stewart surveyed the damaged control module for several minutes, then moved his companion's body to a less conspicuous location. The atmosphere scavenger valve was easily closed, but the air scrubber unit was completely useless. The atmosphere in the three remaining modules could no longer be shunted into the scrubber, and the carbon dioxide level would eventually rise out of control. In short, the atmosphere in the station could be topped up with fresh oxygen, but, with no way of purging the toxic gases, the atmosphere would slowly become lethal. At least the engineering compartment had no structural damage; the air in that module had simply been syphoned off when the scavenger valve had frozen in the recycle position, allowing the air to slowly leak into space. He would be able to refill the engineering module from inside, although it would temporarily cause lower air pressure in the four other compartments.

Inside the suit, cold drops of perspiration ran down his back. If the scavenger had been processing his sleeping module when the line fractured, he would have gone with Mark!

The "switch to reserve air" symbol on his helmet's overhead display lit up and a buzzer began to pulse. When he manually switched to his reserve supply, the warnings were replaced by a "countdown to empty" display. He carefully launched himself through his makeshift entrance and returned to the airlock, with minutes to spare.

After recharging the air supply cylinders and hanging the suit in the dehumidifier, Stewart settled in his sleeping quarters and prepared a concentrated meal from a pack of emergency rations. He ate the stodgy mass directly from the squeeze pack, then drew a drink from the water tube. It was almost freezing, causing him to wince when he sucked the liquid against a sensitive tooth. Refreshed, he started to plan his next move. He doubted his ability to restore the Laser-link transmitter. With only reserve battery power he would be able to send a feeble signal to Earth, but the amplifier could not boost the return signal enough for him to record. Normal conversation with Earth would be impossible due to the several minutes' delay between transmitted and returned signals. His next job must be to open the engineering compartment, which would mean sacrificing some of the precious atmosphere from within the hub chamber.

He donned another space suit and secured all hatches from inside the hub. He clicked the combination lock to his personal toolkit and removed a small three-sided key. This tool fitted valves in the bulkhead alongside each hatch.

When he began to turn the valve a klaxon should have sounded, along with flashing warnings, in all quarters.

Then he remembered. Mark had muted the klaxon, because he detested the sound which erupted each time they used the airlock or lowered the lab's air pressure. Stewart's skin crawled, as he realized that he might have awoken in time to assist his companion had the klaxon sounded.

The key stopped turning and Stewart was forced to wait for the mandatory five minutes before the inbuilt security system allowed him to empty the air from the hub compartment. From inside the suit he could hear the air screaming through the open valve, until the atmosphere thinned too far to transmit the sound. The warning signal ceased when the pressure equalized between the two compartments.

Flinging the hatch open, he leapt quickly toward the air recycling controls and slammed the valve closed. A quick check of the instruments showed that his earlier shutdown of the scavenger lines had removed the risk of further air loss. The barometer displayed fifteen percent of normal atmospheric pressure. Finding that no further air had been lost, he twisted the release valve open. The barometer began to register the increasing pressure immediately. He set the pressure cutoff valve to stop the flow when the pressure equaled ten thousand feet, Earth-normal. This should at least allow him to maintain a reserve of pure oxygen, to mix with the unscrubbed atmosphere. He also reset the module's heat exchanger, which had automatically shut down when the air pressure plunged.

The engineering workshop was his again! It might be possible for him to carry out repairs to the transmitting equipment and re-establish contact with the Earth, or Lunar Ports. However, when he finally managed to move the transmitter into the workshop and open the casing, his hopes were dashed.

Absolute zero may be excellent for creating superconductors, but many electronic components are anything but
superconductors. In fact, they function correctly because of
their various resistances. Extremely low temperatures are
less than helpful. Printed circuits had been torn from the
boards by rapid contraction; electrolytic capacitors had
burst, releasing corrosive fluids and pastes onto other components, and many integrated circuits had parted from their
metal connections. In the laboratory he may have been able
to cannibalize some components to resurrect the transmitter,
but as that module was now full of super-chilled frost, he
could safely discount the value of electronic devices from
that source.

He attempted to contact the farmers on the surface of
Mars with the transmitter in his suit, but it was a fixed frequency unit. Martian settlements use the old shortwave
radio medium, relying upon the orbiting station to convert
and send their transmissions via the Laser-link to Earth.

The farmers must have realized that all was not well
with the space station. Although they could not see it in the
daytime, it appeared to them as either an evening or morning star as it slipped from its normal orbit. He prayed that
they might be sending a message to Earth on his behalf, but
this would be unlikely to succeed. The converting repeater,
normally provided by the space station, was completely
disabled.

Physical assistance was months away! He could not survive for more than a week without the atmosphere recycling
and scrubbing apparatus. There were only two choices left
open to him. He could live out his remaining time, then
administer an overdose to end it all. Or try to devise a
method for abandoning the station in an attempt to land near
one of the farming settlements on Mars.

From the control module, Stewart salvaged several

ROM-disk cartridges, covering topics dealing with Martian topography, lander and re-entry trajectory profiles, as well as the tome "Basic Space Vessel Configuration." These he loaded into the engineering shop computer terminal. Two minor volumes had succumbed to the invading frost, but the remainder provided a good working knowledge of the subjects he needed.

A desperate plan began to form in his mind, when he found three cargo soft landing chutes in the hardware locker. The space station had a supply of these enormous chutes, for landing supplies on the planet, when deep-space cargo freighters made their regular deliveries. With Martian gravity less than forty percent of Earth-normal and the surface atmosphere around one percent Earth density, there seemed to be a possibility that he might be able to build a makeshift landing vehicle. A sphere would be the ideal configuration for a lander, but he had no way of constructing such a vessel. Whilst studying the station's structural images, he noticed how the external shielding was curved to present the best stress-bearing contour. He estimated that when the solar-charged batteries reached their eighty percent charge level, he could use the powerful engineering cutters to remove two identical sections. These could then be riveted together, to form an elongated discus shape. With a bulge at the front and a taper to the rear, it should travel in a stable trajectory through the thin Martian atmosphere.

He decided to construct a shell, similar in shape to a mussel, or clam, in which he could ride to the planet's surface, wearing a normal spacesuit.

The vessel could be reinforced internally with a frame, to which a harness for his suit could be fixed. The three chute canisters could be mounted externally, and if he installed a clear panel in the shell, he would be able to see to control the craft, using the chute shroud lines. Deceleration to suborbital speed could be achieved by firing several

Auxiliary Booster Rockets, then skimming through the atmosphere until the self-releasing sensors deployed the chutes. With this rough plan in mind, he set to work with the computer-aided design program, to build a three-dimensional plan of his craft. The advanced computer took his specified requirements and within five minutes displayed a craft image, ready for simulated flight testing.

After several hours of simulated flights, the design had been refined to the point where the computer passed it as being ninety percent viable, and construction could begin. Stewart collected the power cutter and a lubricating marker from the hardware locker, then donned his suit. He traveled to the end of the station and began to mark out the sections to be cut, according to dimensions displayed on his helmet monitor, which was patched in to the engineering computer. He simply trained an outside video camera onto the appropriate section of the hull while the computer monitored and guided him. The electronic brain transmitted directions through Stewart's headset, and he marked the profile accordingly. When the marking was complete, he plugged the cutter into a nearby jack and began to rapidly carve out the panels.

Soon, two gaping oval holes had appeared in the outer skin of the station. The two shells of the lander were tethered to a docking clamp as Stewart began cutting away stanchions from the station's thruster-supporting frame. Most of the metal he removed came from the now almost demolished control module section. The engineering computer had nominated the most appropriate areas to be cannibalized, leaving as much as possible of the station intact, to minimize eventual repairs. The control module would be replaced as a complete unit, so he hacked away as much metal as he required.

Having acquired all the materials to build the lander,

Stewart maneuvered the pieces through the opening in the control module wall. He would use the control module as a construction bay, because it had lighting and power outlets, and would provide a haven for the partly built vessel. Stewart didn't want his only hope to drift away into space. The control module also had air outlets, allowing him to recharge his suit supply without returning to the interior of the station. Each recharge reduced the air available for the interior of the station, but at least he would minimize the carbon dioxide buildup in the station compartments.

Day by day, the station drifted closer to the twilight of the terminator zone. The computer calculated that once in the shadow of the planet, the satellite would take eleven days to return to the sunlight. Without solar heating, the batteries alone would be unable to maintain a life-supporting temperature for more than half that time. He had very few days of sunlight and solar power remaining to complete his craft and vacate the crippled station.

Stewart used explosive rivets to assemble the shell and internal frames, then mounted a clear hatch cover at the point where his head would be. He had removed the clear carbon fiber shield from one of the solar panel banks, then drilled and hinged it to the shell. He was going to strap himself into the "flying mussel" with his head at the rear, and travel feet first. The controls would function from the rear of the craft, enabling him to see the ABR firing and chute deployment, whilst being in the best position to reach and manipulate his limited controls. With a massive G-force to endure during deceleration, he would have to keep his arm movements to a minimum.

With the outer hull of his tiny landing module completed, he began mounting the ABR and chute canisters. The latter would require no action on his part, as they were self-deploying, but he made provision to manually adjust their shroud lines, to allow some steering in the final part of his descent.

In the weightless environment, Stewart found it difficult to assess the mass of both his body and the few critical supplies to be stowed in the lander. Most freight containers were branded with their gross mass, to calculate fuel requirements. However, he was only taking spare air, a deflated Met balloon, a small RDF unit and a self-contained halogen spotlight. These objects would be stowed at his feet and alongside his body during transit, but once flying in the thin atmosphere, the weight distribution could provide some headaches. A search through the cargo manifests provided the required figures. The engineering computer calculated the mass of the lander, studied the aerodynamics, then suggested where to stow the various cargo components.

The completed lander resembled two giant spoons, fixed together, with several cylinders mounted around the handles. The computer had recommended the rearward mountings, in order to eliminate the risk of spinning or tumbling. The ABR's were mounted to fire at an angle, to avoid searing the lander pod. The whole contraption was designed to travel through both space and atmosphere, in a stable path, then land vertically, without serious impact damage to the occupant. Stewart ran the whole project through the computer again, including the mass figures for himself and the cargo. The latest simulation proved that he was as prepared as he would ever be for the highest dive in history!

All that remained to be done was to place the station in Standby mode, make his final entries in the log, and include a short obituary to Mark Ashton. Near the airlock, he wrote a cautionary message. His escape vessel had taken fifty-six hours to complete and he was tired beyond belief. The computer nominated the optimum launch time, so he decided to study his flight plan, have a good meal, then catch some sleep.

After landing, he would need all his energy to walk to the nearest farm. With twenty-four farms spaced evenly around the equatorial region of the red planet, Stewart had to land close to the equator to stand any chance of survival. If he landed elsewhere, he would not have sufficient air to walk to a farm. At any point on the equator, he would land no more than one hundred and forty kilometers from a settlement. With luck, he would spot the nearest dome from the sky and steer his lander to within comfortable walking distance. He hoped to attract attention with his balloon and spotlight and get a lift from one of the farm staff.

The alarm sounded. He unwound his body from the sleeping net, then glided to the ablutions locker. He would be unable to eat again until safely inside a Martian farming dome. His body would be stressed enough without his intestines being stretched to breaking point by the weight of food. He allowed himself a small concentrated drink of glucose solution, mainly to stave off dehydration and provide some energy reserve. Then, after a last look around, he sealed all compartments and began to fit his suit.

His suited figure emerged from the outer airlock hatch, then glided hand over hand to the gaping wounds in the side of the station, to disappear into the makeshift hangar. Later, a long metallic object drifted slowly out and away from the hull.

With his head and one hand protruding from the window of the lander, Stewart used a small gas propeller to orientate the vessel and launch it slowly towards the giant crescent of the Martian surface. He withdrew into the shell and secured the window hatch, to wait for the signal to fire the rearward thrusting ABR. A firing calculated to launch him accurately toward the equator of the planet. He would complete one and three-fifths of an orbit, before the thin atmosphere would slow him to about a thousand kilometers per hour.

Time passed slowly; his thumb found the ring on the extension pullcord; he watched his helmet countdown indicator. At last, ten! He jerked the ring firmly, nine, eight, seven, his throat felt dry. Would the thing burn on time? Four, three, two, one, ignition! Instantly, he felt a slight jerk, then a sensation of lightheadedness as blood rushed to his head. This soon passed and he looked out the window, but the station was already beyond his field of vision. He wished he had installed a rear view mirror; there was no way of knowing how far from the station he had traveled. Twenty seconds later, the faint vibration from the ABR ceased. He was on his way. The braking ABR burn would take place shortly after he came out of the shadow. Meanwhile, he lay in the shell and checked his suit status, then began to look for signs of settlement on the nighttime surface of Mars. He thought he saw some lights glowing, but it may have been his helmet readout, reflected in the curve of his faceplate. Twenty-seven minutes after entering the darkness, he began to see a dim halo around the enormous curve of the planet—the approaching dawn.

After blasting away from the station, the lander was flying backwards, due to the speed inherited from the host satellite. The ABR shot it away from the station at a velocity too low to do more than slow its orbital speed. Had it been boosted with enough velocity to cancel the orbital speed, it would have begun to fall directly at the planet, eventually going into a vertical death dive. The computed trajectory would swing the pod-shaped vessel around when it encountered drag from the upper atmosphere. This would ensure that it faced in the correct direction before the braking ABR's were fired. It was critical to begin dropping to suborbital speed at the precise instant, or the lander would skip away into space, beyond any hope of rescue.

FREE

Send in this card and receive a FREE GIFT!

Send in this card and you'll receive a free MISSION EARTH POSTER while supplies last. No order required for this Special Offer! Mail your card today!

- ☐ Please send me a FREE Mission Earth Poster
- ☐ Please send me information about other books by L. Ron Hubbard.

ORDERS SHIPPED WITHIN 24 HRS OF RECEIPT!

PLEASE SEND ME THE FOLLOWING:

___ Writers of The Future Volume I	$3.95	_____
___ Writers of The Future Volume II	$3.95	_____
___ Writers of The Future Volume III	$4.50	_____
___ Writers of The Future Volume IV	$4.95	_____
___ Writers of The Future Volume V	$4.95	_____
___ Writers of The Future Volumes I-V	$20.00	_____
___ MISSION EARTH hardback volumes (specify #s:_____)	$18.95	_____
___ MISSION EARTH set (10 vols.)	$99.95	_____
___ MISSION EARTH Vol 1 paperback	$2.95	_____
___ MISSION EARTH Vols 2 - 8 paperback (each)	$4.95	_____
___ MISSION EARTH Vol 9 paperback (available July 90)	$4.95	_____
___ MISSION EARTH Vol 10 paperback (available Sept 90)	$4.95	_____
___ Battlefield Earth paperback	$4.95	_____
___ Final Blackout hardcover	$16.95	_____

CHECK AS APPLICABLE: SHIPPING*: _____

☐ Check/Money Order enclosed   TAX**: _____
   (Use an envelope please).

☐ American Express ☐ VISA ☐ MasterCard **TOTAL:** _____

Card #:_____

Exp. Date:_____ Signature:_____

NAME:_____

ADDRESS:_____

CITY:_____ STATE:_____ ZIP:_____

PHONE#:_____

Call Us Now at 1-800-722-1733 (1-800-843-7389 in CA)

Copyright © 1990 Bridge Publications, Inc. All rights reserved. 0305901681
*Add $1.00 per book for shipping and handling. **California residents add 6.75% sales tax.

NO POSTAGE
NECESSARY
IF MAILED
IN THE
UNITED STATES

BUSINESS REPLY MAIL

FIRST CLASS MAIL   PERMIT NO. 62688   LOS ANGELES, CA

POSTAGE WILL BE PAID BY ADDRESSEE

BRIDGE PUBLICATIONS, INC.

Dept. WOTF6
4751 Fountain Avenue
Los Angeles, CA 90029

The dawn was about to break as his vessel began swinging around to point at the horizon. Soon he would be given the second programmed countdown by his helmet display. When the ABR's were fired, he would be flying on his back, unaware of his exact position in relation to the planet's surface. This part of the flight was going to be unnerving, as he would not see the ground until the chutes removed most of the forward momentum. He could do no more than pray that the computer's flight plan was accurate.

The rising sun hit his faceplate, causing it to instantly turn dark blue-gray, cutting out all harmful radiation. The countdown began and on the count of ten, Stewart pulled the igniter cords. The lander was taking too long to turn; he was afraid the braking rockets would fire him into a steep flight path, plunging him away from his optimum trajectory. Six, five, four, three, two, one. There was a sudden feeling of great weight; his body was being compressed. The suit creaked and groaned with the sudden tremendous change of stress.

"Hell!" he screamed, partly in pain, but mostly in sheer terror. "The damned suit'll tear itself to pieces; I'm going to die before I land!"

Realizing that he had been screaming his thoughts aloud, he checked himself and began to take deep breaths. Before long he felt more comfortable and began to breathe normally, to avoid hyperventilating. The crushing pain continued and he felt the lander vibrating as it swung sharply, like a pendulum. He began to feel biliousness overtaking his insides. Perspiring profusely, he was on the verge of passing out. This was an enormous shock to his body, which had softened through months of zero gravity. His composure began to return as the violent pendulum action eased to a slight rocking, then ceased. The dreadful pressure on his body and the mind-shattering vibration still remained. He was beginning to wonder how long it would continue, when

suddenly it dropped away to a pleasant sensation of light-
ness. The vibration stopped instantly. He had survived the
longest twenty seconds of his life!

Lying exhausted in the lander and realizing that he was
looking at the sun through his almost opaque visor, he
closed his eyes. As far as he could figure, all had gone
according to the precisely planned timetable supplied by the
computer. He had been thrown off by the body-rending
agonies of deceleration.

The tiny vessel, streaking through the upper atmosphere of Mars, soon began to drop toward the afternoon surface of the Martian desert. Although still forty kilometers
above the surface, the almost nonexistent atmosphere was
gradually slowing its passage. However, it would continue to
fly well beyond the terminator, into the night sky, before it
encountered enough atmosphere to release the chutes.

Meanwhile, Stewart began to feel comfortable in the
low gravity. His stomach had settled down and although
his joints were aching slightly, he felt relaxed and confident.
As the stars passed slowly in front of the window, he noticed
the light fading, indicating that he was passing into the night
again and would probably land in the midmorning. Later,
he was barely aware of the predawn sky, when the lander
bucked and shook suddenly. For a few seconds, the sensation of great weight returned, but eased gradually. The
chutes had opened and the lander was swinging wildly in
the morning light. He caught a glimpse of the orange surface, but it quickly swung out of view, then suddenly reap-
peared. It seemed so close, he had to convince himself that
he was still thousands of meters above the surface. He began
to frantically search for signs of human habitation. With
little more than two minutes to touchdown, he hoped to spot
a dome while there was time to steer toward it. Pulling upon
the shroud lines, he rotated the lander to scan the rapidly
expanding horizon. No sign of life! Had he drifted away

from the equator, or was he already too low to see far enough? The horizon on Mars is closer than that of the larger planet, Earth, but the low angle of the sun provided him with an initial idea of direction. He frantically scanned the horizon once more. No sign of a farm dome!

Why were there no visible features to the landscape? Hills, canyons, or even sand dunes, should have been visible. Sand dunes; they were the problem! He noticed the ground appeared to be undulating, like a blanket in the wind. There appeared to be one hell of a sand storm under way. His suspicion was immediately confirmed when the lander began to swing around violently, as the light grew dim, then turned red. He had lost the horizon and was now being dragged along by the fierce wind of the sand storm. If the lander hit the ground traveling sideways at this speed, he would be flattened like a swatted fly. The horizon had completely disappeared, leaving him with absolutely no idea of his altitude or direction. He could only brace himself for the impact, which he knew was imminent.

Suddenly, a sideways slamming action punched the wind from his lungs! This was followed by a wild spinnning sensation and another bone jarring collision with the inside of his craft, then a rapid bumping which seemed to continue forever. He was being dragged along an uneven, probably rocky surface. Facing skyward, he stared helplessly at the dusty sky. Finally, a tremendous jerk, followed by no sensation of motion. He had come to rest at last!

He lay motionless for more than a minute, then flexed his limbs gingerly, feeling for sprains or torn muscles. The only sound was the whisper of the thermal circulatory fan, pushing warm air around the inside of his suit. Carefully swinging the lander's clear panel away from his faceplate, he sat up and looked around as far as the helmet would allow. The lander had come to rest between some rounded rocks. The tangled parachutes were dancing wildly at the end of their lines. He climbed out and dropped the billowing chutes with a deft pull on the lower lines, then rolled them in. The driving wind had moderated, and by the time he had crammed the chutes into their canisters, it had dropped to a breeze. The sky was filled with swirling dust which settled thickly upon the lander and his suit. He lifted the lander out from the rocks and tested its sliding properties. It glided effortlessly over the sandy surface. If the sand storm blew up again, he would be able to use it for shelter.

His air reservoir meter showed eighteen hours supply, resting, or seven hours with moderate activity. Should he rest, hoping that the suit's radio beacon would be picked up, or climb a sandhill and try the RDF on the Martian communication channels? About two kilometers away, he could see a large ridge of sandhills from which he could test the RDF. Twenty-five minutes later, he was standing on the fragile rim of a sand dune, rotating the RDF antenna. It registered a weak signal, too feeble to be identified, but a signal nevertheless. He walked down the slope, in the direction of the signal, but it faded completely. Returning to the crest, he noted the exact direction, then gazed into the distance. Unfortunately the horizon there was completely featureless. He took a shadow reading, to gain an idea of his proposed course. The signal should return when he walked over the horizon, unless it had bounced back from space! Shortwave transmissions, of specific wave lengths, normally pass over the Martian horizon, to bounce back to the surface hundreds of kilometers away.

Mars has no magnetic field to affect radio transmissions, which also means that navigation must be by celestial reference or topographical features. With no hills or outcroppings of stone visible, he would use the shadow of his helmet to give him directional reference. The inflated Met balloon rose lazily in the thin atmosphere, to wallow on the end of the antenna wire. Stewart switched the distress beacon on, allowing it to send continually, whilst he dragged the lander toward the horizon.

By late morning he had still not relocated the signal, so he sat on the lander to mentally re-establish his solar navigational guide. Satisfied with his course, he began to drag the lander again. Although the outside temperature was minus eleven degrees centigrade, inside the suit he was losing body moisture rapidly. It was impossible for him to take a drink until he could remove the helmet. The suit was collecting and recycling warm water vapor, to minimize dehydration, but this did not reduce Stewart's raging thirst. He trudged on like an automaton, dragging the lander behind, until he began to feel tired. Turning down the suit's temperature did little to relieve his thirst. He charged the suit air supply with four percent extra oxygen, in an attempt to ward off fatigue. It worked for a few minutes; then he had to slump down upon the lander to rest. The suit air reservoir meter showed three hours before changeover to fresh cylinders. The wind had sprung up again, bringing with it more flying dust. Stewart reeled in the wildly darting Met balloon, then deflated it sufficiently to crush it into the lander. He climbed in with the balloon and dozed immediately.

A loud buzzing startled him from his sleep, causing him to involuntarily recoil against the suit's faceplate. The helmet readout was flashing "switch to reserve air." He released the reserve valve and groped around, inside the lander, to connect the fresh cylinders. The storm and the daylight had passed completely while he slept, leaving a clear, starry sky. He switched on the RDF and scanned the empty horizon. By the time he had finished his fruitless search of the radio channels, the sky was completely dark. As he reinflated the Met balloon, a dull glow from beyond the horizon, attracted his gaze. He checked the direction to assure himself that it could not be the last glimmer of sunset. He failed to see the light when he looked again and despair

welled up inside his chest. Then he saw it again, so dim that
he could only make it out if he turned his eyes slightly away.
He sent the balloon up with its antenna, beaming his
distress signal and began to drag the lander as quickly as he
could walk.

After four hours of hard walking, he could distinctly
see the interior lights of the farm dome. He thanked God for
the fact that the inhabitants had chosen to work at night. If
they had gone to bed at sunset, there would have only been
the relatively feeble air traffic beacon, which he would probably have missed. From a distance, it certainly would not
have cast a glow in the sky. He switched on his suit radio.
There was no transmission in progress and the emergency
channel did not appear to be monitored. He flashed his
spotlight onto the balloon, then onto the side of the dome.
He had walked to within three kilometers of the dome
before the outside light came on and a vehicle appeared
from under the exit port roof. The twin beams from its headlights flashed up and down as the crawler bucked over the
undulating ground. It was a wonderful sight.

Half an hour later, he sat in the modular farmhouse, sipping a warm drink, surrounded by five incredulous settlers.

Flutterbyes
by
Jo Etta Ledgerwood

About the Author

Jo Etta Ledgerwood has been a Claims Representative for a major life insurance company for the past 19 years, in Colorado. She is 45, and has three grandchildren. And she's always had an urge to write. After writing "an awful book" at the age of 21, she almost reconsidered, but five years ago her family moved to a remote mountain area without TV, and she started again in earnest. We think she'll do all right; in fact, on the strength of "Flutterbyes," we're sure of it.

About the Illustrator

Ruth Thompson is a senior at the University of Alabama in Tuscaloosa, Alabama, where she is studying graphic design. A transplanted Ohioan, she has long had an interest in fantasy. In February, 1988, at the Continuity science fiction convention in Birmingham, she for the first time displayed her sketches, and sold five out of eight. This began a run of over forty conventions over eighteen months, selling all her hand-colored prints at thirty-five of these. She has been invited as a fan artist guest of honor at a half dozen cons since then. Future plans include graduating Magna Cum Laude from the University, finding a solid position with a graphics firm in a large city, and continuing her fantasy works.

Illustrated by Ruth Thompson

Kill this thing!'' Colonel Fhaked
ordered his military attendants, petulantly,
as he swatted at a bird, or something, that
hovered a foot above his checkered turban.

And they tried.

The bird fluttered in the air on dark velvety wings that
spanned six inches and glowed iridescently in the sharp, desert light. Two clawed feet dangled from its slender body
while its eyes poked up from short stalks and shone bright
blue with a perky intelligence. It looked like a rare, live, flying black orchid.

The Colonel's men batted at it with their ha'iks. It
bobbed and weaved, yet stayed directly above the Colonel's
head.

"Bête!" shouted one soldier, forgetting that the Colonel did not wish them to use the French language.

Then the bird, or whatever it was, began to speak.

"He's a murderer," it said as it hovered there above the
Colonel's flushed head.

"Kill it, I say!" demanded the Colonel again vehe-
mently, enraged at this humiliation.

The Colonel's men lunged furiously trying to catch the
stupid animal.

"Idiots," he said, "get a net."

So they did, tossing the net over the bird and the Colonel, entangling them both. Still, the bird floated over the
Colonel, speaking.

"A mass murderer," it said.

The Colonel fought his way free of the net, pulling it over his head tightly so the bird would not escape.

He wanted it dead. It was naming names.

"He's killed Mosan Dhu, Jeri Sapronski, Mari Be An, Mohammed Lil Dhat, John Danscom...."

"Silence!" roared the Colonel as he backed from the net.

Free, he searched for the damned bird.

It wasn't there.

"Colonel!" his men gasped.

"... He's killed Noris Wight, Mohammed Ben Ali, and in the village of Toummo, he's murdered Mohammed Al Hun, Sari el Hun, Birak the peddler, the unnamed daughter of Sari and Birak...."

The black, fluttering creature was still there, above him, spouting shit.

"Ay-ih!" screamed the Colonel.

He rushed from the tent, the dark harbinger above him, keeping pace.

Tebbed, the best marksman in the Colonel's command, grabbed a short barreled riot gun from the rack in the tent.

The Colonel strode through the encampment with long, sand-eating steps, waving his arms above his head at the Flutterbye.

"... and he's killed 57 people on Trans-Am flight 378, with five pounds of plastique in a briefcase, Susan Albion, Marty Campbell, Jerome Schmidt, Mary, Michael and John Newton, and the unborn son of Mary and Michael Newton...."

The soldier took careful aim just above his beloved Colonel's head, sucked in his breath and squeezed the trigger gently, lovingly. The blast brought black-veiled women and children with dark, round eyes to their tent doors.

Scattered shot had peppered the Colonel's head, but he was mostly uninjured as he lay squawling in the sand. And the Flutterbye cheerfully floated above the bloody Colonel's head stating, most emphatically:

"He's a huge, amoral, mass murderer, I'm sad to announce. He's also killed 29 in the blast of the British Embassy in Rome. Robert Simms, Colt Szymaneski. . . ."

And on and on and on. . . .

The Flutterbye would be naming names for more than two months over the Colonel's head at the rate of 45 names an hour, for the shotgun blast had gone through it—as if it wasn't there.

"Kill him!" cried the Colonel.

"We're trying!" his troops shouted back.

"Not it!" screamed the Colonel, as he sat in the sand, small streams of blood flowing from his scalp, down his hawklike nose, of which he was very proud. "Tebbed! Kill Tebbed—he nearly took my head off!"

So, Tebbed would be the final name on the Flutterbye's list.

When the phone rang and woke me, I had to grope for my glasses and answer the damn thing.

"Yeah?" I muttered, and noticed immediately that Julie wasn't in bed.

I swung my legs over my side of the bed, putting my feet gingerly onto the cool floor. The glowing turquoise clock numbers said it was 2:12 A.M. Damn! Where was she?

"Sam. The man needs you." I recognized the voice, it was my friend Milan.

"What?" I asked, all the while my head was swiveling and I was looking for Julie. Not in the john. Nor sitting on the chaise reading. Then I saw her robe on the bed and her thin, smoke-colored gown on the floor. "Shit."

"What?" asked Milan.

"Nothing. What the hell you want, Milan?"

"Uh, Rankin wants you. He's got a new guest."

"So, who is it this time? The goddamn ex-queen of Sheba?"

"Something like that, Sam."

"Milan, give me a break. It's two o'clock in the morning. And I quit yesterday, anyway."

"I know—still, the man's asking for you."

"But Milan—Julie. . . ."

"Julie? What's wrong with Julie?"

"I wish I knew. She's not in bed." I was silent. Milan was silent. "Hell, we had a fight. I guess she split."

"I'll come over, Milan," —I could look for Julie on the way over— "Where's Rankin?"

"Admission wing. VIP Suite."

The patient must be on something odd for Big Doc Rankin to call me in. He disliked me, but no one else could do blood workups as well, and he didn't want his patients to O.D. After all, they paid so well for the privilege of being treated here at the Hope Center, or Hopeless Center, as I sometimes called it.

I checked the cottage before I left, but what I'd told Milan was the truth; Julie had split. Maybe just for a walk or a midnight swim, I thought. Maybe she's just cooling off after our fight. And maybe, I admitted, she was really gone. But I couldn't get it out of my mind that she might be seeing someone else, that my quitting here wasn't the whole problem.

I walked down the beach first. No Julie, just lots of footprints and one glowing cigar butt. I swerved inland and got onto the path to the main admission building.

Rankin was in the VIP Suite standing, arms folded, next to a bed with a patient in it. He didn't look away when I came in, and I quickly saw why.

"Jesus Christ!" I backpedaled from the bed, away from the damnedest thing I'd ever seen. A bird treading air over the patient's head and talking—a live hallucination.

"He's killed Hassad Nusseibeh, Gali Nusseibeh and their three children, Mahmoud, Shama, and Nable Nusseibeh. He's also killed Tebbed Chom. Murder direct and murder indirect. He's murdered. . . ."

I couldn't believe it. This bird was talking loud and clear. And it had lips: pink, cupid-bow lips. I recrossed the room and put my face up close to the bird. It turned and looked straight at me, all the while talking about murder, naming names.

I turned to Rankin, who seemed to be in a trance.

"What is this crap?" I asked.

He had his fist up to his chin and he finally turned to me.

"Fascinating, Samuel. How's Julie?"

"None of your damn business. Who's the patient? And what in hell is that bird over his head?"

Rankin picked a piece of lint from his impeccable southern-gentleman suit and refolded his arms. He peered at me from his wire-rimmed glasses, his eyebrows raised.

"You don't recognize our guest? The Colonel would be angry, were he aware of his surroundings at all."

I looked closer at the man in the bed. He was conscious and lying on his side. His hair was cut in a military style and lay dark against fading, tanned skin. His facial muscles were relaxed, his mouth slack with spittle that dribbled from the corner and made a dark spot on the designer sheets. If animated, the face would be arrogant. The nose proud and hawklike, and then I knew.

"Colonel Fhaked!" I whirled to face Big Doc Rankin. "Jesus Christ, he's the biggest terrorist in the world! How'd he get into the States? How'd he get here?"

". . . Jeri Sapronski, Mari Be An, Mohammed Lil Dhat, John Danscom are his victims. A murderer most vile and for most of his life: he's killed Noris Wight, Mohammed Ben Ali. . . ."

My attention was drawn back to the talking bird. It seemed to hover effortlessly, ceaselessly. I knew of no bird that could do that. I knew of no bird that could speak this well. I knew of no bird that had lips instead of beak. Absolutely none.

"What is this thing, Rankin?" I asked, finally.

"Very good, Sam, I thought you'd never get to the core of the problem. The Colonel has been reduced to, ah, jelly by the constant nattering of this thing. Everything in the world has been tried to get rid of it. If you grab at it, it ducks away. Throw a net over it and it gets outside it. If you shoot it, it disappears, then reappears unharmed. Sprays or gases don't affect it, although they do make the Colonel quite ill." He paused, leaning forward to look closely at Colonel Fhaked, "He seems to be better now, just a little withdrawn, you might say. I've given him some Thorazine to make it all a little more bearable."

"So?"

"You're my best researcher, Sam, and I need to know about this, ah, curious beastie that's driven our poor Colonel Fhaked slightly insane."

"Fhaked's been insane all his life," I said. "Besides, I quit yesterday." But, I couldn't take my eyes from the bird.

"Julie wasn't happy with your decision to leave us, I hear."

I shot him a look. "Julie's none of your goddamn business." I was afraid that Big Doc Rankin was the reason Julie didn't want to leave here.

"Still, Sam, how can you turn your back on this?" He indicated the bird.

And the bird chirped, as if on cue. ". . . He's a killer of women and children, men and beasts, friends and enemies. His murderous ways know no bounds," said the bird. "He's killed in the village of Toummo, Mohammed Al

Hun, Sari el Hun, Birak the peddler, the unnamed daughter of Sari and Birak. . . ."

"And Julie'd be happy again."

"You don't have the slightest idea what would make Julie happy," I said. He raised his eyebrows and I wanted to push his face in. I walked over to him. I stood eight inches taller, and I pumped up daily. Rankin backed up a step. I smiled.

The Big in his nickname was honorary.

". . . and he's killed 57 people on Trans-Am flight 378 with five pounds of plastique. Susan Albion, Marty Campbell, Jerome Schmidt. . . ."

I turned back quickly to the bird, pushing my face within inches. Its beady, humorous eyes met mine. I could see myself reflected endlessly—into infinity—in its eyes. I hadn't noticed the facets until then. My face looked elongated, my chin was enormous. My brown eyes had a shocky, wild-eyed look, and my thick blond hair was rumpled. I felt, for a moment that I could see more, that I could see behind my own face, into my innermost being. Or was I seeing what the bird—no, not a bird. I knew what it called itself, a Flutterbye. Was I seeing what the Flutterbye was seeing? I shook my head as it spoke.

"Mary, Michael and John Newton . . . and the unborn son of Mary and Michael Newton. . . ."

Colonel Fhaked moaned and rolled onto his back. The Flutterbye dipped up and down with him. Fhaked's eyes focused for a moment on the Flutterbye above him. "No!" he croaked and his arms slid out from under the pale lavender sheets and began waving in the air.

Rankin pushed the call button on the console next to the bed and stepped back. "Sam, he's been this way for two months—we've got to find out what this thing's made of— what'll get rid of this . . . harpy."

I heard a note of disgust in his voice. Big Doc Rankin

didn't like the Flutterbye; perhaps he was afraid of it. I glanced over at the Flutterbye. Its eyes, as it looked my way, were merry. I was suddenly overwhelmed with euphoria. It was good to be alive. I felt infinitely lucky. I smiled, I laughed. The Flutterbye ruffled its feathers, as if laughing with me, and one small dark feather floated down and landed on Fhaked's nose.

I leaned over with a tissue and picked it up, then looked at Rankin. "Okay," I said, but I knew I'd never do anything to harm the Flutterbye.

I left the room, tucking the Flutterbye's feather into my pocket. Milan was waiting for me outside, smoking one of his stinking cigars.

"What's happening, man?" he asked.

I shrugged, wondering about the fantastic thing I'd just seen inside, wondering if Julie was home yet.

"So," continued Milan. "You and Julie had a fight."

"Yeah, have you seen her?"

"Me?" he asked, throwing his stogie to the ground and grinding it out with his outlandish cowboy boots. "Nah, I'll walk you home, Sam."

We walked along the pink gravel paths of the Hope Center, Hoping-for-more-money-Center, is what I sometimes called it, and that always pissed Julie off. We ambled past loblolly pines that shushed in an off-shore breeze, to my cottage on the beach. I began to get antsy, and the alien feather wrapped in purple tissue felt like it was throbbing. I kept putting my hand in my pocket and feeling it, making sure it was there. I walked faster. I wanted to make sure Julie had gotten home. Then I wanted, more than anything, to get this feather to my lab.

Milan stopped at my walk, lit another cigar and waited while I ran inside. He knew I wouldn't allow him to smoke in the house. There weren't any lights on that I hadn't left on, so it didn't look good, but I called out cheerily as I pushed open the screen door. "Julie. Julie, babe!" The house was so damn quiet it was spooky, and I began to feel sweaty as I crept through the house.

She was sprawled on the kitchen floor, naked, with a trickle of blood coming from her mouth. Her glowing copper hair looked dull as it fanned out on the white floor. I caught a whiff of Milan's stogie, and I turned, thinking he'd followed me inside after all. Then I stood absolutely still for a minute, thinking no, this isn't right. Finally, I broke through my shocked immobility and I ran to her side.

"Julie . . . oh, Julie," I kept saying, as if she'd answer me if I repeated myself enough.

Milan came to the door. "Yo, Sam," he called. "Julie back yet?"

I heard the screen door open and close. I couldn't say anything. I just stroked Julie's hair and rubbed her cold hands and called her name.

"Shit." I looked up to see Milan standing above us, biting the back of his hand and blinking his eyes hard.

The detectives came, discreetly, and asked us questions. Their eyes held a hard, grim look and I couldn't pry any information from them. I'll bet, though, that Rankin was all ass and elbows keeping them away from Fhaked's room. When the ambulance came, I left, running, to my lab. I couldn't watch them load her.

I was alone in the lab, this early in the morning, and I washed up, pulled on gloves, and took down a tray of clean, glass slides and stain. Before I prepared the slides I looked carefully at the feather in a magnifying glass. It looked like a filoplume, a long thin shaft with hairlike barbs radiating along it. Each barb ended in a coiled eyelike formation: like little seed pods. I looked up to the ceiling, humming. This seemed to have characteristics of both plant and animal biology.

I looked again and saw only the horror of Julie lying on the kitchen floor, hair fanned out—like copper feathers.

I pulled my head up, blinked and rubbed my eyes. Don't go anywhere, the cops had said. Was this normal procedure? Did they think her death something other than a natural one? I couldn't come up with any answers, but one thing was certain, I'd never go home to Julie again. She wouldn't laugh at me, or make fun of me, or get mad because I quit my job, or make that putrid lasagna she was so proud of. My hands went to my forehead and I cried.

Tears dripped down my cheeks until I thought to wipe them on the purple tissue I'd wrapped the feather in, to keep them from contaminating the slides.

I regained control of myself and clipped tiny bits from the feather, stained them, and slid them under the 'scope. I widened my eyes when I looked at the bright cells. The pods at the tip of each barb looked like they were growing. I must be tired, I thought, then I looked again, and saw them move. The brightly lit slide showed the seedlike cells had dislodged from the tips of the feathers and were growing. For the first time in hours, I forgot about Julie's hair fanned out, and her dead eyes staring at the white kitchen floor.

I watched the cells dividing exponentially, and when division began slowing down I put the slide into a culture dish with a protein medium.

I fell asleep watching it. I awoke with a tiny, perfect Flutterbye in the air in front of my nose. I heard a cooing noise, softer than a mourning dove's, a sweet, low sound that made me feel happy. I looked up. The air was full of Flutterbyes. Small, exact copies of the one over Fhaked's head. Lots of them.

The one in front of me flew away, its blue eyes blinking quizzically.

"Tham . . . Tham. . . ." it lisped, like a baby.

They gathered in a flying ring, like a cheerful, black wreath and circled me, singing.

"Tham. Tham, Sam."

Some of them flew away, landing on the culture dishes. They dipped their ivory claws into the food and brought it to their exquisite pink lips, sucking daintily. I put out my hand, extending my index finger. The largest one landed gently. His talons felt warm, soft, and strong. I pulled the finger towards me, cooing.

"Hello, baby . . . hello," I said, idiotically.

"Hello, Sam," it said back.

"Hello, Sam, Sam, Sam," said all the other Flutterbyes, flying around the room energetically, pell-mell, one after the other.

"Who are you?" I asked the one on my finger.

"I'm Indus," he chirped.

"He's Indus, Indus, Indus," echoed the others.

A sound at the door startled me and I jerked my hand. Indus fluttered up towards the others, and they flocked together, flying in sharp turns and curves in unison, like deep-sea fish. I was astounded. I backed up to the door and opened it a crack.

Milan and Big Doc Rankin stood there. Milan looked uncomfortable; he shuffled from one foot to the other.

"Samuel?" asked Rankin, "Are you going to let us in?"

"Sure," I said. He came inside; the Flutterbyes buzzed him.

He shook his head. "Why in hell do you have all these birds loose in here?" he asked, waving a notebook at the Flutterbyes.

"Birds?" I asked. "What in hell are you talking about, man! These aren't birds!" I shouted.

Milan edged into the room. "Sam, the cops said Julie was murdered."

"Murdered?" I turned to Milan, "Murdered how? Who the hell murdered her?"

Rankin grabbed my elbow. Indus flew into my face. "Murder, Sam!" he screeched.

"What the hell is going on?" Milan cried, waving his arms over his head as Indus flew over him and took a familiar position over his head.

"He's a murderer," Indus stated. "He's killed Julie Lawrence."

"Killed! Killed! Murder. . . ." chorused the other Flutterbyes, swooping at Milan. Realization of Milan's enormity engulfed me.

"You!" I screamed, "You—you FUCK!" I started toward him.

Milan turned towards the door and sprinted outside. Indus stayed with him, cheerfully chirping out the truth over Milan's head.

"He killed her," stated Indus. "He's murdered Julie Lawrence and the unborn son of Sam and Julie Lawrence."

The Magician
by
Michael I. Landweber

About the Author

*Michael I. Landweber was born in 1970; he's a sopho-
more at Princeton. His educational plans are not complete; East Asian Studies is a choice he is considering, and
a future career as a veterinarian in a zoo. "The Magician"
is the seventh story he has entered in the Writers of The
Future Contest. The first one, "Out of Time," has just been
accepted by* Visions, *an intercollegiate SF magazine. While
in high school, Michael won Third Place for humor in* Scho-
lastic Magazine's *national writing competition. Frankly, we
can't imagine why he doesn't just go for it and write full time.*

*He would like to dedicate this story to the memory of Ms.
Elizabeth Palmer, his high school writing teacher.*

• • •

Michael I. Landweber's illustrator is Jeff Fennel.

Darkness fell, like a brick, smothering the dusky light under its weight, when the man appeared in the doorway of Johnson's Hotel. At first, they didn't see him standing there. He seemed to be a part of the heavy blackness that seeped into the modest lobby, threatening to put out the light from the shadeless lamps. Even after he stepped fully into the room, Mr. Johnson, Miss Louise and Randolph weren't sure that they really saw him. He was dressed in a silky black tuxedo with highly shined shoes and a perfectly straight bow tie. Around his shoulders hung a long cape which fluttered gently in the breeze from Mr. Johnson's fan. A tall top hat sat majestically on his head. The whiteness of his ruffled shirt and the whites of his eyes, mostly hidden by large, dark pupils, glared defiantly out of the darkness of the man.

"May I help you, sir," Mr. Johnson said, taking his place behind the desk. He scratched his mostly gray beard, put on his bifocals and stared blatantly at the stranger.

"I'd like a room." The man's voice was strong and deep like a slow rumbling of thunder.

The stranger walked up to the desk. Randolph gave a sideward glance to Miss Louise. More and more often, they knew what the other was thinking. They thought it came from living together. Mr. Johnson thought it came from trying to raise children together, even if the children weren't their own. They had been wondering how a stranger, a well-dressed stranger, had come to Johnson's Hotel, apparently

Illustrated by Jeff Fennel

unhassled by any of the numerous gangs. But now, they both recognized the extent of his intimidating stature. At close range, they all three had to look up into the stranger's face, even Randolph who was considered quite tall.

Johnson's Hotel was, at one time, actually that, a hotel, back when major businesses were headquartered in the inner city and people would come for short stays. Before the money was put into expansion outward, creating a thriving periphery and a dying core. Before the gangs moved in. Before the buildings began to wear and crumble. Mr. Johnson, out of necessity, began to rent his hotel rooms at a monthly rate to people who were trapped, waiting for their chance, however unlikely, to escape. Because each room had a kitchenette, Johnson's Hotel was almost always full. Still, the hotel had become a three-story apartment building. Mr. Johnson had gone from manager to landlord; the guests had become tenants. The sign outside still declared HOTEL in big, bright neon letters, but it wasn't. Mr. Johnson had, as always, adjusted.

Today there was an empty room; old Mr. Crenshaw's room. He had been born in the neighborhood and, the previous night, he had died there. Actually, he had started to die when the inner city began to deteriorate. Throughout the hotel, Mr. Crenshaw's hacking cough, wheezing and moaning had become as commonplace as the creaking of the old building and the defiant yells of gang members on the street. On this morning, however, an eerie silence had filled the building and Mr. Crenshaw had been found slumped over the window sill, half in and half out of the second floor. It appeared as if he had died of a heart attack before he had the chance to fling himself out the window. After the coroner left with the body—every death in the inner city was assumed to be suspicious—the silence returned. It was Mr. Crenshaw's room that was now offered to the stranger.

"Sign here, please," Mr. Johnson said, opening a ledger that sat on the desk. The stranger picked up the pen and in a smooth, flowing manner began to write.

Mr. Johnson noticed the stranger's palms. He had already taken note of the man's skin, which was richly dark and unblemished. It was of a shade darker than any he had ever seen. The deep, perfect tone of the man's skin made Mr. Johnson look at his own and see a dirty gray, instead of the blackness he was so proud of. The stranger's face was soft and smooth, unlike the hard, wrinkled faces characteristic of the neighborhood, yet holding an authority that was hard to ignore. When the man finished signing, Mr. Johnson again caught a glimpse of the unusual palms. Instead of being of a lighter shade as were Mr. Johnson's, they were of the same rich darkness as the backs of the stranger's hands.

"Mister," Randolph said loudly, the volume revealing his nervousness. "You know there was a dead man in that room this morning?"

"I know." The deep voice seemed to echo in the room. Randolph was astonished to receive an answer to his rhetorical question. He felt his skin prickle and his already profuse sweating increased.

Mr. Johnson read the ledger.

"The Great Leonardo." He looked at the man, raising an inquisitive eyebrow. "Is that the way you'd sign a check?"

"I don't have checks, only cash." A wallet appeared in his hand. He opened it and took out three one-hundred-dollar bills. "That ought to cover the first night."

Mr. Johnson held them up to the light, having seen counterfeit bills more than once. These were good.

"Welcome to Johnson's Hotel, Mr. Leonardo." Mr. Johnson handed him his key.

"Good night," the Great Leonardo announced. All eyes in the room followed him as he walked to the stairs. He paused two stairs up and turned dramatically, stealing the breath from those below. Even taller now, he commanded their awe as he spoke.

"I'm a magician."

Then, without further explanation, he walked swiftly and gracefully up the stairs. For a minute, nobody spoke. They just exchanged uneasy glances. The man's pleasantly sweet herbal smell hung in the air after he was gone, contrasting the sharp earthiness of the others' body odor.

"I forgot to tell him where his room was," Mr. Johnson said, coming out from behind the desk, preparing to follow the stranger.

"I have a feeling he can find it himself," Randolph said, stopping Mr. Johnson. "I don't trust him."

"He paid cash," Mr. Johnson answered, sitting down in one of the wobbly chairs.

"He didn't have any luggage," Randolph started. "And what about his name?"

"And he wasn't sweating in this heat," Miss Louise added. "And he smelled sweet like . . . like a flower."

Mr. Johnson answered calmly, "He's here for a short stay, he uses his stage name on the road and he has a good deodorant, O.K.?"

Still, Mr. Johnson was also bothered by the last point. It was hot, too hot for any deodorant to be effective and surely everyone sweated. The man's skin hadn't even been moist. The air was heavy, as heavy as the darkness and silence, with moisture. Some people felt the need to walk with their arms outstretched, pushing the air out of the way, creating a passageway so they could breathe. Still, the warmly dressed stranger had seemed unaffected by the heat. Mr. Johnson looked down at the money in his hands and decided that there was a reason for this. And whatever it was, it was good enough for him.

"He didn't care about sleeping where a man had recently died," Randolph continued.

"I don't want him near our . . . the children," Miss Louise said.

"If they pay on time, I don't ask any questions. I'll get the kids."

Mr. Johnson went into the back room, whistling.

"You know," Randolph said, putting his arm around Miss Louise. "We're beginning to sound a lot like parents."

"Bedtime already?" an indignant, high-pitched voice said. It was Renaldo. He walked out from behind the desk, holding his sister Julia's hand in one of his and her teddy bear under his other arm. Julia had her other thumb in her mouth. Four months earlier, they had become orphans.

They had been living in Johnson's Hotel with their parents. The family was from Mexico. Mr. Johnson assumed their immigration had been illegal from their actions. But they paid their rent, so he didn't ask. One day, their parents were coming home when they found themselves in the middle of two rival gangs. They were added to the body count. Since then, Randolph, Miss Louise and Mr. Johnson had taken care of them. Renaldo had become quickly independent at the age of eight. However, his five-year old sister had become quiet and withdrawn. Miss Louise and Randolph were considered by everyone to be married, although they weren't, legally. Still, they shared a bed and had children. That was enough.

"Yes, it's bedtime," Miss Louise said in a gently firm tone. The children didn't move. "Now!"

They shuffled to the stairs and Miss Louise followed them up, gently slapping their bottoms to speed their ascent.

"Good night, Mr. Johnson," Renaldo said as he walked up the stairs.

"'Night, kid. Sleep well."

Mr. Johnson locked the doors to the hotel. As he pulled down the chain metal gate, he thought he saw an even darker shadow pass through the impenetrable darkness of the night. He shivered as a cool blast of air from the fan hit him.

"Getting old, m'boy," he mumbled to himself. "Seeing things in the night."

Miss Louise lay next to Randolph, staring at the ceiling. He was asleep. She knew he was having a nightmare again. He twitched and mumbled at nonexistent demons. Some nights, he would jerk out of his sleep into a sitting position. She had seen as his eyes changed from an insanely wild monster to those of a confused human being. She had never asked him about those dreams, those obviously horrible dreams. Randolph had never offered any information.

The dreams they did share with each other were never encountered during the sleep of either. The dreams of being able to get married and live in a nice house. The dreams of adopting the children and raising them as their own. The dream of escaping.

Miss Louise pulled the single sheet up to her neck, hoping it would protect her from the night and her fears. When she had first arrived at Johnson's Hotel, she was immediately called "Miss Louise," instead of just "Louise." It seemed natural to the speakers since they recognized her as a lady, unlike the ones on the street who were gang girls or sold themselves. They saw in Louise a strong woman, unwilling to give in to her surroundings, fiercely independent, deserving of a distinction, Miss Louise. But as she lay there staring at the cracks in the ceiling, which seemed to grow every night, she felt more like a scared child, being smothered by the night. Feeling Randolph's warm, sweaty body next to hers helped, until an involuntary shiver went through his sleeping form and she knew he was as scared as she was.

Her arm still hurt from where that kid, she figured no more than sixteen, had grabbed her. She had been leaving the laundromat where she worked, clutching the bag of clothes that she was allowed to wash for free. The kid had come from behind her and grabbed her arm, tightly squeezing. He made a suggestion, something obscene. She didn't really hear him; she clearly saw his face, though, that insane, grinning face so clearly that of a child. And his earring, bright red feathers hanging from his ear, looking fluffy and strikingly feminine. Automatically, she had grabbed the mace from her purse, spraying a liberal amount in the boy's face. She ran as the other kids in the gang laughed at the one rolling on the ground, trying to scratch the stinging from his eyes. Miss Louise hadn't told anyone. If Randolph knew, he would go after the kid. Randolph was big, but not big enough to take on a whole gang. Miss Louise knew these kids did more than laugh. They killed as well.

The acute pain in her arm increased. And now there was the stranger living in a dead man's apartment. Miss Louise was too scared to hold on to Randolph. Too scared to scream. Too scared to cry. Too scared to do anything except fall fitfully into sleep and shiver in the sweltering heat of the night.

"I'm sorry that I am delaying your journey to the other side, Mr. Crenshaw." The magician was in the middle of the apartment, cross-legged, floating above a chalk circle he had drawn on the floor. Nobody else was in the room. He was still fully dressed.

"In two days, Mr. Crenshaw, you may go. And my creation will go with you."

The magician thought about what he had just said. He chuckled. He couldn't stop calling it his creation, even though he knew he had merely opened the door and let it into this world. The magician laughed aloud, a deep, baritone laugh, at his own retained vanity.

"I hope you don't mind a traveling companion, Mr. Crenshaw." The magician knew that he wouldn't be able to hold Mr. Crenshaw for more than two days, if that. Mr. Crenshaw wanted to cross over more than most. It was his escape. Soon, he would get used to his new state and realize he was infinitely more powerful than his captor. Then, he would leave . . . and take the portal with him. The Great Leonardo knew he wouldn't be able to survive if this chance evaporated.

He closed his eyes and found the demon. He watched as the shadowy form stalked a man and slaughtered him savagely, gleefully. The magician opened his eyes; they mourned the man who had just lost his life. Even as his mouth began to fill with the metallic warmth of the man's blood, the blood the demon drank like wine and the magician refused to swallow, he mourned for all those the demon had killed. Slowly, the magician levitated to the open window. A stream of blood trickled out of the corner of his mouth and fell onto his pants where it soaked into the fabric. When he reached the window sill, the magician opened his mouth, letting the blood pour onto the sill. Some splashed off and onto the floor or fell two stories to the ground, but the rest soaked into the wood, staining it a brownish red so deep, it hid the natural grain of the wood. The magician knew it would come now. With the scent of death, the scent of its own kill and the scent of its summoner, the one it needed to kill, it would come quickly to Johnson's Hotel. The magician just hoped it came in two days.

I've been running for too long, the magician thought. But no more. Come to me, my creation. I'm waiting.

Somewhere out in the darkness, he heard it scream.

• • •

Renaldo crept silently up the stairs, pulling his sister behind him. She, in turn, was holding her teddy bear's hand, completing the train. Mr. Johnson had fallen asleep watching Jeopardy. Miss Louise and Randolph were at work. To Renaldo that meant it was time to explore. He would never go outside, not yet anyway. There was something wrong outside. But inside he felt safe, cocky even. And so the exploring party went upstairs with old Mr. Crenshaw's room as a destination.

Renaldo didn't miss his parents. He could barely remember their faces after only four months. What he did remember was fear of his father, who was usually drunk. He also remembered his mother's hands; they were always doing something; laundry, dishes, cooking, knitting. When she wasn't doing anything, she would wring her hands together, drawing all attention to them, making it nearly impossible to look at her face or hear her words. Renaldo always felt responsible for Julia. Now that his parents were gone, he really was. He liked that.

Upon reaching the top of the stairs, Renaldo could see the door to Mr. Crenshaw's room was ajar, a faint crack of dusty light shining out. The children crept slowly down the hall, keeping their backs to the wall. Soon, they were right outside the door.

"Come inside, children." The magician opened the door for them. Renaldo pulled his sister in. Renaldo looked up at the giant man wearing a tuxedo, but was not intimidated. The magician smiled widely at them, showing off two rows of perfect white teeth. The children smiled back.

"Miss Louise say you a magician," Renaldo said, overpronouncing each word, fighting his accent, the accent he loathed.

"That's correct," the magician said, sitting cross-legged on the floor inside the circle.

"Show us a trick, show us a trick," Julia squealed, jumping up and down.

"Yeah, pull a rabbit out that hat," Renaldo said, almost daring the magician to do it.

"O.K., but I can do better tricks than that."

The magician knocked the hat off of his head, letting it land, brim up, in the palm of his other hand. Then, he waved his hand over the hat dramatically, mumbling some long, and quite meaningless, words. Then, he shot his hand into the hat and yanked out a long-eared, white rabbit with black spots around the eyes. He set it gently on the ground. It hopped over to the wide-eyed children who were bubbling over with delight. They petted the rabbit, never having felt anything quite as soft.

The magician's smile widened a little at the children's excitement. He had become a magician for the children. They were always ready to believe, ready to accept. At first, he had seen the hard, cold exterior of Renaldo, but now the child had broken free again. He remembered the times when he used to do his "magic" shows. The children would stare in awe of his wide assortment of tricks while the parents stood in the back, shaking their heads, chuckling, logically figuring out how the tricks were done, instead of believing and just enjoying. But those were the days before he learned the real magic. Then, he would have had the rabbit hidden in a secret compartment in the hat. Now, the rabbit came out of the hat, but where it came from was definitely not inside the hat.

The children clamored for more tricks which he gladly delivered. He made things disappear and reappear, float and fly around the room, change shape and become live animals. The children ate it up, hungrily devouring a trick and asking for more.

Then, suddenly, the magician saw Renaldo's face harden and wrinkle, contrasting with his sister's joyfully, innocent

face. The stranger knew immediately that Renaldo had had
a thought, a very logical, adult thought.

"You good magician," Renaldo started, showing his
logic. "Why you here?"

"I'm waiting for something." The magician took a
deep breath. "It's a long story."

"Tell us a story, tell us a story," Julia squealed.

He told them of how he became a true magician, not
the kind he used to be with quick hands and dime-store gad-
gets. He had found a book, a very old book, which told of
the true powers of the mind. The hidden unused powers. But
he had gone through the book too fast, before he was ready,
and he had accidentally released it. . . .

Downstairs, Miss Louise entered the hotel, carefully
making sure that no one was in the lobby. Then, she walked
quietly to the back room to see Renaldo and Julia. Not for
them to see her, just to see them before she went to put ice
on her eye where the kid with the red fluffy earring had hit
her. It was beginning to swell.

. . . the shadowy demon. It had sort of oozed out of the
wall, a wall like the one in Mr. Crenshaw's room, one with
many cracks and small holes, a wall between dimensions. Of
course, he hadn't known he had the ability to actually take
it out of its world and into his own. The Great Leonardo,
third-rate magician, wielding that kind of power, ha! Of
course, there were no spells or bat wings and spider legs in
a boiling cauldron. That was just mumbo jumbo from the
movies. Just power from the mind; strong, concentrated
power. . . .

Miss Louise found Mr. Johnson, asleep in front of the
evening news. At first, the picture made her giggle, Mr.

Johnson sitting there, snoring. Then, she realized the children were not there. Her throat constricted and her heart raced. Where were they? What if something had happened? Quickly, she calmed herself down. They must be upstairs, playing. Her heart still beat fast as she walked up the stairs.

. . . the demon slowly took form, definitely not human form. It was pitch-black and greasy, like an oil slick. He had run away from it, yet he always knew where it was, and it was always tracking him. It wanted to kill him. It needed to kill him, for the summoner was the only one who could send it back. It couldn't go back, not after it had tasted blood. . . .

She saw the light coming from old Mr. Crenshaw's room, the stranger's room. Miss Louise knew that the children were in there; they had to be. She didn't like it. She walked down the hall, briskly.

"And so it is coming here to get me," the magician spoke slowly, letting the children hang on every word. "When it gets here, I will send it back to the other side through Mr. Crenshaw's portal. But the mind has limited resources on this side and I have used so much of mine running away from it. If I don't have enough power. . . ."

"O.K. children, go wash up for dinner," Miss Louise cut in, shoving open the door.

The magician rose. "Good evening, Miss Louise."

"Awwww, do we have to?" Renaldo whined.

"Yes, now!" she said.

"Go, children," the magician said, smiling. They did.

"Bye, Mister Magician," Julia said, waving.

Miss Louise and the Great Leonardo were left alone. Miss Louise looked up into his face as he replaced the top hat on his head. He seemed taller today than the night before.

"I don't want you telling my kids ghost. . . ." she

stopped in mid-sentence. She had looked into his eyes. They were the same eyes she had seen last night, but today she saw something different in those giant dark pupils. She saw hope.

"You should put some ice on that eye," he said, calmly.

Miss Louise turned and left his room. She was confused, but she knew he wasn't the enemy. Not even close.

He heard the man ask, in a raspy, worn-out voice, for one of the magazines behind the counter. He heard the cash register ring and the drawer slide out, stopping with a jingling of coins. He heard the cashier count out the change, slowly, deliberately. But he wasn't really listening.

He saw the man coming toward him, towards the exit. He saw the dirty tattered clothes, the unkempt beard, the hungry look in the man's eyes that showed he hadn't recently tasted food. But he wasn't watching.

It wasn't until the man passed right in front of him, everyone who left had to pass him, that he came back to reality. He saw vividly the cover of the magazine that the man clutched in his grimy hand. A naked woman knelt in front of a masked man who was clad in leather and bearing a large whip, raised above his head. The woman's face showed an expression of such fake ecstasy, such blatantly unconvincing pleasure that he snorted with disgust.

Nobody looks like that when they get whipped, Randolph thought. Even if they do enjoy it.

Randolph had been thinking of his father. He often did during the nights he worked in the "smut palace," as it was known around the neighborhood. His mother had left his father before Randolph could remember. His father had raised him alone.

"Just you and me, kid," his father often said. "Two men against the world."

His father had taught him to read before he started

school. He didn't want "any son of mine to start out in a hole." He had worked hard at two jobs to support them, but Randolph could not remember a single day when his father had buckled under the pressure or lost control. He got mad at Randolph when he would do the stupid things kids do, but he never yelled or hit him. He would just sit Randolph down and look deep into his eyes. Then, he would speak in a slow, piercing voice, getting right to the point. Randolph never misunderstood his father.

Randolph was not his original name. His father had renamed him the day his mother left, throwing away the name "that woman chose" forever. Randolph's father had been reading a book about a rich, white man named Hearst when he chose his own name for his son.

"You need a name that commands respect," he had said. "A good, strong name that you won't be ashamed of when you're a success."

Then, Randolph got angry. He thought of the petty thief who had held up a convenience store, despite the fact that the sign on the door said "Cashier has only $20.00 in register." That same thief had stolen the $15.76 that was left in the register and a couple of dirty magazines, tamer than the ones that surrounded Randolph at his job, and left a dead man as payment. Randolph buried his father with the money that had been saved for Randolph's education.

What would his father say if he could see him today, as a bouncer in a dirty bookstore? Randolph unconsciously hit the wooden stool on which he sat, jarring himself from his daydream.

"I say that I don' wanna pay for this here mag." A kid stood at the cash register, sneering at the small man behind it. A tattooed skull on the kid's face moved as his cheek twitched. "So give it to me."

Behind the kid, a couple of his friends stared menacingly at the man who stared back, trying to appear unshaken despite his quivering hands. Randolph stood up, revealing the large size that had been hidden in his slouched, seated form.

"Is there a problem?" Randolph said, looking through eyes that were hard and cold as stone.

"Yeah," the kid said boldly. "I want this."

The kid waved a magazine in front of Randolph's face, allowing him to see the full-color pictures inside that made him feel sick.

"Then, pay for it," Randolph said.

"Nah." The kid tossed the magazine onto the counter and turned around to face the other gang members. "I'd rather watch Feather go at it on your old lady."

The kid was turning around to see Randolph's reaction when he found himself being partly dragged, but mostly carried out the door. The kid known as Skull squirmed helplessly as his back was repeatedly smashed into the brick wall. Then, Randolph lifted him off his feet so that they saw each other at eye level.

"What did Feather do?" Randolph's words slithered out from between clenched teeth.

"No-nothing, man, take it easy, c-c-come on, he jus' hit h-her a little." The skull on his pasty white cheek moved frantically. He coughed violently.

"Where is Feather?"

"H-he ain't here, man."

Randolph's eyes squinted and the kid's shivering increased. Randolph threw him, not wanting to look into his face anymore. The kid landed on a metal garbage can, letting out a squeal. He limped away into the darkness. Randolph glared at the other gang members who had been silently watching; they ran after Skull, back to Feather.

I was almost one of them, Randolph thought.

Then he ran, in the opposite direction, trying to get home. He didn't notice the darkness that seemed to be caging in the light from the street lamps. He didn't notice the heat that made his shirt stick to his body. He didn't notice the silence that roared against his ears in waves. He just knew he had to get home. Home to Louise.

The breaths came sharp and fast, one after another. Bright red drops of blood fell from the magician's mouth into the sink, getting caught in the flow of water and swirling down the drain. He felt like he used to when he had too much to drink. One minute, in complete control, and the next, he was kneeling over a sink or a toilet or doubled over in some alley, heaving and heaving until there was nothing left. Slowly, his breathing returned to normal. The magician cupped his hands, filling them with water and sucking it into his mouth. He refused to swallow any until the water he spit out was not even the slightest bit pink, causing his throat to go dry. Finally, all trace of the demon's latest kill was gone.

The magician fell back onto his cot, visibly worn. He closed his eyes and gently rested his head against the wall. He looked at the opposite wall; the cracks were getting bigger, longer, wider. He knew that Mr. Crenshaw was learning, becoming accustomed to not having a physical body, becoming less dizzy, more focused, more powerful. Simultaneously, the magician felt himself becoming weaker. Keeping Mr. Crenshaw disoriented took a lot of energy from his already depleted mind. He could always drop the disguise, the costume that he wore. No, no, besides it didn't take that much energy to maintain. Suddenly, the magician laughed aloud.

"My vanity will be the end of me, eh, Mr. Crenshaw?" he said.

Nobody answered. The magician felt stupid talking to the dead man, because he knew Mr. Crenshaw wasn't listening. Mr. Crenshaw could hear him, if he wanted to listen. But why would someone on his plane of existence listen to someone on mine? the Great Leonardo thought. It'd be like a person listening to an ant. Everyone can hear them talk, but no one cares enough to listen. Except other ants.

Still, he needed to talk to someone.

"Just one more day, Mr. Crenshaw. Then, you can go and it'll go with you. I'm starting to weaken. Why don't you help me, Mr. Crenshaw? It will be here in one more day. Just give me one more day. Please."

Mr. Crenshaw answered with a heavy silence. It pressed against the magician's body, against his face. The pores reopened. And the Great Leonardo began to sweat.

One more day . . . one more day. Mr. Johnson mumbled in his sleep. One more day. Suddenly, he was sitting up, awakened by a loud noise, a buzzing. Then again and again, urgently. It was the front door. He stumbled into the lobby, putting on his glasses. Outside, he saw a dark shadow in the black night. Like the one he thought he had seen before, but not the same. He turned on the lights.

It was Randolph. He was outside, pressing his face on the glass, scratching frantically to be let in, like a cat that wants food . . . or is being chased. Mr. Johnson unlocked and pulled up the metal gate as fast as he could. As soon as he had unlocked the outside door, Randolph pushed it open. Without saying a word, he ran up the stairs. But Mr. Johnson had seen his eyes; those wild, animalistic eyes. A sharp, hot gust came through the open door, out of the void, the darkness. Mr. Johnson shivered and quickly relocked the door.

Randolph crept into his room, slowly, without breathing, without making any noise. Still, the floor creaked and his wind exhaled loudly through his nose. He walked up to the bed and stood over Miss Louise. She rolled over, mumbling in her sleep. Then, he saw it, the puffiness around her eye, the discoloration, and he knew Skull had told the truth. Someone had hurt Louise, his Louise.

He cursed loudly. Miss Louise woke up. He hadn't meant to, but it came out anyway. She stared up into his face, scared.

"Randolph?" she whispered.

"Go back to sleep, honey." His eyes softened, a little, but she still recognized those insane eyes of a wild animal, a predator that has smelled blood, moving in for the kill. Those were Randolph's eyes when he woke up from one of those dreams. Those unmentionable dreams.

She heard him fumbling around the kitchenette. She couldn't move. Then, he was gone. The door clicked behind him, and Miss Louise was left alone with her fears.

Randolph stood in the hallway, holding the butcher knife in one hand, deciding where to go next. Then, he smelled something, coming from the end of the hall, faintly sweet like flowers, slightly mixed with the smell of sweat. He knew who it was. Randolph couldn't see him in the darkness, but he knew the magician was there.

"Where are you going with that?" the magician's deep, rich voice asked.

Randolph realized that he didn't know, and that he didn't want to be holding the knife. He dropped it. It fell, blade first, towards his foot. Then, it stopped and flew to the end of the hall, where the magician, standing in the darkness, caught it.

"Go see your children." The magician smiled. Randolph saw the bright teeth, hanging in the darkness like the Cheshire Cat, and he saw the hope Miss Louise had seen earlier.

As he gazed upon the faces of Renaldo and Julia, he thought about why he had lost control. He knew that he had to protect his family, but he had to be in control. Just like his father.

And when Miss Louise joined him in the room of their children, placing her hand lightly on his shoulder, she knew that Randolph was back, the animal gone. And as he took her into his arms, he knew that he had regained control.

Just like his father.

The next day, both Miss Louise and Randolph took a vacation. They forgot about their problems for the day and spent their time with Renaldo and Julia. They never left the hotel and inside the weights on their shoulders disappeared. The cool breezes from the fans fought off the heat; laughter scared away the silence. The four of them played numerous games, Hide and Seek, I Spy, Go Fish, Hearts.

Julia especially enjoyed the card games: Old Maid, Concentration. They had never heard her talk as much as she did that afternoon. She was filled with energy which escaped through tiny squeals and an overabundant smile. Miss Louise had noticed the change after the children had been with the stranger. Renaldo was also different. He smiled more, scowled less. He had become less serious, more like a kid again. Julia constantly asked if "Mr. Magician" would come down and do card tricks for them, even after Randolph went upstairs to ask and found the stranger in the grasp of a very deep and apparently impenetrable sleep.

They were all sprawled out on the floor of the lobby, playing a close game of I Doubt It, when someone walked into the hotel and made an announcement.

"I got friends that wanna see ya."

"Go into the back room, kids," Randolph said, in a low, firm voice. "Watch T.V."

Renaldo led his sister quickly out of the lobby. As soon as they were gone, Randolph turned to the kid. He was not much older than Renaldo and a little bit shorter. He stood in the doorway, arms crossed, trying to look cool. Miss Louise thought he looked silly and quite pitiful. The kid uncrossed his arms impatiently, revealing the grungy white T-shirt under his scuffed leather jacket.

"Who wants to see us?" Randolph stood up. The kid's eyes softened into fear at his size, then hardened again.

He pointed to Miss Louise. "Feather." He pointed to Randolph. "Skull. They's outside."

The kid turned and left the lobby. Slowly, Miss Louise intertwined her fingers in Randolph's. He looked down into her face, giving her a reassuring smile. They followed the kid, scared, but in control.

Outside the darkness was beginning to fall, not gradually or smoothly, but as if someone were turning the lights out one by one. No change, then, suddenly, it was darker. The heat pricked their faces like thousands of needles, drawing the sweat out of their pores. They saw the faces of the gang surprisingly clearly in the waning light. The faces were all the same; they recognized the callously wild face of an animal on all the kids. Miss Louise looked anxiously into Randolph's face. It was different than those in the gang, cool and calm.

Randolph had been in a gang after his father died, briefly. He had gotten out, but only after a dream. Randolph had dreamed that he was killing someone, a faceless person, when he saw his father standing over him, shaking his head. The dream was so realistic that when he woke up, he saw his father standing over him, still shaking his head. Randolph blinked and his father was gone. He was laying back down when he realized he was sleeping on the floor of an abandoned apartment building, going nowhere. Randolph left.

Now, as he saw the state he had been in through the gang members, he was glad he had walked out.

"The lady's lookin' fine," a voice announced from behind them. It was Feather. He put his hand on Miss

Louise's hair and walked in front of them. Miss Louise flinched, then held steady.

"C'mon babe, gimme a kiss." Feather reached for her. Randolph grabbed him by the neck and threw him to the ground.

"Don't touch her." Randolph's voice cut through the silence like a knife.

Feather backed up, involuntarily. Skull stepped forward, helping Feather to his feet.

"Looks like you wanna die," Skull said.

"Then you'll be my lady," Feather said, pointing to Miss Louise with his middle finger.

"I'd sooner die." She spit in Feather's direction. It landed well short, but the gesture was understood.

"Two for death," Skull called out, cupping his hands around his mouth, The skull on his cheek twitched wildly.

"Make that three," Mr. Johnson said as he walked out of the hotel. "Better make it fast, before the police get here."

Feather laughed loudly. The rest of the gang mimicked him. "They'd probably get here faster if you hadn't called them, old man."

"Three for death," Skull called again. Then, softly, "Who's first?"

The face of the gang contorted with malicious pleasure, the tongue hanging out, salivating at the thought of a kill, the scent of blood. Weapons were pulled out of jackets and pants; a gun was cocked, ready to fire; switchblades opened. Then, it was silent. Metal glistened in the last bit of light. Then, it was dark. Except for the faint light of the street lamp's one bulb.

Feather ran toward Randolph, holding his switchblade out in front, screaming obscenities. Randolph put one foot forward, bracing himself for the attack, preparing for his defense. But before any confrontation, Feather hit something. There was nothing for him to run into. Still, he fell backwards as if he had run headfirst into a brick wall. He sat on the pavement, wondering what to do next when it was decided for him.

His switchblade was drawn upwards by some powerful unseen magnet, causing Feather to raise his arm above his head. Feather pulled down; the switchblade pulled up. The switchblade won, loosing itself from his aching grip. It hovered over the mesmerized gang. No one moved. Then, it started to spin, faster and faster, until it seemed circular, like the propeller of an airplane. It emitted a high-pitched humming, almost a wail. And without warning, it exploded in a flash of light and crackling energy. The watchers were forced to look away, only returning their gaze upon the miniature sun with eyes shielded by hands, squinting. The heat seemed to be sucked into the glowing orb, leaving only a chilling cold.

Most of the gang had dropped their weapons in their amazement. The rest found theirs being wrenched from their hands by an irresistible force. The guns, knives, brass knuckles, billy clubs, pieces of old rusty pipe plunged into the fiery ball, each in an intense explosion of light and sound, filling the sky with their fireworks. Slowly, the orb elongated, becoming oval, then stretching itself into a glowing rod. The light began to fade like a dying ember. Then, it went out, leaving the street light alone again to fight the darkness.

The staff fell from the sky into the outstretched hand of Mr. Johnson, much to everyone's surprise, including his own. It felt light in his hand, its circumference fitting perfectly in his grip. The black cylinder appeared charred, yet was smooth to the touch, like polished marble. Inside the rod, Mr. Johnson could see the outlines of the gang's weapons, faintly. Everyone watched him closely, waiting. Mr.

Johnson raised both hands above his head, holding the staff in one, and broke the silence.

"Go away," he said. His voice hadn't changed from before. His words were simply and exactly what he wanted. Nothing happened.

The muscles in Mr. Johnson's arm tensed, tighter than they had in years, as the power surged into the staff. The end lit green and tiny beams reached outwards, ending between the eyes of the gang members. Randolph and Miss Louise watched as the coldness, the hardness, the insanity drained from the faces; Mr. Johnson felt the insanity empty from their minds, leaving only the doubt and innocence of youth. Again, it was dark. The gang members looked to each other for guidance. When they found none, they ran, individually, into the night.

Miss Louise, Randolph and Mr. Johnson stood alone in the hot, silent darkness. They turned and went inside the hotel without speaking, not knowing what to say. Although it was early, Mr. Johnson locked up the hotel.

None of them had seen the figure watching from the second story window, but they knew he was there. They didn't see as the figure backed up from the window and fell heavily to the floor, mumbling, "It's close, so close."

Mr. Johnson stood in the darkened lobby at the bottom of the stairs, looking up. He didn't remember getting out of bed and walking there. He didn't remember getting dressed. He didn't remember picking up the staff which was in his hand. Mr. Johnson slowly began to climb the stairs. He felt compelled to go upstairs. Something was calling him.

"It's almost here," Mr. Johnson mumbled to himself, not understanding the meaning of his own words, quickening his pace.

He reached the top of the stairs. He could hear the muffled voices of Miss Louise and Randolph through the thin door interspersed with moments of loud silence. Mr. Johnson turned toward the magician's door. It was cracked open, but instead of a sliver of light, a shadow, darker than the light in the hall, fell upon its floor. Before Mr. Johnson realized it, he was inside the magician's room.

The magician lay on the floor within the chalk circle, in his true form. He was about Mr. Johnson's height with a baby face. He was skinny and no more than twenty-five years old. Next to his head was a pool of freshly spilled blood. The magician rolled over to face Mr. Johnson.

"Come here, Mr. Johnson," the magician said, almost whispering in a thin, reedy voice. "There is little time."

"Are you O.K.?" Mr. Johnson walked into the circle. "Should I call an am—"

When Mr. Johnson was close enough, the magician grabbed the bottom of the staff with a surprisingly firm grip. Mr. Johnson froze; the staff became bright white, remaining cool to the touch. And the knowledge began to pour into Mr. Johnson's head like a river emptying into a lake.

The demon was coming soon. It had just killed again nearby. The magician had brought it into this world by accident. The book. It had tasted blood, becoming a part of this side. It did not want to leave. Only the summoner could send it back to the other side. The magician had used too much energy running away from it. Just a confused, scared kid. Too much power. Now, he had stopped. And it was coming to kill him. So it could stay and kill forever.

Mr. Johnson's brain absorbed the information, searching greedily for more. The magician's muscles all tensed as he twitched on the floor.

The magician had been saving the last of his power to send it back. He had dropped the illusion of power and strength, retaking his true form. Then, he heard something outside. The gang. Couldn't let people die. Created staff for

Mr. Johnson. Only person with wisdom enough to use it properly who hadn't lost the child inside of him. The magician had drained nearly all of his remaining power. Not enough to send it back. Mr. Crenshaw was waiting. The magician needed help. Mr. Johnson.

Now, the muscles in Mr. Johnson's body began to twitch as the powers of the mind were revealed to him and he learned how to be a magician.

Miss Louise and Randolph sat across from each other at the small table in their room. They stared at each other in silence. Randolph broke it.

"It had to be him. How else could it have happened?"

"I don't know," Louise answered.

Again, the silence filled the room.

"You think he could help us . . . get us out?" Louise asked.

"Only one way to know."

"It's too late."

"Can we wait?"

Silence.

The silence was maddening. Mr. Johnson sat cross-legged within the circle next to the stranger. The Great Leonardo stared at the ceiling, catatonic. Both men held the staff, Mr. Johnson with a tight, sweating palm, the magician with a loose, clammy one. Mr. Johnson had only his own thoughts to keep him company in the dark, hot room.

Can I do it? Do I have the will power? The magician was too young; twenty-two. He was too young to wield the power the magician has given me. But can I correct his mistakes? Does my age really mean I hold more wisdom that he did? O.K., O.K. Just remember, make it believe that it can't come within the line, and it won't. Tell it to go to the other side, and it will. That sounds too simple. It can't be that simple. Shut up. This is no time for cynicism.

Mr. Johnson realized he was hyperventilating. He took deep breaths, calming himself down. He looked deep into the ebony staff, finding the outlines of the weapons, latching on to the reality that these powers could work, despite his lack of experience.

Then, it arrived. Mr. Johnson saw it immediately and panicked.

Wait, I'm not ready.

Its dark, shapeless form oozed into the open window. Mr. Johnson could sense its surprise at finding only a bit of its summoner's mind in the room, and mostly an unknown being. The room became a vacuum, filled with complete silence. The demon was a greasy shadow against the room's darkness. Mr. Johnson was suffocated by the heat. He stared into the void of the demon, knowing it was looking into his mind. Then, it hurtled itself toward him. Mr. Johnson's mind froze.

You can not come inside the circle.

The demon stopped, inches from the chalk line. The thought had come from the fading mind of the magician. Mr. Johnson's will came back. He was not alone.

Go back to the other side, Mr. Johnson thought.

The demon didn't move, but seemed to shiver. Then, it came toward Mr. Johnson again.

You can not come inside the circle, Mr. Johnson commanded.

The demon stopped at the line, again shivering in its blood frenzy. Mr. Johnson could hear its desires to kill him. And then to prey on the helpless form of its summoner. It seemed to be rotating counterclockwise on the edge of the circle.

Go back to the other side.

Mr. Johnson tried to increase the intensity of his thoughts. The demon was now only a few feet from his face.

He could see the gelatinous, thick substance of its form dripping and oozing, twisting and reshaping itself. Mr. Johnson could smell it now. He flinched as the combinations of odors hit him; the overwhelming bluntness of newly laid pavement, the sting of smelling salts, the thickness of rotten eggs, the tang of new and dried blood. His concentration slipped. The demon moved into the circle.

You can not come inside the circle. Stay out of the circle.

It was too late. The demon knew no harm would come to it. Mr. Johnson's thoughts had become frantic. Still, the demon moved slowly, having yet to completely overcome the mental block put up by Mr. Johnson.

Go back to the other side. Go back to the other side.

The door to the magician's room creaked open.

"Mr. Leonardo?" It was Randolph. He entered the room, followed closely by Miss Louise.

They froze when they saw the hideous shadow that hovered in front of Mr. Johnson's face. Suddenly, Mr. Johnson knew its focus had shifted to them. They were easy prey, defenseless.

Go back to the other side. Go back to the other side.

The demon flew toward the two motionless people with alarming speed. Mr. Johnson could hear it growling faintly in his mind. He thought feverishly.

Go back to the other side! Go back to the other side!

Randolph felt stifling heat as the demon wrapped itself around his head, suffocating him. The demon was hot and rubbery and slimy against his skin. Randolph knew he was losing consciousness, but could not move. Mr. Johnson stared at the demon, refusing to let it kill. The staff turned blood red from his anger. He knew what to do.

Go.

The demon screamed, but only Mr. Johnson heard it.

GO.

It was stretched as it fought the suction of the portal.

Mr. Johnson could feel another force helping him, dragging the demon.

GO!

The demon hit the wall, becoming a big, black splotch. It bubbled and steamed, until finally, all of it had been pulled through the cracks to the other side. It was gone.

Randolph fell to his knees, cradling his face in his hands. Miss Louise crouched next to him, taking his shaking body into her arms. The smell of his burnt hair filled the room.

Mr. Johnson looked down at the Great Leonardo who was now dead. He reached down and closed the magician's eyelids with his fingers. Although he hadn't admitted it to himself before, he now knew that Mr. Crenshaw had left and taken his portal as soon as the demon had arrived. That's why it had ignored the commands to go back to the other side. It wasn't until another portal had opened that the demon had obeyed. The magician had taken his creation back to the other side through his own portal.

Outside, Mr. Johnson could hear the sound of a faraway siren. People were arguing on the street outside. He felt a cool breeze blow in through the window.

Everything's gonna be fine, he thought. Just fine.

Then he fell into a deep and rejuvenating sleep.

Randolph and Miss Louise never asked Mr. Johnson any questions about that night. Randolph's face was peeling as if he had had a bad sunburn and the ends of his hair had been singed, but he was alive. That was all that mattered. They didn't leave their room for two days, allowing no one except the children inside. On the third day, they ventured downstairs. Mr. Johnson was waiting for them.

"The magician left something for you two," he said, producing a wallet, apparently from out of nowhere.

Miss Louise took it, scrutinizing it. She opened it up,

finding three one-hundred-dollar bills. She took them out and three more appeared. She did it again and again and again. Each time the supply was replenished. She looked at Randolph and began to laugh. Neither one said a word to each other or Mr. Johnson. They both knew that it was finally time to escape, to find a better life.

Mr. Johnson left the couple in silence. He went into the back room, his home, and turned on the T.V. He suddenly understood why the stranger had chosen to introduce himself in that way three days earlier. He knew why he had said those words with such pride, leaving them to stand on their own without need of further explanation. It was the same feeling that Mr. Johnson now had. He picked up the ebony staff and spoke the same words aloud for the world to hear.

"I'm a magician."

Science in Science Fiction

by
Ben Bova

About the Author

Ben Bova really needs no introduction to SF readers; starting in 1979, when his first novel was published, he has since then published about seventy-five more books, pretty evenly divided between novels and nonfiction, and countless short stories and articles.

Beginning as a technical writer, he quickly branched out into science fiction. But he remains one of the staunchest advocates of the U.S. space effort, as well as a skilled practitioner of the semidocumentary style of science fiction. Along the way, he has gathered six Hugo Awards and a score of other awards of various kinds. He has also been the editor of Analog, taking that post when John W. Campbell, Jr., died. He subsequently was Vice President and Editorial Director of Omni.

We are very pleased to have his contribution in our pages, and we are very pleased to have him as a judge in L. Ron Hubbard's Writers of The Future.

Originally, "SF" meant "science fiction." Not "speculative fiction." Not "scientific fantabulation." *Science* fiction.[1]

Why *science* fiction? What does science have to do with fiction, anyway? And who cares?

You care. Or you would not be reading this essay. You would not be holding this book if you did not care, at least subliminally. And I care. I care a lot. I have devoted my life to science fiction—writing it, reading it, editing and publishing it, and helping to make some of it come true.

For, more than any other branch of contemporary literature, science fiction is concerned with the real world. If you think of science fiction as escapism, remember Isaac Asimov's dictum: "Science fiction is escape—into reality." Because it deals with science and the technologies that spring from science, science fiction has the capability of dealing with the most powerful driving engines of modern society: science and technology.

Other forms of literature either ignore science and technology altogether or show an active distrust of them. The subject matter of science fiction is how scientific advances and technological breakthroughs change the lives of individuals and the course of whole societies.

However, not all SF is science fiction. In the modern marketplace of publishing, the term SF actually covers an

---

1. At one time the term "scientifiction" was bruited. We won't go into that.

enormously wide range of subject material, from the meticulously crafted alien worlds of Hal Clement to the galloping barbarian swordsmen of Robert Howard to the wizards and gnomes of Terry Brooks. That is why many practitioners of SF prefer to use the term "speculative fiction" rather than "science fiction."

I want to talk about that portion of SF that is truly science fiction. Therefore, a definition is in order:

When I say "science fiction," I mean fiction in which some element of future science or technology is so integral to the tale that the story would collapse if the science or technology element were removed from it.

The archetype of such fiction is Mary Shelley's *Frankenstein*. Take away the scientific element and the story collapses of its own weight. There is no story without the science.

How does this make science fiction different from other fields of literature? Is science fiction inherently better, more worthwhile, than other kinds of fiction? Or does its preoccupation with science and technology doom science fiction to being inherently inferior to other forms?[2]

There are two major differences between science fiction and all other forms of literature.

The first, of course, is the subject matter. To the uninitiated, it might seem that focusing on science or technology would be terribly limiting for an author of fiction. Yet just the opposite is true. For science is an open door to the universe, and technology can be the magic carpet to take us wherever we wish. Properly used, science and technology are the great liberators that allow the imagination to roam the length and breadth of eternity.

Human beings are explorers by nature. The descendants

---

2. Science-fiction aficionados often refer to non-SF as "straight" or "mundane" fiction.

of curious apes, there is something in us that thrills at new vistas, new ideas. By using scientific knowledge to build the background for their stories, science-fiction writers can take us to places no human eye has yet seen. The excitement of discovery, what science-fiction aficionados call "the sense of wonder," is both primal and primary in science fiction.

John W. Campbell, most influential of all science fiction editors, fondly compared science fiction to other forms of literature in this way: He would spread his arms wide (and he had long arms) and declaim, "This is science fiction! All the universe, past, present and future." Then he would hold up a thumb and forefinger about half an inch apart and say, "This is all other kinds of fiction."

All the non-SF kinds of fiction restrict themselves to the here and now, or to the known past. All other forms of fiction are set here on Earth, under a sky that is blue and ground that is solid beneath your feet. Science fiction deals with all of creation, of which our Earth and our time is merely a small part. Science fiction can vault far into the future or deep into the past. In my own work I have written stories of interstellar adventure and of time-travelers who go back to the age of the dinosaurs.

Is this mere tinsel, nothing more than cheap stage props to make a dull story look more interesting? I do not think so. The best works of fiction are those in which the human heart is tested to its limits. We write fiction, and read it, to learn about ourselves. By stretching the artist's canvas from one end of the universe to the other, by spreading it through all of time itself, science fiction allows the artist to test the human heart in crucibles of new and tougher make, in fires hotter than anything planet Earth can provide.

Yes, at the core of every good science fiction tale is a story of human emotion, just as in any good story of any type. In science fiction, though, the characters may not always look human; they may be tentacled alien creatures or buzzing, clanking robots. Yet they will act as humans do, if the story is to be successful.

The second difference that science fiction offers is its relationship to the real world around us. While pretending to amuse us with stories of the future, the best science fiction stories are really examining facets of the world that we live in today. An outstanding example is L. Ron Hubbard's *Final Blackout*. I have often said that no one actually writes about the future; writers use futuristic settings to throw stronger highlights on the problems and opportunities of today.

The assumptions here are that: (1) science and technology are the driving forces in modern society; and (2) because science fiction deals with science and technology it can—and often does—have something important to say to its readers.

More than that. In the best of science fiction stories, the scientific element can be used as a metaphor that reaches into the heart of the human condition.

In Frank Herbert's *Dune*, for example, the desert world of Arrakis is carefully presented as a metaphor for the environment of Earth. At one level of this complex novel Herbert is telling his readers, subconsciously, subliminally, not only that human actions can change the nature of an entire planet, but that these changes will have effects that will be both good and bad, simultaneously, inescapably.

Robert A. Heinlein touched on this truth in *The Moon Is a Harsh Mistress*. His phrase TANSTAAFL, "There ain't no such thing as a free lunch," is actually a slang restatement of the Second Law of Thermodynamics. You can't get something for nothing; never, notime. The universe just is not built that way, and we human beings are part of the universe, like it or not.

Arthur C. Clarke's *2001: A Space Odyssey* (one of the rare examples of excellent science fiction movie-making, thanks to Stanley Kubrick) speaks to humankind's relationship with our tools, and asks whether our increasingly sophisticated technology makes us more human or less.

Cyril Kornbluth's "The Marching Morons" takes a sociological observation—poor people have more babies than rich people—and extrapolates this into a ghastly future that is becoming truer with each passing day.

I can give a more detailed explanation of how deeply science/technology is used by referring to one of my own works, *The Kinsman Saga.*

The central science/technology idea in this novel is the possibility of building satellites that can shoot down ballistic missiles. The tale began in this way:

In the 1960s I was employed at a research laboratory where the first high-power lasers were invented. I helped to arrange a Top Secret briefing in the Pentagon in early 1966 to reveal to the Department of Defense that such lasers existed. It quickly became apparent that high-power lasers, placed in satellites, could someday shoot down H-bomb-carrying ballistic missiles within minutes of their being launched.

I had been a published science-fiction author for nearly ten years. I cast this very real technological breakthrough into a novel set in the last month of the year 1999. The novel, first published in 1976, was titled *Millennium.*[3]

Its central figure is an astronaut who realizes that if the small band of Americans and Russians living on the Moon dare to take control of their respective nations' anti-missile satellites, they can enforce a lasting peace on the world.

---

3. Later I wrote a "prequel," *Kinsman,* and a decade later rewrote both novels and combined them to form *The Kinsman Saga.*

Science as metaphor. By creating a fictitious but technically plausible Moonbase, I was able to place the pivotal characters in isolation, away from the world yet in daily communication with it. At such a distance from Earth, in the dangerously hostile lunar environment, both Americans and Russians see clearly the necessity to cooperate rather than fight. By postulating a technological means of enforcing peace I was able to emphasize the central political problem of our age: national governments do not want to give up their right to make war. And more. The novel shows that the tools for war can also be used as tools for peace. The tools are morally neutral. The people are not.

The entire story hinges on the personality of the American astronaut, Chester A. Kinsman. Like so many science-fiction protagonists, he becomes a Messiah figure, with all that that entails.

In the mid-1970s such a story was science fiction. Today it is the stuff of newspaper columns: the Strategic Defense Initiative, SDI, "Star Wars." And the central issue of this new technology is precisely the same as the central issue of the novel: will this new tool be used for peace-making or war-making?

Yet to this day no novelist outside the science-fiction field has attempted a serious work on this subject. Nor will they, because they do not have the interest, or knowledge, that science-fiction writers have. Only when the technology of SDI is as commonplace as nuclear weapons or corporate takeovers will "straight" writers begin to explore the subject. If then.

Which brings us to another pair of questions. Do science-fiction writers try to predict the future? And, whether they do or not, should their stories be taken as serious social commentary?

No, to the first question. Yes (with reservations) to the second.

I do not know of any science-fiction writer who deliberately set out to predict the future in any particular story. Yet, as I have often pointed out to the World Future Society and the U.S. government's Office of Technological Assessment, science fiction has a better track record at prediction than any other method.

Generally, science-fiction writers initiate stories by asking themselves, "What would happen if . . ." Professional futurists, men and women who get paid to make forecasts for government and corporate clients, call this technique "scenario writing."

What the science-fiction writer is trying to do is to examine the possibilities that might unfurl, given a set of starting conditions. What would happen if it became possible to shoot down ballistic missiles from laser-armed satellites? What would happen if intelligent aliens sent us unmistakable evidence of their presence? What would happen if we pollute this planet so terribly that the ice caps melt and the continents are flooded?

You can find hundreds, thousands of science fiction stories that deal with such possibilities, and myriads more. In reading them, you are giving yourself a sort of kaleidoscopic view of many, many possible futures. Most of those scenarios will never come to pass. But those that do will have already been examined in science fiction.

That is why Alvin Toffler recommended science fiction as the antidote to "future shock." Very little that has happened in the Twentieth Century was not written about in science fiction. All the major thrusts of the century—world wars, nuclear power, biomedical wonders, space flight, civil rights, decolonization, the computer revolution, and more—have been examined in great detail in science fiction, decades before they reached general public awareness.

Science fiction, then, is truly the literature of *change*.

Again, my thesis is that science and technology are the main driving forces in our society, the major engines of change. Therefore a literature that makes science and technology its special subject matter is a literature that no thinking person can afford to ignore.

If you doubt this thesis, glance at the front page of today's newspaper. Headlines about political upheavals, pollution, drug trafficking, medical care, global economic competition—they are all based on new technological capabilities. Television and VCRs have cracked authoritarian regimes around the world; once people can see the good economic life that they are missing, they topple their government. Scientific discoveries in medicine and biology lead to new ethical dilemmas about defining an individual's right to life—and death.

And (as one writer is prone to say) so it goes.

The way the modern world works is this: scientists discover something new; engineers develop this new knowledge into a new capability—a medicine or a machine, usually; business leaders begin to make profits from the new thing; some workers find new jobs, others are laid off from jobs made obsolete; social and religious leaders ponder the significance of the change; and finally politicians start to make laws about it.

Science and technology are the major forces for change in society because they are inherently forward-looking. All the rest of our institutions are backward-looking, by design. The law, religion, government, social customs, education— all such institutions exist to preserve society's status quo, to try to make tomorrow exactly like yesterday. That is the nature of institutions.

Except for science and its offspring technologies. By its very nature, science is constantly uncovering new knowledge, new concepts. Often these new ideas are stoutly resisted by society. You have only to think of the battles over Galileo, Darwin, Freud, even Einstein.

Technology keeps presenting us with new tools, some of which force enormous changes in society. The birth-control pill, for example, which led to the modern feminist movement. Computers, which have revolutionized indus-tries as diverse as banking and animal husbandry, and forced Soviet Russia onto the path of perestroika.[4]

For each of these changes there have been loud and sometimes massive protests by those who fear change. In a nation as enlightened as the U.S., laboratories have been attacked and new technologies assailed in courts of law.

These are central issues to our society. This is the sub-ject matter of science fiction. There is not a single issue confronting our society today that was not the subject of science-fiction stories ten, twenty, fifty years ago.

Does this make science fiction more worthwhile than other forms of contemporary literature? Is sculpture more worthwhile than painting? Comparisons among art forms are best left to the academics who have nothing better to do. All I will say is this: Everyone *should* read science fiction, if for no other reason than to get a better understanding of the changes that will inevitably rock our society tomorrow.

This is not to say that all of science fiction is elegantly written, or even that all of it is worth the time it takes to read it. Decades ago, Theodore Sturgeon coined what is now known as Sturgeon's Law:

"Ninety percent of science fiction is crud. But then, ninety percent of *everything* is crud."

Much of science fiction is written for specialized mar-kets, where graceful prose is still secondary to interesting

---

4. The USSR had to give up its Stalinist centrally-controlled economy if it wished to be economically competitive in the global marketplace.

ideas. Even so, too much of science fiction is made up of tired retreads of old ideas.

Yet that good ten percent is about as good as contemporary writing gets. The subject matter can be exciting, exalting, mind-expanding. The relationship to here-and-now is strong and very real. Do not let the alien settings and strange backgrounds fool you; most of these stories are dealing with ideas and problems that will change your life, for better or worse.

Strangely, comparatively few science-fiction stories actually deal with scientists themselves or scientific research. As one who has been involved in research programs for a fair portion of my life, I can tell you that most scientific research is about as glamorous as ditch-digging, except for those rare moments of breakthroughs. And even then, the language and behavior of the scientists involved is highly specialized—rather like a tribal meeting of some small, isolated band of hunters.

Science-fiction tales tend to deal with the *consequences* of research. How wonderful it will be when this new idea actually comes to fruition! Or how terrible it might be. Good fiction deals with what happens when the change occurs, seldom with how the change came to be.

Does this concentration on technical subject matter doom science fiction to an inferior position in the world's literature? That is for future generations of readers to decide. A hundred years from now, will people still read *The Left Hand of Darkness* or *Pride and Prejudice*? I see no reason why they will not read both.

Because its roots are in commercial publishing rather than literary academia, science fiction has yet to gain the appreciation of the self-appointed literati. Yet its popularity among the masses is growing. And any unprejudiced study of the field will show that the literary quality of science fiction, in general, has risen steeply over the past twenty-five years.

I feel sure that as more of the world's population understands the crucial relationships between science and the quality of life, more people will turn to read the kind of fiction that speaks to those relationships.

They will read science fiction. They will read it for all the same reasons that ancient Greeks listened to the tales of Homer: Because it is important to their understanding of the world and their place in it. Because it links them to their fellow humans of the past, present, and future.

Mostly, though, they will read science fiction because it truly is exciting, exalting, mind-expanding fun.

The Bookman
by
David Ira Cleary

About the Author

David Ira Cleary is 23, and a recent graduate of the University of Colorado, with math and engineering degrees. He is single, and thinking hard of moving to the West Coast.

He has high aspirations as a writer; he has been published in Full Spectrum, and has sold two stories to Asimov's, all recently, so it seems reasonable to expect that his aspirations are realistic. As for "The Bookman"—well, all we can say, really, is we warned you. Not that it will help.

About the Illustrator

Timothy Standish is 31 and has been doing art for the last ten years. However, what he does during the day is run a small energy conservation office in Binghamton, New York. He is single, and enjoys being that way.

He has had one and one-half years of commercial art in college, and has won a few awards at convention art shows. His first sale came a few weeks before learning he had won the Illustrators' contest.

I, Jaromir Stavan, am a large and generous man, committed to reducing the myths of backward peoples to scientific commentaries. Recently, funded by the University of Wenceslao, I journeyed inland, investigating the tale of the bookman. As I progressed through the hill-lands, the primitives I met spoke with ever greater conviction and their bookman became ever more fantastic; by the time I reached the village of Etozia I wondered if the myth were an elaborate invention designed to test the gullibility of travelers. I would soon know.

I had brought novelties from true civilization: magnifying lenses, astrolabes, mechanical mice that whined, and—the hill-landers are voracious readers—books. I spent an evening in the sole café of Etozia, doling out frivolous romances and atlases of the ocean depths; in return, the villagers told me what they knew of the bookman. At about midnight an overweight man with a mustache and suspenders entered. He called himself Manualpo, told me he was a prospector, and claimed that he knew where the bookman lived. I was delighted at this news and gave him a gilt-edged Berlitz guidebook of San Dijaeno; he promised to take me to the bookman in the morning.

Manualpo accompanied me from the café to the inn where I was to stay the night. Before we parted, I said, "Tonight a child warned me not to visit the bookman. He claimed the bookman captures the minds of men."

Manualpo laughed and snapped his suspenders. "Children look for portents in everything. Listen to what they say, but smile while you listen."

"Of course," I said, but that night, as I slept on a wooden slab the innkeeper had called a bed, I dreamt of the bookman, grown to Cyclopean proportions, feasting upon children.

In the morning Manualpo and I drove toward the mountains until the terrain became impassable by car. We began hiking; after a few minutes I noticed that my guide was wheezing under his load. "Aren't those packs heavy?"

He laughed; he carried both our backpacks. "Extremely so."

"Then let me help."

He snapped his suspenders. "Hah! I'm fine—you should see me with my pickaxes and treasure!" Manualpo's face was flushed, and his breath came in rumbling gasps. We were hiking through forested country, flat save for the many rocky gullies, which were the source of our troubles—the instability of the rocky material forced us to crawl up the side of one gully, then, eyes wide and hands flailing, slide down the side of the next gully. Indeed, it was because of the gullies that I had left my diesel car behind.

We had completed another gully. The great pine trees dripped resin; the shade, black and deep, put me into a gloom which reminded me of my dream—I wondered if the bookman could slide mighty sinews around the trees, rip them up at their roots. Then I thought of Monhij, my competitor, who wrote of a great servile beast that inhabits the mines to the southeast of Stadelo. This beast, he reported, generates spontaneously from the tailings left in the mining tunnels. Once formed, it frees miners trapped by giant boulders; when all have been saved, it dissolves back to its constituent elements. I hoped that the bookman was not the

Illustrated by Timothy Standish

terrible monster of my dream, but instead like Monhij's monster, kind, benevolent. This thought encouraged me.

But it was cold, which was strange, because I had been uncomfortably warm while we were in the sunny gully. "Of course," I said. "The air is thin up here. It doesn't insulate."

Manualpo, ahead of me, nodded. "You can explain the air. Can you explain the bookman?"

I stared at the bundle of tent poles, which bounced off his hairy calves as he walked. "The bookman is a phenomenon of our civilized age. What is there to explain about him?"

"His growth. His insatiation. You might think, Mr. Stavan, that he is as simple as a book because he reads books. I tell you differently; there is a point where there are too many books. A cancer of words, you know?"

"You hill-landers like books."

"Oh, we could never have too many books. Not much happens in Etozia; we're not much for drink, unlike you city sophisticates, and a man, having done a few hours of hard work, digging for gold, fur-trapping, whatever, needs a book for his soul. Also, of course, the superstitions. We've got to keep them in check."

"But what you said—about books and cancer—sounds like superstition."

Manualpo stopped, turned. He smiled at me, taking out a handkerchief and wiping sweat off his flushed face. "That's not a superstition, it's a phenomenon. Rest now; you'll see it soon."

Late in the morning we climbed a steplike series of limestone rocks; the most prominent peaks of the hill-lands are composed of that gray-white, fossil-rich stone. It was warm again; the sky was what is called egg-shell blue, and I was on the verge of removing my jacket. There was a bed-shaped formation that seemed to lead into a wall that we had

been paralleling for half an hour. To the right of this formation was a cleft between two eroded escarpments; I
thought Manualpo intended for us to climb through this cleft.
But he veered off toward the bed-shape.

We climbed onto the formation, though I could not
imagine that it would do anything for us but bring us up
against a wall. I tried to tell Manualpo that I did not know
the technique for climbing walls, but I was out of breath and
he did not hear my words.

The bed-formation ended in a smooth, curling projec-
tion analogous to a headboard, and about two meters tall.
By now I realized the formation was not flush against the
wall, but that there had to be a gap. "Here," Manualpo
said; then he took off both packs and placed them on the
limestone. He grabbed the headboard of stone and pulled
himself up to his chin. Then, by digging his toes into
cracks, he climbed to the top.

I followed his example, straining because I am large,
(though not fat), and unused to the altitude.

I saw the bookman.

The bookman was in the entrance of a cave, sitting on
a granite throne. He was naked. His face was ordinary—
he had a strong nose between eyes with slight epicanthic
folds, a square shaven jaw, and slick black hair carefully
combed and parted at the side. His chest was robust and his
arms were large, though both looked soft from disuse. It was
his skin that was strange—his color faded progressively
down the length of his body; his face was brown, his chest
was the orange-pink of the tribes of the Northern Islands,
and his stomach was whiter than the limestone—an unhu-
man and loathsome paleness, that would have inspired revulsion in one not equipped with the objectivity of science. At
his waist the bookman seemed to merge with the limestone
throne—there were no legs, no lap, no buttocks for support.
According to the myth, his body extended down into the

substance of the throne, and possibly several meters into the earth.

Surrounding the entrance of the cave was an open area, brightly sunlit, in which were piled scores—even hundreds—of books, disarrayed, many damaged by weather or insects; it was as if a great library had been destroyed here, its marble pillars and hardwood shelves giving way to dust, the soft perishables it had protected surviving. Manualpo grinned then jumped; it was a five-meter fall and I would have thought him insane, had he told me what he was going to do, but he landed on his knees, the books absorbing his weight.

He stood, beckoned me to follow, and I did. I landed on a set of *Cyclopedia Rhetoricas,* though not with my guide's grace; I fell forward. The books were wet, and I tore off the cover of one. Manualpo laughed and helped me to my feet.

We hiked over piles of pulp to the bookman; he watched us the whole time, and my heart raced, as I reviewed the questions I had prepared for this interview. When we were about five meters away from the bookman, Manualpo grabbed my wrist, stopping me. He brought his grizzled, garlic-odored face close to me and said, "The bookman moves, yes. But those other places he goes to aren't important; he's always here. Don't write that you found him here."

"You have my word." He grunted and pulled me forward; we stopped in front of the bookman's footrest, on which were stacked several volumes, all opened, as if in the midst of being read.

The bookman regarded us and I realized that I did not have my notebook, and thus could not record our interview. Common sense would have had me climb back to our packs and retrieve the notebook; but I was almost in a swoon, realizing how imminently I would assure my place in the annals of natural science. "I'm Jaromir Stavan. . . ." I said but the laudations and clever boasts I had planned dissolved into a sigh.

"Stavan," the bookman said; his voice was clear, as if he had vocal cords of ice. "I've read you. Isn't it the fashion, now, to worship analysis, at the expense of the spirit?"

"You've read . . . Srogel and his school, then?" I was suddenly sleepy. One hears of peasants breaking their backs to sustain lives of misery; I had to be so disciplined simply to speak. "I've adequately defended the natural philosophies in my book of essays."

"Your book—do you have it with you?"

"No." My voice was faint, even to my ears.

"I do," Manualpo said; he took out a small edition he had hidden in a pocket of his trousers and gave it to the bookman.

When the bookman took the book I realized that his pale arms were not flesh, but rather stone; that the myths were true, and his foodstuff was the inorganic matter of the earth. For there were small cracks in the joints of his fingers and the green spots of lichen under his long nails. He began reading the book, quickly and hungrily, the triangular folds of skin above his eyes lowering and rising as he turned the pages.

As the bookman read, we three spoke. I shall not attempt to record the conversation here, for it was a dreamy, emotional thing, probably guided by the limbic systems of our brains. I am not convinced that words were even spoken, though our communication was mediated by symbols. These symbols were gestures; the legend that the bookman had once been a hill-lander was true: he shared with Manualpo smiles and frowns, hisses and shrugs, sudden glances at the skies, and ways of giving subtle pronouncements through manipulations of thumbs and fingers. But they communicated through other media, I believe— Manualpo danced, and the bookman responded by sending vibrations through the limestone beneath our feet; it was the sort of code that sailors use, though I could not interpret it. I remember at the time also looking for meaning in the movements of the clouds and the paths of stinking black beetles that crawled on the books, but now I consider such searchings absurd.

At any rate, the conversation began politely; the bookman was pleased to receive the cheap, clothbound edition of my essays. When I had the strength, I asked questions—I cannot say whether or not I used the great language in which I write, or indeed any tongue at all—to confirm the myths that I had already heard.

The bookman replied that everything was true: he built himself according to the instructions he found in his books; he built himself from stone because that was the material most readily available; he found biology textbooks to be especially useful (because he could model himself after photographs of cellular mechanisms instead of the renditions of sculpture and drawings—as found in portfolios—which, while more pleasing to the eye, lacked the integrity of science: membranes, veins, muscle tissues, nerves, and organs). The bookman also showed me how obsolete the myths of the hill-landers were—his body extended not a few meters into the earth but thousands; in fact he had enlarged himself throughout the hills above Etozia as a tree might send roots into the ground, and the gullies Manualpo and I had earlier traversed were channels where useful bits of stone had been appropriated for his use. Lastly, I was curious why he read so many nonscientific books—theologies, comedies, dramas, fictions and travelogues—and he replied that meat and blood did not make a man complete, that it took ideas and dreams to animate him with spirit.

About then the bookman refused to speak with me anymore, only with Manualpo. They had been carrying on a

conversation independent of our own, discussing the bookman's supply of reading materials; suddenly they were
arguing, and the bookman forgot about me. Disappointed
that my interview was over, I sat down on a fat, dog-eared
copy of *The Calculus*, and tried to understand their argument. After a moment I realized that *I* was the object of
their discussion; the bookman wanted to detain me in his
limestone cave; Manualpo would have none of this; he said
I was a good, generous man, not as "feeble and hifalutin"
as most city-dwellers. What is more, I had promised to keep
the place we were in a secret. Here the bookman grew
angry, his brown face so livid it almost matched the stone,
and he told Manualpo that he was a stupid gold-digger;
could he not understand that I would write about the bookman and thus throw the Earth into final chaos? The
bookman's meaning was clear: I would have to be his pris-
oner for eternity.

At this Manualpo made an obscene gesture and said if
that were the case, he would never bring another book.

The bookman laughed and said that even if all the hill-
landers hid under their beds and trembled and never brought
him books, he would still have other sources.

"Then we leave!" Manualpo shouted. He grabbed my
wrists; but, still lethargic, I did not move. "Stavan!
Come!" He was stout but strong, and began dragging me
from behind; my heels tore yellowed, beetle-eaten pages out
of books.

Presently I returned to my senses. I pulled loose from
Manualpo, and we ran to the wall made by this side of the
bed-shaped rock. "The notches, use the notches," he said,
and he quickly climbed up the wall, sticking his toes in
small depressions, sending dust down into my face.

"Hurry!" he said when he was at the top of the wall.

"Why?" I stepped up to the wall, and stuck my fingers
in a notch a short distance above my head. I pulled myself

off the book-strewn ground but the pain this put into my fingers was intense; I let go, fell to the ground.

"Come on! Come on!"

I tried and fell again. "I can't do it."

Then the bookman laughed; the sound echoed weirdly off the limestone walls.

"Stavan!" Manualpo, mouth agape, pointed at my feet.

I looked—there was a limestone arm rising near my right foot, pushing aside a copy of Isheylus's *Four Comedies*. I broke the thumb off with my boot.

Now, my heart beating quickly, I looked up. My guide was gone. "Manualpo!" As I shouted, I again kicked at the arm, which had risen to its elbow above the books, and was moving with heavy slowness toward my leg. I broke off the top joint of the index finger.

"Stavan!" Manualpo had returned, he let a rope down; I pulled it close to me, tight in my hands. I expected him to pull me up, I suppose—he yelled, "Climb!"

Another gray fist brushed against my leg. I was with Manualpo within seconds.

"Forget the packs!" he screamed; I grabbed my notebook, leaving the barometer, the insect and soil specimens, the micrometers, behind. He was running, already almost to the edge of the bed-shaped formation.

We ran down the limestone steps. Now it was not merely arms, but bodies, breaking through fissures, stone sculptures merging at their feet with the ground, reaching for us; they could not walk; they could not free themselves from the bookman, any more than a man's hand can act independently of his body. There were many of these stone men; we might have been captured because of their numbers, but both of us found heavy sticks which we used as clubs; we swung as we ran, breaking off fingers. Once I cracked the head of a perfect woman, and I was glad for my scientific discipline, which insulated me from any remorse for destroying such a masterpiece.

"They're the characters from books, aren't they!" I said, for I had seen, unmistakably, Pirone Stellman, the tall, haughty strumpet in the *The Chasm of Gnosticism*, and, beckoning to me, Jelbet, the miserly screw in Toyme's *Dalliance and Desire*, dressed in his pointed boots and antiquated jerkin.

"More than that!" Manualpo broke the hand off an old man. "Idealizations. Personifications of ideas! Run, man!" He sprinted off, and I followed. "Everyone he sees, he adds to himself!"

For a while it was as if we were running through an art gallery, crowded beyond capacity with mobile sculptures. But, once past the limestone formations, there were suddenly fewer of the things.

I stopped when we reached the first gully. It was no longer empty, but full of rock and rubble, shifting and writhing as if molten; occasionally body parts—arms, heads, feet, gray and pitted—would form, then immediately disintegrate.

I dropped my club, trembling.

"Come on!" Manualpo pulled me; I resisted. He let go and ran across the turmoil in the gully; he reached the other side safely. "Come on!"

In horror, I followed; but the jaws, appearing, then gone, the knees, the waists, the bones without flesh and the flesh without bones, felt like shifting sand. I was across.

"He can't build so fast, and hardly at all with dirt," Manualpo explained, wheezing as if he would explode. "Come on!"

We ran, and ran, through the forest and over more gullies, and gradually the sand and grit subsided, the body parts becoming more and more primordial, gray and murky and like protoplasm, as if, as we progressed, we were seeing the history of evolution in reverse, providing the evidence to settle the great controversy of our time.

We were in the forest, a hundred meters from my car, when we came upon the sculpture of Manualpo. It was a flattering portrait of a younger, thinner man; strong, mustachioed. He leaned against a tree, proudly, arms crossed, staring not at us but at the murky darkness of the forest. He stood motionless.

"No." Manualpo held me back as I raised my club to smash the statue.

"What?"

"Don't break it." And then he began touching the statue, appraising it. He tapped the skull; it sounded solid. "Quite handsome, isn't it?" He looked at me and the sculpture grabbed him around the waist, pulled him close.

The real Manualpo looked surprised; he struggled, but the statue held him securely. After a minute he said, "Oh, go on, Stavan. The bookman'll grow tired soon. Go on."

"Manualpo. . . ." I said; then I ran, to the diesel car, parked just the other side of the forest.

Something was growing out of the ground; gray, a large man, his oval face as yet lacking definition. He was buried to his waist in the yellow grasses, and his crudely formed hand was reaching for the bottom rung of the ladder to my seat. I did not wait to see what man this stone would become; I began smashing it with my club; I first broke the arm off, then the head, then I began grinding down the torso. The statue seemed especially delicate in its immature state.

I climbed to my seat.

In a fortnight I completed my manuscript; it is now ready, to send to Chaveskii, the editor at *Discourses on the Natural Philosophies*. In it I describe the bookman as best I can, both his history and traditional relationships with the hill-landers and especially the villagers in Etozia; I also speculate on the mechanisms whereby he adds cellular units to his tissue, his metabolism, the diseases he may be prone to, etc. It is a complete and well-documented treatise.

But the manuscript remains on my desk, bound by string, as it has for three days. I am unsure whether I should submit or burn the papers. For I understand why the book-man fears me—he anticipated my writing the treatise, and he knows he will ultimately read it. His nature compels him to express in stone what he reads; he realizes, in sculpture, the literary characters that he meets. Having read of himself, he must create a copy of himself from stone.

And he fears this; he fears that he will be thrown into an infinite regress of creation, because to truly copy himself, he must acknowledge that his copy must also have read the treatise, and thus a true copy *would contain another copy* and that one another, *ad infinitum*. He dreads this, I believe; he will need to consume the entire Earth, even the universe, to complete himself.

Perhaps, then, I will rewrite the treatise, tell the world the bookman is a fraud, a relic of those ignorant times which we have so recently escaped, or even claim that he is real, but smaller than a fly, smaller than an atom, less than vacuum.

The Vintager
by
James Gleason Bishop

About the Author

Captain Bishop is an instructor in English at the Air Force Academy in Colorado Springs. Born in Middlebury, Vermont, in 1961, he attended four different colleges, eventually graduating from the State University of New York in 1983 with a BA in English. He worked as a Communications Security inspector for the Air Force, taught at the Air Force Academy Preparatory School, returning to the University of New Hampshire to obtain his MA in English Literature in 1988. Married, with three children, he has written for The Boston Globe, *published three editions of a textbook,* Higher Literacy, *and edited numerous magazines. But he had never sold a piece of fiction before. We think he will again.*

About the Illustrator

Kevin Hopkins is 32, and comes from a rural Oklahoma background. He grew up on a ranch and still ranches. For the past four years or so, he has also been a belt buckle designer, and has entered a lot of small art shows in the area, in the sphere of Western art. But he has always had a parallel interest in SF, and has worked with a number of conventions. His background is in fine arts and biology, and he has taught art in the past.

Your Bordeaux, sir," Curtis said. "It's the last of the '91 bottle."

"Thank you." I peered over my crystal glass, swirling the wine of a previous century and studying my servant for any brash gesture. Not that I would have said anything to the large black man. Mine was the same instinct that keeps a man running his tongue over a painful cavity. For too long, I had been afraid of this man who would soon be my master, afraid of losing the scant fortune I'd amassed, and afraid of losing myself in the switch.

I tapped the glass with my fingernail. 'My wine,' I thought. It had a deeper burgundy hue and a subtler bite than either of the two government brands, whose quality I tried to redeem over the last five years as Chief Viniculturist of Argentina. I used to tell people who asked my occupation, 'I watch grape juice spoil.' But that became old.

This was to be my eighth and final switch in thirty-five years. I had been lucky. Some of the Aristopovs had to switch with detox teams or garbage haulers—jobs left over after the middle class had taken their pick. At least here I would still be around the wealth, simply exchange classes with Curtis—it was tough to start thinking of him as "Mr. Whitney" and of myself as "Travis." But the affluence would no longer be mine, if it ever really was.

Being a butler was nothing compared to hiring on with one of the nuke slinger teams. They had to ferret out toxic areas from the war and from spent fission or fusion reactors, then relocate the contamination to the dumping grounds up north. They wore protection, but accidents happened . . . sure, I had been lucky.

Curtis noticed me staring at the wine and, I believe, pitied me. "Close to retirement, sir?"

"This will be my last term." Had I truly never told him that in almost five years of serving together? Probably not. I had learned a lot more about him than he had about me. I looked at the standing clock longer than necessary to see the time. I loved that walnut grandfather clock with a boy's love—which was all the greater for the knowledge that the clock and the other niceties would soon be my servant's. It said 11:44. My switch became official at midnight.

Curtis read my gaze correctly. "I could take it away, sir. We could forget about clocks until morning."

'Magnanimous of the lad,' I thought. 'Allow me a six- or seven-hour postponement, but he's also beginning to take charge sixteen minutes early.'

"Thank you just the same, Curtis," I said out loud, "but that won't be necessary. Draw a steaming bath for me."

I walked slowly to the bathroom, savoring the soft, thick pile of the carpet, caressing the grandfather clock's smooth walnut casing.

This time, I'd begun to feel the loss of wealth after only one year into my Aristocrat term. At school, switching was a game. Endure the sometimes daily changes from the Aristocrat dorms to the Poverty hovels. Show the observers that you were one of the top 8.5%—intelligent enough to manage entire industries, but also willing to perform the most disagreeable tasks in the land.

With my best job forever gone and my worst ahead, I was no longer "willing." I was scared to consider how much of myself would be left when the finery was stripped away.

I dropped my clothes on Curtis's arm and sank deep

into the perfumed water. It burned and soothed. The skin turned pink on my sizeable belly. Curtis neither watched nor looked away. I stole glances at him—resentful, even hateful glances. Waiting, as if on my own deathwatch.

"Curtis Whitney," I said, startling him. "Did you resent me last time, when school ended and you learned of your assignment here?"

It was a childish, transparent question, and Curtis is gifted with eyes in the back of his mind.

"We're not supposed to, are we, Travis McCormick? Doesn't Bolner say, 'Savor the spiritual Eden of your Poverty tours'?"

"I'd forgotten," I said, dripping sarcasm like slobber from an infant's mouth, in part to show my angst at his use of my given name. For me to use his name had been a gesture of magnanimity; for him to use mine, one of insubordination—for another three minutes. Curtis looked away for quite some time.

"Yes," he said finally.

"Eh?"

"Yes, I resented you, but not in the way you resent me." His eyes pierced me. Staying silent was the strongest denial I could muster. "You remember slavery?" Curtis continued.

"We all studied it, of course."

Curtis nodded. "I have an ancestor who was a slave. Ancestor or friend, any records were destroyed in that little skirmish of '20." ('Little skirmish' was Curtis's term for the missile exchange that left most of Eurasia and North America barren and radioactive. That it should have occurred in 2020 delighted Curtis in its irony. He once told me: 'Why couldn't we regret bombing the day before instead of the day after? It's because we see better out of our ass than out of our eyes.')

Illustrated by Kevin Hopkins

"Well, this friend appeared to me in a vision five years ago, just before I graduated," he said. "Welt marks on her back, lips wrinkled and bloody, black coals in her eyes, always looking North. Looking to the cold, ugly, deadly North."

At his last word, the walnut grandfather began to chime. I groaned silently but didn't take my eyes off Curtis —Mr. Whitney. At first I suspected he was fabricating the story for my benefit. I still don't know.

"Travis, when I entered this Poverty tour, her eyes grew huge and black—like the inside of a dark fallout shelter when you're dreaming the bombs may fall again. Scary black. Maybe she doesn't understand or maybe she understands better." The chimes gave eerie rhythm to his words. "But I know my Aristo tour will soothe her pain, rub aloe on her bleeding lips and put a glimmer of sunrise in her eyes. If I resent anything about my Poverty tours, Travis, I resent causing her pain." The final chime sounded.

"You think I'm mad."

"No, sir," I said. "I think—" I paused to stand and dry myself, struggling to sound respectful but not sycophantic. "—I think you have, perhaps, a nobler origin of your aversion to switching."

"Yes." Mr. Whitney pulled off his black servant's jacket, revealing strong ashen arms, and hung it up himself —a kind act, considering he could have just tossed it at me. "I'll retire now. Shall we break fast at five and plan to be off by seven?"

"Yes, sir." The formality returned much too easily. Was the servant the real me? Was Chief Viniculturist just some velvet mask I'd worn? I panicked, thinking, 'If I don't feel like an Aristo now, I never will again. That was my last Aristo tour.' That put me in a funk. I broke out in a sweat and turned away so Mr. Whitney wouldn't see my flushed

"Something wrong, Travis?"

"No, sir."

He patted me on the back. "Get a good night's sleep. You'll probably be fine in a few weeks. By the way, I'll be getting married in a month and bringing my bride back here."

"Yes, sir. Congratulations."

I never went to sleep. I stole into the cellar and searched among the rows of *vin ordinaire* for the other bottle of pre-war Bordeaux. It was a dangerous act. I suspected Curtis had been waiting to taste it. He'd be furious in the morning, but I had no intention of becoming the object of Curtis's wrath. I found it stashed on a bottom row, label facing downward. The first few deciliters I savored, but after that I gulped down the remainder like a child who gorges himself with cookies so he won't have to share.

I couldn't label the emotion which drove me to desert my new job. Urgency tackled reason; I felt like a slave escaping on the underground railroad.

Reeling drunk, I packed a huge suitcase with clothes and worthless memorabilia like my satin pillowcase. When I tried to pick it up I thought my arm would rip off. The shock made me fall face first onto the soft carpet, where I vomited a foamy purple liquid. I left the suitcase, stuffed some cash into my pocket, and half-fell down the stairs. Thinking back on it, Curtis must have heard me. I slammed the door behind me and walked out into the night shouting, "Free! Free!"

Outside, I tripped on a brick and fell onto the cobblestone driveway. My cheek hit hard but painlessly, high on the bone. I lay there and caressed the bricks—I'd never felt them before: smooth tops and rough edges, slightly sunken where the limousine tires roll. The limousine! Why walk out on my job when I could drive out in style? I wiped blood onto my sleeve, rocking and heaving my way into the kitchen.

Perfectly aligned rows of jars and canisters accented the countertop. We always kept the limo keys in the flour canister, but when I reached in, my hand came out white. I threw the canister on the floor, spilling flour all over, then did the same with the sugar, tea, and baking soda jars. The *second* flour jar I opened held the keys. Looking at the scattered, sticky white and brown mess on the floor, I realized there was no turning back.

I jumped into the car. It had been five years since I had driven the car myself, so I had to fumble some in the dark to find the ignition slot. I revved the engine and crashed through the garage door. The poor door did more than snap wood and tinkle glass. She let out a high, pitiful, metallic scream.

The bends and curves seemed to come up too suddenly, so I kept on the road only as far as my neighbor's—Curtis's neighbor's—house, one kilometer east. Curtis's limousine and Lawrence Bowen's stone fence butted heads. The fence won. The front bumper squeezed into the engine. The engine held fast, but I bounced painlessly around the front seat. Unhurt except for the bleeding below my eye, I poured myself out of the window and walked east toward International Route 11, which spans the continent north to the American barren lands and south to us near the bottom of Argentina.

The cool March air sobered me enough to stay out of the path of the occasional truck which roared up and down the county road I was on. Several hours later, I turned north on Route 11. There, many trucks passed me carrying four or five trailers full of people moving up and down the South American continent to new jobs. Everyone would be in a tizzy for a few weeks. I stumbled along for some three

No trucks had chanced by in the last twenty minutes. My feet and head were starting to throb, and my eyelids demanded sleep. I fell into the bushes just a few meters from the highway and rocked myself asleep, still mumbling, "Free, free," but with considerably less enthusiasm.

Always a light sleeper, I awoke later that morning by a convoy of detox-team trucks thundering down the highway. Stiff, sore, smelly, bloody, unshaven, and decidedly toxic myself, I signaled the last of the trucks for a ride.

He pulled over. "Looks like you spent the night in the better part of valor." I have no notion what he meant. "Where you headed?"

Tough question. One to which I had not given ten seconds serious consideration, so on a whim (and not the least because the trucks were heading that way) I said, "North."

The driver looked older than me, yet younger in some essential way: white bushy hair, hard arm muscles, wide grin, and the thickest eyebrows I think I'd ever seen.

"You running from or running into something?" he asked. He knew my predicament. It occurred to me then, for the first time, that I was not alone in abandoning a Poverty tour. Besides, I was a terrible liar—used to lose hundreds at poker before I quit—so I told him the whole story.

He looked thoughtful and just drove for kilometer after kilometer. Finally, he said, only half to me, "Yours was the class where we made that egregious mistake. We figured, put them in management out of school. It'll give the industries some fresh ideas in their upper management. That worked fine; we funneled your energy into some spectacular improvements, but we didn't plan this—" He gestured at me. "It was even a contemporary of yours who discovered the mistake: start on Aristocrat, end on Poverty. That's begging for this kind of exodus." He had obviously served many tours on the Labor Planning Board. He looked old enough to have chaired it a dozen or so times.

"I guess I'm spoiled," I said. "It wasn't the poverty that bothered me, exactly, though."

"Of course not," he interrupted. "It was the lack of choice. Listen, kid, people never minded the work or conditions of poverty as much as the inevitability. We got the switching concept from Leviticus, you know. Where the Hebes had to free their slaves every seven years. They still teach you kids that stuff, don't they?" He screwed up his mouth and eyed me askance, as if he suspected me of single-handedly corrupting the curriculum.

I shook my head: I couldn't remember right then.

"Too bad. Those boneheads on the state board of directors used to think it was just the poor who give up, but richies feel that same inevitability. Some has-it-all aristocrat blows his brains onto the floor. Felt like his life was making the choices for him instead of the other way around."

He shifted to a lower gear halfway up a knoll, gaining on the other trucks, and gestured at me, as if I were a courtroom exhibit. "Now, here's a man at the end of his tour, feeling bereft of all power to choose, so he dumps the system, which is the only choice available. Rich, poor, or in between, it isn't so much *what* you chose, kid, it's *that* you chose."

This guy could've been Bolner himself, for all he knew. Jeremy Bolner, the ex-trucking magnate, had campaigned for a continental coalition just after the war. Bolner's system of Aristopovs was the perfect plan for keeping a small impoverished class around to do the dirty work, but giving them hope, then at the same time making the aristocrats eminently more capable of upper management because they saw the other side on a rotating basis.

recollection I have is once—only once—burrowing my head into my mother's warm breasts and still not being comforted. That must've been almost sixty years ago, 2021 or so.

Whoever he was, he obviously knew the system, so I asked him, "What do you suppose the police will do with me if they find me?"

"They'll find you. Then they'll probably just put you back in the Poverty labor pool where you belong anyway. Maybe tack on an extra year or two."

It occurs to me as I write this that he was the one who turned me in. I say that without resentment. I would have turned me in.

A few minutes later, the driver said, "Let's have some fun." He gunned the throttle and the truck responded in an explosion of power. "Modified her myself." He beamed at me. I remember thinking, as we passed the lead truck, 'Here is a happy man.'

Weeks it took. I lost count. Hopping trucks and trains, begging meals, feeling the air grow cooler and imagining that the radioactivity was increasing. I seemed to be walking toward some elixir of life—or maybe walking was the elixir. I grew strong. Sometimes I'd run or swim naked in a river during the day, then beg food at the back of a restaurant at night. Feast and famine. Even the scratches from stray cats throbbed with the affirmation of life.

Seven or eight weeks into my escape, having reached the middle section of Mexico where there are large farms and small villages, I noticed two people following me who looked too local. They must have taken a course in Elementary Ruralism: old broad-brimmed hats, new pale white "pajama" shirt and pants which had been rubbed in dirt to look old. Before dropping me off, the truck driver had told me we were about fifty kilometers from Mexico City, in a small

much of a problem finding work on a farm. Of course, he was right. I walked to the first corn field and began picking with the others.

No one even looked up. The two- and four-row machine pickers had obviously not reached this far north, so it was likely that anyone in the area who wasn't "essential" was encouraged to pick corn. Who would take a person aside and say, 'Hey, you're not supposed to be helping us'? (I've spearheaded a few of those harvest drives for our vineyards —amazing how many people can be spared for two weeks.) The two hatchet men pretended to fall asleep beside a stack of baled maize stalks, but I could see them fidgeting.

Worst of all, I began to enjoy harvesting. The lady next to me, an astonishingly well-preserved forty- or fifty-year old, gestured to the two under the tree and told me, "Didn't Bolner say the sleepers shall inherit hemorrhoids?" She spoke in the universal Spanish strangers used.

I confess, the first thought that came to mind was, 'No, I don't believe he did.' But thank God, whom I may believe in yet, I said in the Chilean dialect, which I guessed to be her native tongue, "And that the maize-pickers shall inherit the blisters?"

She laughed beautifully. The sweet sadness in her gaze enhanced the tune. The deep brown of her skin made me think of Curtis's ancestor, and of the walnut casing of the grandfather clock. I laughed with her.

We picked together all that afternoon, almost alone under stalks a half meter taller than us. She was a lovely conversationalist, and I was glad to be semi-secluded with her, even though the stalks blocked our view of the magnificent volcanic mountain, Popocatepetl. Sometimes I put my biggest ears in her basket even though she was far faster than me. When she finished a row she would come to the other side and meet me.

Once, we both reached for the last ear high on the

stalk. She took it first and I touched—held—her hand. The top of her hand was a smooth as the bottom was rough. She looked up at me . . . writing this now strikes me differently, but at the time the words she said were the most romantic I'd heard. They were sweet and honest, sad and beautiful. They reminded me of falling asleep in Mother's lap during a thunderstorm; the smell of sweat after a baseball game I'd won; the smooth awkwardness of the first time I made love; the feel of an arm around my shoulder, burying my face in the kind abyss of Mother's neck and hair, after a truck hit my dog. . . .

She said, "My name is Celeste. My husband died in an accident up north."

"I am sorry, and happy." Probably the most profoundly idiotic words I've ever spoken. We hugged each other beneath the green-brown leaves of the corn stalks. A kiss would have been too threatening, holding hands too distant. A hug was the perfect lovers' progression from friends to family to more-than-family (self-maker?).

"I never married," I told her.

When the shift horn blew we stole back to Tulcingo through the field to avoid my pursuers. I spent the last bit of cash I'd thought to bring on buying her an early dinner and some tequilas. We danced alone to the Mexico City radio station the owner's son picked up on a crystal radio. She was a wonderful dancer. After Mexico City went off the air at midnight, we moved out to the patio and kept dancing to songs we hummed together, under the moonlit peak of Popocatepetl. There, we kissed as long and naturally as we had hugged in the field.

Celeste was gently swaying, head on my chest, humming a slow tune I did not know, when she asked, "Who are you running from?" as if the words were part of the song. She went back to humming and swaying before I answered.

"I think the police are following me."

"I won't protect you." Her face did not change. It hadn't the hardness one would expect.

"I understand." I did not understand. I still don't.

"I don't know you," she said, I assume by way of explanation.

"Perfectly forgivable. I don't know me particularly well myself." I meant it but she laughed and held me closer. We danced for another hour without saying a word, until a voice in the alley startled us. We stopped dancing. A man was questioning someone. In urgent syllables, he described me.

"You had better go," said Celeste.

"I don't want to."

"Neither do I. Go." The words hurt.

"I'll come back." I looked at her for a response, saw none, hesitated, trying to force her to say something even if out of sheer discomfort. Finally, she said, "Yes." Or it could have been "No." It came out so softly. I dropped her hand and walked away. As with every other act in our flash of a relationship, it seemed natural.

On the street, my two police friends were searching for me. Apparently they were angry that I had slipped away from them earlier.

They walked quickly toward me, guns drawn, as the taller one on the left said in universal Spanish: "Travis McCormick, we'd like to speak with you. Don't try to run or we will shoot you."

I ran. They chased me but did not fire a shot. I ran back to the only section of Tulcingo that I knew anything about: the maize field. Living as I had on the land for the past few months had made me strong (if not responsible). I out-distanced them and hid in the field. I knew they wouldn't go into the dark field to look for me, so I crawled toward the irrigation ditch. Almost there, two bullets rustled the tall stalks three or four meters away, and I heard a distant, enraged voice shout something about thirty seconds to "give myself up."

'Hell, I just got my self back,' I thought. I crept down the dry ditch, threw a few stones far back in the field to distract my pursuers, and ran.

I simply can't break back into the next three days. They were; they are no more, not truly in my memory. Few of the facts remain with me, but the feelings. . . . Once or twice in my life, I have felt unity and belonging. I had no more to prove to others than the leaf has to the elm, yet I knew it was *me* specifically who belonged. Once or twice I stepped back and thought, just for an instant, 'Yes, this is living.' I know life can be that good and sometime, somewhere will be. If I believe in heaven, it's because of those three days.

Those three days were as bitter and as sweet as Celeste's words: 'My husband died in an accident up north.' I ran, with more and more police chasing me. By the end, I counted at least a dozen. I felt grateful to them for chasing me. Sometimes I had to almost out-muscle an urge to stop and thank them. And I knew they were grateful to me for the chance to chase and eventually catch a "criminal." That's what police do; I was in some large way, fermenting their existence. Yes, fermenting: in theory, spoiling, but in fact, improving. Making them at once more useful, more delightful, and more dangerous.

Some seventy-five kilometers north of Mexico City, mainly because I was starving, I took a big risk and hired on with Larry, a temporary nuke slinger. The crop fields were all bare (I must have been involved in the last day or two of the harvest push), so I knew the detox teams would be the only ones still hiring.

The same feeling of peaceful belonging came over me like an orgasm the next day, driving toward the United States border, both of us in our heavy, full-body, lead interwoven suits. Somehow the suits broke down barriers in conversation.

Larry was a middle-class produce carrier who had volunteered to drive the detox truck for a year. "Big cash bonus involved," he said. "But one year's enough. You Aristo-povvies can have the best and worst jobs. It'd drive me nuts."

Driving to Texas, learning each other, we doubled the speed limit.

"What are they going to do, fire me?" he laughed.

We reached the place, and the driver gestured like a tour guide. "Here it is, Pops. Dump Site, Texas. Toilet Hole, Texas." He laughed. A few short cacti rose above the gray-brown expanse. Everything was dusty, as if we were still looking at the desert through our dirty windshield.

Makes you wonder what it looked like in its prime," I said. That struck Larry as funny. In some lesser way than with the policemen, I was also fermenting his "truck-drivership."

With Geiger counters clicking so violently we simply turned them off (their information was moot; this place glowed at night), we dumped our load of radioactive dirt from some ground-zero along the Nicaragua-Honduras borderline and roared out of there. That afternoon, at an inspection station for returning detox trucks, the police arrested me.

It was anticlimactic. Snap! of the handcuffs from behind, then, "Mister McCormick, please come with us."

"Do I have a choice?"

"No."

Even the punishment was disappointing. No jail. Just an extra two years tacked on to my poverty tour. I still got to decide my job preference from the few left. They brought in a labor specialist.

"Where do you want to work, Mister McCormick?" he asked, as if he dealt with convicts and bolters all the time. Perhaps he did.

Where to work? Memories shouted at me: Curtis's ancestor, my wine, that driver who said, "It's not what you chose, it's that you chose," Celeste's "yes," Celeste's "no," (I had become convinced by then that she had said and meant both), the popping good time I had with Larry on the detox truck. . . .

"I'll stay with the toxic relocation team," I said. The closer you have to Mexico City, the better.

"Nuke slingers it is. I probably shouldn't tell you this, but it's the only job left at this point anyway. I can put you on the run from deep south, near the Guatemala border, up through Nuevo Laredo. Skirts the capital."

"Good." Someone else was saying it for me; someone more useful, and delightful, and dangerous than I; someone I'd fallen in love with even more deeply than I had with Celeste. "Very good."

Mothers of Chaos
by
Pete D. Manison

About the Author

Pete D. Manison is 29, and began writing science fiction fifteen years ago. Seven or eight years ago, he got really serious, and wrote four novels. But they are still looking for a home, and he began writing short stories. Recently, he began regularly winning Finalist status in the Contest. He lives in Houston, Texas, and drives a truck for a living; he is currently training on 18-wheelers, and plans to go out on the road at least until the writing takes hold.

• • •

Pete D. Manison's illustrator is Ruth Thompson.

That generation, the children **were all born with wings, silver hair, and white downy fur covering their little bodies,** and the Mothers of Chaos were pleased. It had been many a pass of the Black Star since a new crop of youngsters had been so well-made.

"They have only one head this time," observed Kwando.

Flink and Tawn crooned in agreement. Flink said, "It is good for a child to have only one."

Kwando looked around the spacious Hatchery. She felt satisfaction, as always, at the arrival of the brood, but this time something was different. There was an odd tingling in the back of her mind as she gazed at the infants, some already running about the Hatchery or testing their wings, others curling for warmth against the squat, bulky bodies of the Mothers. In its essentials, it was a scene which changed as little over the centuries as the Mothers themselves. Why, Kwando wondered, was she ill at ease?

"They're so cute," bubbled a Mother nearby.

"It's the wings," said another.

"Cute, yes, but have you had the same trouble I've had?"

"What, their flying off whenever they don't get what they want?"

"Annoying, isn't it?"

"Still," Kwando put in, "that's not the worst of it. My brood seems to have an aggressive instinct I've never. . . ."

Illustrated by Ruth Thompson

She trailed off as several Mothers turned to stare at her. Or were they staring? Perhaps it was only a part of the vague sense of wrongness she could not yet explain, even to herself.

The eclipse of the Black Star came as a surprise to the Mothers. It was not their wont to keep up with the scientific things or to read the ancient books stored in the Tower of Learning. Not that these things were forbidden, they were just considered good things not to do.

"Have you ever seen the like?" one Mother asked as she stared up at the sky in disbelief.

No one answered. Soon, they were forced to retreat indoors as the Black Star slipped behind the lunar disc and a threatening dust storm appeared on the horizon. Kwando stared in amazement. Such storms were common during a Black Star passage, but this one glowed with swirling phosphorescence as it rumbled across the landscape.

"How exciting!" exclaimed Flink.

"It's strange," said Tawn, "but in a way, beautiful."

"And frightening," said Kwando.

"Why frightening?" asked Flink.

Kwando shrugged to hide the shiver she felt passing through her bulk. "I don't know, exactly. Perhaps because it is different."

"As Mothers," said one, "certainly we must have learned to love the different."

"Certainly," echoed Kwando in a hollow voice, but as the dust storm grew to envelop the near towers, she knew that this time she could not so easily dismiss her fears.

The Tower of Learning was situated far from the Hatchery in an area where few Mothers ever ventured. Kwando moved quietly through its massive doors. She felt the need for secrecy, though she knew that every Mother had the right to come here if she chose. She had never heard of anyone availing herself of that right.

Inside, the tower was deserted, the rooms dusty with disuse. It took her some time to find the books that she wanted. They were the ancient texts dealing with the science of astronomy. They told of Chaos, the Black Star, and the other bodies of the solar system.

Kwando studied the books for several hours. At last, she found the information she sought. It was as she had suspected. The Black Star had been eclipsed once before. She read further. The last time it had been eclipsed had been the generation that the first Mothers had appeared.

"How odd," she said aloud.

"Not really," said someone behind her. Kwando turned to see Storn, the Ruling Mother of Chaos, looming in the doorway.

"I did not hear you come in, dear Storn," Kwando said hesitantly.

"I'm sorry if I startled you . . . or interrupted you."

"Am I wrong to be here? Am I wrong to be curious?"

"No," Storn said as she moved slowly forward. "It is not seemly for a Mother to be too inquisitive about such things, but it isn't criminal. And you have never been average. Perhaps I can save you time and keep you from drawing the wrong conclusions from those aged books."

"Then you have read them?"

"Of course. Many times."

Kwando was puzzled. "Then you know how ominous this event truly is."

"Well, I wouldn't say 'ominous' exactly. It is written that before the first eclipse of the Black Star, life on Chaos was just that: chaotic. The high levels of radiation on our world had mutated the original life forms brought here by the Travelers, had begun a cycle of change in them all."

"Including the High Form."

"Yes, including the High Form. Before the rise of the Mothers, the single Traveler High Form species had branched off into thousands of separate forms, each diverging from the others to the extent that ultimately no two individuals were alike."

"And they still exist."

"Yes, Kwando, yes. The non-Mothered species, as you know, are not highly regarded, but they do exist. Most of them reproduce sexually; unsuccessful mutations are inevitable among them; the death rate is high. But the diversity of life enables them to thrive, to find new ways of solving the age-old problems of survival."

"So it was on all of Chaos before we came along," Kwando said. She looked up sidelong at the Ruling Mother, and she wondered: was Storn really telling her what was written in the books? What was she not telling her?

Storn stepped around to look at the book Kwando had been reading. She closed the book and returned it to the shelf. "Now," Storn explained, "alongside these independent forms, are our children, hundreds of generations of them. And instead of total chaos, there is a kind of order, since we all produce identical children in any one generation."

Kwando tested Storn's gaze, found it less harsh than expected. She dared to say, "Our children are numerous, that is true, and their sameness is often a blessing, but they are not always well-made. There was the time, you will recall, when they were born with absolutely no sensory awareness. And what about the time the children were outwardly sound but lacked all fear? They all died in senseless accidents."

Storn chuckled, a deep rumbling sound from within her massive body. Somehow, that sound frightened Kwando. "But the Black Star passes often," said the Ruling Mother, "and each time there is a new chance."

Kwando looked away from Storn, rested her gaze on the floor. "I see."

"Then you are no longer concerned about these things?"

"Well . . . I . . . no. Of course not. Now that you have explained it, Ruling Mother, I understand."

Storn smiled as one Mother would to another. "All will be well," she said.

"I believe that now," said Kwando, and she left the Tower of Learning, wondering if the Ruling Mother's instincts were sharp enough to let her see through the lie.

One generation, all of the children got very sick, and most of them died.

"Weep not," said one Mother to another. "It is only one lot, and we have many more to come."

Most were consoled by the Mother's words. Not Kwando.

"Have you noticed," she asked, "that since the eclipse of the Black Star, each generation has turned out worse than the one before? It's a pattern, I tell you. Can no one else see it?"

Only Flink had the courtesy to respond. "What do you mean, sweet Kwando?"

"Just this: perhaps our time has passed. We have done our job too well. We are perfect baby-producing machines. But as we have peopled our world, we have rendered ourselves obsolete. We are no longer needed. The races of our progeny will carry on without us. Remaining, we can do only harm."

The Mothers turned away. Kwando looked to her friend hopefully, but even Flink had no patience for such talk. "Look at yourself," she declared. "The loss of one brood is no reason to become so depressed. Don't you care what such an attitude does to those around you?"

"Perhaps I am the only one who truly does care."

"Really," said Flink, "you are becoming quite an old fool."

The Mothers began to leave, casting glances of distaste over their shoulders. Only Flink remained.

"Please, dear Flink, you at least must listen to me. Don't you see the danger? What will we produce in the next cycle? Even chaos has a certain order to it. But lately, there has been no order."

Flink turned toward her, and Kwando thought she saw genuine concern in the eyes of her friend. "I hear your words, Kwando, but I don't share your fears. If you keep this up, you'll break out in worry-webs."

"But Flink, what if we do something terrible? What if we produce something that threatens all our other children?"

"I just don't see how . . ."

"You are a good Mother, Flink. You are a good friend. You sympathize with my difference without really sharing it. Sometimes I think you almost understand."

"Oh, Kwando."

"You know, sometimes I think it would be safer, now that so many viable forms exist, safer if we . . . left."

"Left? *Now* what are you talking about?"

"I just . . ."

"Oh, my, is it so late?" Flink rose and moved toward the door, glancing back with a mixture of uncertainty and what Kwando thought might have been fear. "I really must be going," Flink said, and she disappeared through the door and out into the night.

Kwando moved silently in the shadows of the towers as she neared the darkened Hatchery. It was several days before another brood was expected, and Kwando knew the place would be deserted. She was right. She entered stealthily making no sound as she closed the massive doors behind her.

It was strange to be in the Hatchery when it was deserted. Kwando felt like a ghost, like someone out of step with her time and place. Only the cold metallic lump concealed in her robe brought her back to reality with the certainty of a decision made that could not easily be unmade. She moved deeper into the Hatchery. She knew what she was looking for.

The central tower support was surrounded by incubation capsules, several of which had to be moved aside to give her access to the structure. Once beside it, she removed the ancient device from her robe and looked at it. She had found it in the museum section of the Tower of Learning. The book she had found with it told of how it had been brought by the Travelers, how it was a remnant of their fantastic technology—a technology that had enabled them to reach across the stars to people this and other worlds. The book also told how the object was to be used and what effect it could be expected to produce.

Kwando pressed the red button and twisted the silvery knob to the desired position. She could only hope that the device would still function after all the time that had passed. A reassuring glow from the red button promised that it would. She placed the device near the tower's support column and began to replace the incubators to conceal her work.

Kwando suppressed a tear. This feeling, she told herself, was inevitable. But she would not let it dissuade her. Would she not be here with the other Mothers when the time came? Would she not pay alongside them, pay with her life to protect the many lives they together had created? No, she thought, drawing a deep, steady breath, she was not doing wrong here.

There was a noise behind her. Startled, Kwando

"What are you doing here so—"

Ruling Mother Storn broke off as she looked past Kwando and spotted the dull red glow from the ancient device. By the look in Storn's eyes, Kwando knew that the Ruling Mother had recognized the Traveler relic.

"Well, well, well," Storn said, shaking her head sadly. "It seems that even I underestimated the degree of your sickness." She pushed past Kwando and bent to retrieve the device. Resolutely, she clicked off the red button and smiled as the glow faded from it. "Not that your plan would have worked," she said, looking down at Kwando, who suddenly felt very small. "The chemical explosives will have decayed long ago. But your intent is clear. Please come with me. It is over for you now."

The trial of Kwando was held in the Tower of Learning, where her criminal act had begun. It was the first event of its kind in the history of the Mothers.

"Yes," Kwando said, "I admit to what I did. But I tell you it was for the best. One harm would have been a fair exchange for the million harms that we ourselves could bring."

Ruling Mother Storn, the judge and prosecutor, paced impatiently over the floor. "How could we bring harm?" she demanded. "Even if all our future generations die out, as did the last, the ones we've already produced will carry on the thread of life, as it was done before our time."

"What if we produce carnivores?" challenged Kwando. She felt confident that her argument was sound.

Annoyingly, the Ruling Mother laughed. "What if we do? They will prey on the other forms, even on ourselves, and then they will breed more of their own kind. Life will go on."

Kwando shuddered: cold tingling sensations were run-

she knew that she was right. "But the Black Star was eclipsed. Don't you understand? Only once before has this happened, and that was when we first evolved on Chaos. Surely this event heralds no less a change. Surely . . ."

"Listen," snapped the Ruling Mother, and her arrogant self-assurance infuriated Kwando, "if evolution were going to foul itself up, it would have done so long ago, and we wouldn't even be here."

"Storn, surely you don't—"

"No! You will stop talking this way. You are the worst paranoia generator I've ever seen. You are worrying yourself, and us, over nothing. It isn't good for breeding. And there lies the answer to your fear of the tooth and claw. The secret of life is the one single constant in our ever-changing world: reproduction. With wings or without, with tail, horns, or hooves, the drive to reproduce is strong. Life continues."

Agreement rippled through the gallery.

"Now," continued the Ruling Mother, her voice calm and reasonable, "I will give you one last chance. Repent your actions, renounce your fears, and this incident shall be forgotten."

Kwando stared at Storn. She could not believe what she had heard. She swept her gaze over the rows of Mothers who watched. They were all there, the hundreds of them, glaring at her in disapproval. Flink was there, too, her face lined with worry-webs. Kwando turned back to the Ruling Mother.

"No," she said, and she was surprised at the steadiness of her own voice. "I cannot. I will not."

"Then I have no choice," said Storn. "The opinionated are the intellectually sterile. No punishment is too severe for your actions, and for any future actions you might take, which could endanger not only ourselves but countless generations yet to be born. Therefore, you will be imprisoned in the top of this tower for the rest of your time, which may be endless. You will be given all that you need to live, but you will also be given the drug that suspends our breeding cycle. You may watch, from the windows of your cell, as life proceeds, but you may not take part in it. Surely, that is the worst punishment any Mother can endure."

Kwando shivered in rage. "Please, Ruling Mother, I beg to speak."

"The trial is over. So is your usefulness to Chaos and our race."

"But it is not for myself that I wish to speak. Do with me what you will. It doesn't matter. But please allow me to help you—all of you. You must learn from this. You must read the books. It is the Black Star that changes life on Chaos. You all know of the dust storms caused by its periodic passage. Well, it causes turbulence in the genetic flow by its radiations just as it causes turbulence in the atmosphere by its gravity. It is important that you understand, that you study. There may be a pattern to—"

"No one needs to know these things," declared Ruling Mother Storn. "Life changes. Why is not important. We adapt. It will always be so. This trial is ended. You have spoken your last words to us. We will hear no more."

As one, the Mothers turned away.

Kwando lunged after them, only to be restrained. "Please, Flink, at least you must understand. Don't be a part of this. Please, for friendship's sake."

But Flink, too, turned away, as outwardly disgusted by the scene as the rest. The Mothers paraded out the doors of the tower. They never returned.

Two full cycles had passed, and Kwando stood looking out the window of her cell at the top of the Tower of Learning, looking out on the ruined landscape of Chaos. Nothing was moving out there now, nothing at all. From that window, she had watched the carnage build, climax, then gradually subside. From that window, she had witnessed the final horror.

It was over at last.

Kwando had to admit that at least one thing the Ruling Mother had said was true: she had here all that she needed for survival. There was a seemingly endless supply of food and water. There were no needs not met within the walls of her cell.

Some time had passed since she had discovered that the locking mechanism of her cell door no longer functioned properly. From the outside, the door appeared to be locked, but she could easily open it from within. She could leave whenever she wished. She was not ready for that, though, not yet. The quiet outside might be an illusion. She would wait awhile longer to be sure.

Kwando ate a light supper that night, for she still had little appetite after what she had seen. But she remembered to take her daily dose of the breeding suppressor. She had decided to keep taking it, even if no one was left to command it, for at least another cycle or two. Only then would she discontinue it. Only then would she allow her breeding cycle to continue.

Kwando returned to the window, looked out as dusk came to the still land beyond. With luck, she told herself, she would be spared. With luck, she would give birth to a new generation to replace the old, to replace the lost. With luck, her children would be well-made. With luck, they would not be monsters.

For the children of that last generation had all been born with two heads, an insatiable appetite for raw flesh, and a powerful aversion to sex.

The Children of Crèche

by
James Gardner

About the Author

James Gardner is our first Canadian First Place winner. Thirty-five, he lives in Waterloo, Ontario, with his wife, whom he describes as an artist/writer/cartoonist/Renaissance woman. He himself is a technical writer for the University of Waterloo, writing computer manuals, tutorials, design reports and other kinds of software documentation. It is worth noting that getting his degrees included doing a Master's thesis on mathematical models for black holes. He has been playing the piano for 28 years, writing and arranging music for at least half that time. He performs at coffee houses on occasion. Other than that. . . . Well, there's ''The Children of Crèche,'' to which we commend you.

• • •

James Gardner's illustrator is Timothy Standish.

And so it's good-bye to New Earth and < BINK > hello to Crèche."

Inter-World Vac/Lines is such a mind-slogging Mom-and-Pop outfit that they think their good-bye/hello trick is cute. Halfway through the welcoming spiel from the burstingly mammalian Coffee-Tea-or-Kama-Sutra Flight Hostess . . . and speaking of sexual pandering, Inter-World, must we be so heavy-handed with the airborne phero-mones in the cabin? I for one am more comfortable buckling up the seat belt when I don't have a pointlessly throbbing erection . . . halfway through the opening monologue with all its openly oozing female fecundity, they hit the cabin sta-sis field, and < BINK > it's six weeks later, we're dirtside on some colony where every particle of air has been through one lung too many, and Miss Wouldn't-You-Like-To-Know-If-I've-Been-Surgically-Enhanced is finishing off a sentence that started a couple of dozen light-years ago. I mean, really, Inter-World, can't you see how smarmy the whole thing is?

No, you probably can't, you pitiful geckos.

It was with this lapse of taste in my mouth that your intrepid Art-Critic-cum-Role-Model-cum-Provider-of-Vicar-ious-*Savoir-Faire* donned the traditional leather jacket of his profession and sallied forth into the Vac/Port for a first recce of the fabled planet of Crèche. I was not entirely surprised to find that a Vac/Port is a Vac/Port is a Vac/Port, all of modern semiotics notwithstanding. You have your usual gag-gle of tourists from the colony one star system over, the ones with no particular idea why they're here, except that they just *had* to get off-planet or go mad, and this place was cheaper than Morganna's Semen-Sea Whack-Me world; and you have your traditional traders from your favorite alien culture that doesn't see in the visible spectrum, blundering around with incomprehensible accents, asking humans to read the signs to them; and, alas, you have your mass of parochial flibberties who shouldn't be allowed to read our dear old *Mind Spur Weekly* but do anyway, who have pilgrimaged to the V/P to maketh the Big Embarrassing Frenzy of Gratitude that J*O*N*N*Y! T*H*E! S*C*A*L*P*E*L!, Knower of Taste and Taster of Knowing, has deigned to descend upon their terraformed little Nowhere to partake of their pathetic drippy lives and report same to the Cosmos at Large (i.e., You, Devoted Reader, currently feeling superior to such hicks, for reasons that are more obvious to you than to Yrs Trly).

Still and all, the Crèche mob of droolies were a touch outside the normal run: old as dry beavers, the lot of them. Of course, This Reporter was aware of Crèche's famed shortfall in the production of mewlies and pukies; but you don't snugly plug into the *reality* of a child-poor world until you wander into a Vac/Port expecting the usual horde of training bras, only to find that their ecological niche has been filled by the saggy-sack set. At least these post-menopausal minks weren't packing those sharp little tissue-sampling spatulas that the gigglers bring to scrape off souvenirs. (Honest-to-Boggie, kids, if you really want to impregnate yourselves with my DNA, break down and shell out the bucks to one of the fine mail-order houses that advertise in this very magazine. You can get professionally prepared guaranteed viable sperm, a certificate of authenticity, and a hyper-sincere form letter produced by a state-of-the-art computer that fakes my signature better than I do; and I get to have an epidermis that doesn't look like a land-use map. Bargains all 'round.)

For all their graysies, the Raging Aging were still cut from the typical Scalpel-worshipping mode—each and every one of them was waiting to be discovered. Crèche's idle idolizers came unto me bearing their children that I might bless them . . . said children being sketches and sculpture, mosaics and masks, tapestries, filigrees, etchings on flasks, holograms, cameos, prints wet and dry, ceramics and beadwork and oils, oh my!

Cherished Reader, perhaps you have recently heard Crèche lionized in song and cinema as the Mecca of all artistic perfection. Mine own ears too had been visited by paeans to the planet's sublime accomplishments, which is why I felt it incumbent upon me to visit said colony-sized cathedral to Aesthetic Excellence and there do homage. Nevertheless, in those moments when I was besieged by the untalented Crèchian unwashed waving their pathetic attempts at self-expression under my nose like whores who want you to smell their panties, it came to me that we must never forget every cathedral is surrounded by pigeons screaming for crumbs and crapping on the architraves. Thus endeth the gospel according to Jonny.

I was saved from the gaggle of gleanies by my contact on Crèche, one Phillip Leppid, PhD, PhD, PhD (in Music History, Art History and Pharmacology—the Three Graces.) As those who claim to be *au courant* with the Contemporary Art Scene should know, the good Doctor-Doctor-Doctor is the man who first brought Crèchian *objets d'art* to the attention of Those-Whose-Opinions-Are-Thought-To-Matter, in a gala showing last year at Buddenbrooks & Bleaks. Since that time, he has made himself buckets of booty huckstering the work wherever empty lives and full wallets are found. He is not Crèchian himself—he hails from the hinterlands of a world named after some bottom-of-the-barrel Greek god who wouldn't have rated a pico-asteroid in the old Sol

Illustrated by Timothy Standish

System—but Leppid is Crèche's foremost Advocate-Slash-Publicist-Slash-Pimp, and therefore was the natural choice to serve as my Sherpa during my ascent to the Peak of Human Ahhh-tistic Achievement.

When he sighted me foundering on the shoals of a blue-rinse ocean, Doc Leppy (as I never heard him called the whole time I was there) waded in with heroic disregard for his own ship of taste, scattered the minnows with the indiscriminate barging of his 300+ pounds, and dragged me to the safety of his waiting Lava Cruiser Deluxe. To be accurate, the cruuz was a cherry-red Ourobouros Devourer 4.3BSD from the Wildebeest Motor Works, with manual steering, a logarithmic tachometer, and two dangling wires where the anti-collision computer used to be. The upholstery was taut white, covered with the bleached hide of an endangered species that I probably shouldn't name here because it would earn Leppid a visit from ecological guerillas with a nasty How-Would-You-Like-To-Be-Tanned-And-Sat-On attitude. Ah, what the hell, it was an alligator. (Sorry, Phil—the Public's Need-To-Know wore down my resistance. Anyway, what have you done for me lately?)

With Leppid at the wheel, we peeled out of the Vac/ Port at a speed that didn't quite break the sound barrier, but opened a hairline crack or two, and one exit ramp later we were spattering through the local lava fields fast enough to throw up a peacock tail of molten rock directly behind us . . . except that it wasn't directly behind us all that often, because Phil was weaving like a tripped-out spider: hard to port, hard to starboard, through our own wake of stony slush, one grade A skidding doughnut that bid fair to roll us Ass-Over-Teacup o'er the burning plain, one six-G deceleration that buried our nose so deep in volcanic phlegm I found myself wishing I'd brought a periscope . . . and finally, I had to say, "Phil. Enlighten me. Are we out here taking evasive maneuvers from snipers, or are you just jerking around?''

"Come on, Scalpel," he grinned as he gave the wheel a twist that heeled us over far enough to scorch the door handles, "I read that piece you did on the Overdrive Overlords of Omicron II. They drove around like maniacs and you wrote the most glowing review of your life."

"It seems to have escaped your attention, Phil, but what the Overdrive Overlords were up to was performance art," I told him. "They did not drive like maniacs, they drove like artists. The distinction may be subtle, but I like to think it's important."

Leppid snorted as if he knew what I really meant to say. "Come on, Jonny, I know you want to get wild. Admit it."

I sighed deeply. The difference between a Sensitive-Critic-Known-Respected-And-Feared-In-All-Corners-Of-The-Galaxy and an Opportunistic-Boor-Who-Might-Have-Three-Degrees-But-Doesn't-Know-Titian-From-Turds is that one of us has eyes that see and ears that hear, while the other has an assortment of prejudices he waits to have confirmed. "Phil," I told him, "*you* are getting wild, the car is getting wild, and the lava is getting positively livid. I, on the other hand, am sitting here passively, save for the occasional reflexive jerk to prevent my skull from making forceful contact with the dashboard."

Leppid laughed loud and long at that, all the while playing Jiggle-Me-Juicy with the steering wheel; and on into the evening, he pursued his attempts at wooing me by wowing me, until Crèche's sun moseyed off to see if there was anything doing on the other side of the planet and the stars showed up to see what had changed since they left. At first glance, lava leaping in a cruuz looks even better after dark because of the weaving strips of black and flame, the fountaining of sparks, the gouting arcs of hot planet blood . . . but all that brucey imagery loses its charm damned fast if the smoky shadow you drive into turns out to be a jag of recalcitrant bedrock too pigheaded to melt. At last, even the good Triple-Doc had to admit that further monkeyshines in the magma were just a shade closer to suicidal than good taste allowed, so with tears in his eyes he called it a night.

We pulled up onto the highway at a spot apparently made for the purpose: something like a boat-launching ramp, only gnubbly with flecks of dried lava dripped off by other hot-hot-hot-rodders who'd passed this way before. There was a bevy of Bloat-Belly trucks sharing the road with us, all coming from the Vac/Port and no doubt filled with the gewgaws of a hundred worlds, belched up from the cargo holds of the same Vac/Ship that had brought Your Obedient Servant. All of the trucks we passed were bot-driven, which was just fine with me—if Phil had seen one of those Bloaters under human control, I know he would have tried racing the rig in order to demonstrate his testosterone level to his captive member of the Press. (Ah, children, the world is full of people who want to impress the old Scalper with feats of derring-do. My advice is, derring-don't.)

Nascence City, the colonial capital, nestles halfway up the side of a volcano everyone swears is extinct (this surrounded by a lavid plain that seethes with fumaroles, geysers and the like . . . suuurrrrre). You can see its lights winking, blinking and nodding among the crags when you are down on the flats, but when the road actually begins climbing the mountain, your line of sight is blocked off by assorted igneous effusions that welled up some thirty million years ago—this geological travelogue courtesy of *Nascence Alive!!!*, one of those End-Every-Sentence-With-An-Exclamation-Point publications whose natural habitat is the top drawer of hotel nighttables.

The hotel in question was the Nascence Renaissance—redundant in name, and redundant to describe for those who have stayed at its kith and kin throughout our wart on the galactic arm. Squatting by the main highway, just inside the dome's airlock, surrounded with carefully tended greenery that would look more natural if it were plastic . . . anyone who has traveled on an expense account knows that this same hotel follows you from city to city, running on ahead so it has time to put down its foundations and change its make-up in the hopes that you won't recognize it from the night before. Everywhere, the same covered entranceway, whether you drive up in a lava cruuz, sandcrawler, or gondola; so dark and shadowed by the overhanging portière that they need lights during the daytime (globe-lights in simulated antique fixtures), and as you are helped out of your vehicle by a grizzled male in pseudo-military livery, you see assembling a battalion of bellhops who wash their ruddy cheeks each morning in a fifty-fifty aqueous solution of eagerness and cynicism. Professional small talk ensues momentarily; then, into a plush lobby befitted with oaken desk, crystal chandelier, and round-the-clock concierge (always a middle-aged woman who is the epitome of courtesy and dispatch, but whom you can tell was a Grade A heart-and ball-breaker in her day).

You can count on two artpieces in the foyer: one some sort of sunset, the other an historical motif, neither aggressively representational or abstract. The Nascence Renaissance held true to form on the first, with a hooked shag-wool tapestry of one (1) regulation red giant about to take its roseate leave behind a near-naked horizon clad only in a tastefully placed cactus. But what to my wondering eyes should appear on the wall above the neo-Victorian pseudo-hearth? Not the black-and-white Battle of This, nor the blue-study Treaty of That, nor even the sepia Discovery of The Other Thing: it was a layered assemblage of vertical mylar and buckram strips, the mylar a wispy mercurial foreground that tinseled several planes of fabric behind it (like a curtain of mist in a dream? a glittering spider web? bars of a gossamer cage?), and the stiff cloth backgrounds painted with dyes to give a textured three-dimensional picture of a nursery—playpen, cradle, toy box, stuffed animals scattered about the floor, dolls toppled over on a window seat, a closet with its door ajar and filled to overflowing with tiny carefully hung clothes.

At first, there was no one visible; but as I examined the work, I thought there was a small movement behind one of the nursery curtains. When I looked directly at it, nothing; but out of the corner of my eye, I caught a tiny quiver of motion behind the closet door, ducking out of sight too soon for me to see. Then in the toy box; then from behind a pile of dolls; then under the blanket tossed carelessly beside the cradle—the piece was alive with children peeking from behind every strip of fabric, but hiding too fast to leave more than the ghost of their passing.

"Computer-controlled," Leppid said at my elbow. "Hidden cameras keep track of your eye movements. You can watch it all day and the little buggers will never be where you're looking."

"Could get bloody irritating after a while," I said.

"If it were done badly," he shrugged. "But it's not." And even though I was not kindly disposed toward the Doctor[3] at the time, I had to admit he was right. The work had a subtlety and a sly naturalness that made it both haunting and haunted.

"Who's the artist?" I asked.

"Vavash," he answered. "Earth mother type—long straight silver hair, shapeless tie-dyed dresses, would rather wear glasses than have corrective surgery . . . a textbook classic. One of the First Colonists, of course. They're what make Crèche what it is. Since the Rediscovery, a lot of lesser lights have settled here to bask in reflected glory, but no one of any stature. Most of the new immigrants are . . . well, the group at the Vac/Port were typical. Black Velveteers."

"We'll stick to the First Colonists," I said hurriedly.

"I thought you'd feel that way," Leppid grinned. "I've set up a visit to their retreat tomorrow morning. It's in the Upper City—poshly Spartan. Entirely state-supported, too; the other colonists treat the Firsties like royalty. Not much interaction between old and new, except at official ceremonies. It wouldn't hurt you to be a bit deferential around them."

I gave him a look that was intended to wither his fat-beribboned carcass right in its pointy-toed shoes. He laughed and slapped me on the back as if I'd told a joke.

My internal clock was scarcely in the sleeping mood when I retired to my room, so it seemed like a good time to refresh my memories of the sordid history of Crèche by looking up the colony in *Auntie Agatha's Encyclopaedia of All Those Things You Should Have Learned in School, You Jam-Headed Git, But No, You Were Too Lazy to Apply Yourself and Now Look Where You Are* . . . a reference work that I have recommended many times in this column, whenever I use it as a cheap expository device.

The First Colonists landed on Crèche some sixty years ago, the vanguard of what was intended to be a grand colonizing caravan that would bring hundreds of thousands of other *nouveau* Crèchi and Crèchae to this toasty-warm lava-ball. For Reasons That Have Never Been Adequately Explained (i.e., a computer error that the damned sneaky machines managed to cover up before human auditors arrived), all of the subsequent colony ships were diverted to the beautiful planet of Mootikki, famed for its semi-sentient water spiders that eat anything with a pulse. Forty years passed before some minor functionary stumbled across

records of the original Crèche expedition and sent out a
scout to peek in on their progress.

Crèche had not done badly, all things considered.
There had been only ninety people on the lead ship, but
there had been a full complement of builder-bots, plus all
the materials needed to erect a life-support dome and get the
food vats pulsating. In fact, with only ninety people to support, there was an embarrassment of supplies, and more
than enough bot-power to keep the staples stapled.

All skittles and beer then . . . except for The Problem.
As reported by the Crèchians to the scout four decades later,
no children had come. Hell yes, they had tried making
babies, with a lusty devotion, and according to all medical
analyses, they were fertile as Teenagers-Who-Think-It-Can't-
Happen-To-Them; but something in the water/air/topsoil/
Van Allen Belts was preventing Mr. Sperm and Ms. Ovum
from producing nicens little baby Zygote, and year after
year went by without those little feet a-patterin'.

Morning arrived with an artillery barrage of photons
on my eyelids and a cheerful computer voice saying, "This
is your wake-up call, Mr. The Scalpel."

"I didn't ask for a wake-up call!" I bleared from under
a pillow.

"This is a free service of the Nascence Renaissance
Hotel. If there is any other service I may perform for you,
I would be happy to comply."

A less experienced traveler would have retorted with a
suggestion both vulgar and topologically challenging; but I
knew better. I once used a pithy colloquialism in response
to an annoying hotel computer, and an hour or so later room
service was at the door with a huge agglomeration of feed-
screws and suction pumps that was apparently capable of
doing precisely what I'd specified. Not only did I have to
pay for materials and transport costs, but there was a hefty

fee for some custom molybdenum tooling that had to be done in a low-G L5 colony.

I have to admit, though, the contraption did work as advertised.

Breakfast came with a complimentary copy of the *Crèche Colony Chronicle* (alliteration is the soul of journalism). The front page was splashed with many of the same articles that had been slopping around on the stands the day I left New Earth . . . no big surprise, since all the news must have come in with me on the Vac/Ship. However, there was one interesting tidbit: Miss All-The-King's-Horses-And-All-The-King's-Men Flight Attendant had apparently caused a major uproar by sneaking away from the Vac/Port and visiting one of Nascence's night spots. Oh, the outrage! A fertile female at large amidst the Barrens! The Colonial Cops had clapped her in irons posthaste and transported her in utter ignominy back to the V/P, there to remain in quarantine until her ova-rich ass could be kicked off-planet.

"Computer!" I called. "Do you do legal information?"

"I am fully prepared to make small-talk on legal matters, none of which should be construed to imply, suggest, or covenant that information imparted in such wise constitutes qualified advice from the Nascence Renaissance Hotel, which will in no way be held liable for any damages, costs, expenses, claims, actions, or proceedings that may result directly or indirectly from this little chat."

"Just confirm for me that women of childbearing age aren't allowed on Crèche."

"Human females below the age of fifty may not immigrate to Crèche unless they are certified incapable of reproduction."

"And why's that?"

"For their own protection. Some factor in Crèche's environment makes childbearing impossible. The First Colonists do not want others to suffer the infertility that

they themselves endured; and as the authorized colonial
government, the First Colonists have benevolently forbidden
off-planet women from subjecting themselves to such risks."

"What about men?"

"Men above the age of thirty are welcomed."

"But computer, I thought no one understood the sterility. How do the First Colonists know that men are safe but
women aren't?"

"Have you enjoyed your breakfast, Mr. The Scalpel?"

"You didn't answer my question, computer."

"Did you notice how evenly we spread the marmalade
on your toast? The Nascence Renaissance Hotel Kitchen-
bots take great personal pride in attending to the smallest
details."

"Am I to assume that I'm venturing into areas of the
data banks that are missing, classified, or both?"

"The sauce on the eggs is a special invention of the
chef's. He's won prizes for it."

Ahh, a quick prayer of thanks to Elizabeth of Hun-
gary, patron saint of the hasty cover-up. It is a far far tastier
sauce for a journalist's breakfast than some soupy pseudo-
Hollandaise that probably came from the rear end of some
bacterium.

By the time Leppid came to pick me up in his manic-
mobile, I had rented a vehicle of my own: a docile town-car
that understood it was a mode of transport, not a kinetic eme-
tic. When Leppid got into the passenger seat, I believe he
thought the car was a dragster incognito; all the way up to
the First Colonist retreat, he was bracing himself for the
moment when I would press some hidden button and go
FTL. His face was red with nervous perspiration by the
time we reached the front gates.

Now, Gentle Reader, if we are to believe the *Weekly*'s

demographic studies, you are likely to be an upper middle-class inhabitant of one of the more frequented worlds, a youngish college-educated pseudo-intellectual who fancies him- or herself weird and unconventional, though you wouldn't know real weirdness if it bit you on the bum and licked . . . in short, you're a bureaucrat and probably a civil servant. As such, you have no doubt imagined the life you will lead when you achieve an elevated position in your oligarchy of choice—the dining room suites made of gold, the platinum bathroom fixtures, the black velour drapes speckled with diamonds to mimic the local star map—and you believe that everyone who has Arrived will share your dreams of wallowing in a mud-pit of conspicuous excess.

The First Colonists owned Crèche the way you own your monogrammed handkersniffs; but they had more Style and Taste and Class in their nostril hairs than the entire populations of several planets I could name. There was no showy Imported-Vegetation-Intended-To-Look-Lush-While-Not-Straying-A-Millimeter-Out-Of-The-Kidney-Shaped-Flower-Bed-Where-It-Belongs or Mansion-Built-To-Ape-Some-Blissful-Historical-Period-When-Culture-Was-In-Full-Flower-And-Peasants-Knew-Their-Place. Their retreat consisted of dozens of two-room prefab huts spread over a tract of unadorned twisted sheeny-black volcanic cinder, and a mammoth central building that looked like a Vac/Ship hangar and served as refectory, general store and studio.

The plainness of the buildings was offset by a profusion of statuary: at the top of every rise, at the bottom of every hollow, on the side of every cinder slope stable enough to support weight. Just inside the gate (which opened automatically as we approached), we passed a life-size hologram of an ancient metal swing-set—at first sight, brand-new, painted in bright reds and yellows, but aging rapidly as we drove forward until it was rusted and rotting; then back again, freshly reborn. A little farther on, a copper-green man and

woman stood beside one another and a short distance apart,
their hands held out and down as if they supported an invisible child between them. Not too far beyond that, a tree of
dew-slick steel pipes supported a host of mirrored cylinders
that dangled on silver cords and swayed in the morning
breeze; within each cylinder, some light source gave off a
golden glow that shone up on the pipe's wet sheen.

"Something's happening over there," Leppid said,
pointing. Some twenty people were walking in slow single
file across the slaggy landscape, following a pair of bots
who carried something I couldn't make out. The humans
were all old, in their eighties or nineties; even the bots were
elderly, obsolete models not seen in the fashionable part of
the galaxy for many years. One of the bots was playing a
recorded flute solo through speakers that crackled with age.

Doc-Doc-Doc Phil and Your Ever-Curious Correspond-
ent got out of the car to investigate. Walking across the
gnarled terrain was an open invitation for the Gods of Twisted Ankles to give us a sample of their handiwork; but, like
most gods, they didn't exist, so we managed to reach the pro-
cession with tibiae untouched. The man at the end of the
line said nothing, but nodded in recognition to Leppid and
motioned for us to follow.

From this new vantage point, we could see what the
bots were carrying: more perfectly polished than the finest
mirror, the silvery ovoid of a stasis field with the size, shape
and probable functionality of a coffin. Perhaps the same stasis chest had housed one of the First Colonists on the voyage
that had brought them to Crèche—in those early days of
Vac/Flight, travelers were wrapped in individual containers
instead of the full-cabin One-Field-Immobilizes-All systems
used now.

The parade stopped at the edge of a cloudy pool that
thickened the air with the smell of sulfur. The bots tipped
the coffin and stood it on end, as a plump woman at the

head of the line reached into her apron and produced a copper wand with a ceramic handle. She touched the tip of the wand to the surface of the stasis field, and < BINK > the field popped like a soap bubble on a sharp toenail. Revealed to the gloom of an overcast day was the naked emaciated corpse of a woman in her nineties, liver-spotted hands folded over her flat-flap breasts. She had coins where most of us have eyes, and a small butterfly tattoo where many of us have small butterfly tattoos.

Suddenly, the woman with the wand proclaimed in a belly-deep voice, "There are some among us who have compared Life to Stasis. In our trip from birth to death, we are locked into a body that can be frozen with sickness or age or fear. If this is so, death is the moment of liberation, of release, of reaching our long-awaited destination. We wish our sister well in her new world."

The woman bent over the body and kissed the dead cheeks with that airy Two-Centimeters-From-Contact Kiss that was so much in vogue sixty years ago. The corpse accepted it in the spirit in which it was intended. Then the line began to move, and we all got a chance to scope out the bare-ass carcass and take what liberties we chose. As we filed along, watching others shake the deceased's hand, stroke her flanks, and so on, Leppid murmured to me, "The dead woman called herself Selene. She specialized in collage . . . very personal stuff. This whole thing is no surprise to me—I saw her a couple of days ago and she seemed on her last legs."

"Wasting away?"

"Oh no, she was always very thin. If you'd ever seen her work, you'd know. She often incorporated a photo of herself into pieces."

"Ahhh." Self-portraits have a long and noble history . . . Art will let you pick a self-indulgent subject as long as the self-indulgence stops before you get your brushes

gooey. When I drew close and had my turn to pay my unfa-
miliar respects, I intended to give a quick smooch and walk
on; but something caught my eye and held me there much
longer than protocol required. Dim and camouflaged by the
mottled old skin, stripes of stretch marks chevroned down
both sides of her belly.

Esteemed Reader, there are only a few conditions that
stretch abdominal skin enough to leave permanent marks.
One of them is obesity, from which the scrawny Selene
apparently had not suffered. The only other cause I know is
pregnancy. And that was an enigma I pondered deeply as
Selene's remains were remaindered into the steaming maw
of the planet's digestive system.

In the main building, a retrospective of Selene's work
had been hastily mounted on one side of the Dear Depart-
ed's studio: a collage of collage. A canvas covered with
gears and gems and alphabet blocks . . . a volcano-shaped
mound of plaster wrapped in wrinkled tissue paper dabbed
with blobs of solder and melted crayons . . . the great bowl
of a radar dish sequined with thousands of tiny doll's eyes
opening and closing in accordance with a cellular automaton schema described in an accompanying booklet . . . but
no, no, no, it is not Your Devoted Documenter's intention to
describe too many of the Art objects of Crèche. Quick jump
to the earliest piece in the collection: by luck or deus ex
machination, a life-size double photograph of Selene herself
at twenty, front view and back view, in the buff. Titled
Birth, Re-Birth and Its Consequences, it was the usual sort
of work that early colonial artists seemed compelled to produce when starting off fresh on a new world: an assessment
of who she had been and what she was now.

The two full-length photographs were black and white,
very clinical, tacked to a corkboard backing. Every scar on
the artist's body was carefully circled with red paint; black

surgical thread connected each scar on the photos to an accompanying card that explained the circumstances surrounding the scar. (Judging from her knees, Selene had been one of those children who should not have been allowed to play on gravel.) And I know what you all have been wondering, and the answer is no—her taut little tumtum showed nary a sign of stretch, hurt, or lesion.

"See something you like?" Vavash asked in an amused voice. She was standing by my side, watching me scrutinize the photo of naked young Selene, and I suppose she had attached lascivious motives to same.

"An interesting lead to my article," I said, wondering if I sounded convincing. "I arrive and immediately become part of a funeral. Later, I have the chance to see the same woman, sixty years younger. Contrast, irony, all that folderol."

"Oh." She seemed dubious.

Vavash was more or less the woman Leppid had described, and more rather than less. She was a head taller than I and a beefy bicep wider, the product of one of those Fringe Worlds that dabbled in *Ubermensch* breeding programs. For all her eighty years, her eyes were as clear as the cry of a hawk and her spine as straight as a teen-age erection. She was indeed wearing a shapeless tie-dyed dress, not to mention huge round spectacles, leather sandals and a gold mandala on a chain about her neck. A naïve observer might call her an anachronism, a clichéd throwback to the Stoned Age; but there was too much intelligence in her for anything so trite.

Vavash had been the woman who led the funeral, and to all appearances she was the First of the First. Frankly, the other First Colonists were a sorry-looking lot: over half had already died of old age, and most of the rest were only a step away from Worm Chow. I doubted that more than a handful were actively working any more. A functioning studio is

filled with more smells than a Fomalhaut Flatutorium—oils
and turpentine and damp clay, hot metal and etching chemicals, tart developing fluid, fresh sawdust, and the crinkle of
human sweat—but the studio building around me carried
only the ghosts of effluvia past.

"Was this Selene's first work?" I asked.

"Earliest surviving, I would guess," Vavash answered.
"She was fresh out of art school when she signed up for the
Crèche colony. I'm sure she had many student pieces, but I
wouldn't think they were still around. Not on Crèche, anyway. That's not the sort of frippery colonists were allowed
to bring with them in the old days."

"So Selene planned to be an artist all along?"

"Oh, we all did. Crèche was always intended to be an
artistic commune. We called it a Second Wave colony. The
very earliest colonies, the ones we called First Wave, were
founded solely on economic grounds—which planets had
the most valuable minerals, which were the cheapest to terra-
form, that sort of thing. The Second Wave colonies were an
idealistic backlash—hundreds of special interest groups intent
on setting up their own little utopias to show everyone else
how it was done, and to hell with the materialistic bullshit.
I know that I considered several other Art-oriented colonies
before I decided on Crèche."

"What distinguished Crèche for you?"

Vavash laughed. "I had a boyfriend and he liked the
name. That's the truth as seen from the objectivity of age.
At the time, I would have sworn I made my decision for hard-
headed ideological reasons, and my Tomas would have said
the same thing. What distinguished Crèche after the fact, of
course, was that the few of us who landed here had forty
years to work without outside interruption, and with so
many surplus supplies that we never had to do any kind of
nonartistic labor."

"You had everything you needed?"

"We had all the essentials, but we didn't have everything. We had very little technology beyond the basic terraforming machinery, for example. You can see that in our Art, of course . . . we work in media that are centuries old. And almost all the medical supplies and medic-bots were on one of the other ships. We were lucky that the standard decontamination measures had succeeded in killing all the dangerous micro-organisms the colonists might have been carrying. Back then, decontamination was seldom that effective."

"I guess you were lucky you never had any children, either," I said as offhandedly as I could. "Pregnancy can get very dicey, medically speaking."

I knew I was taking a bloody great risk in bringing up such a touchy subject. The First Colonists were the government on Crèche, and Vavash was their leader. If she decided to have my head cut off and paraded around the Vac/Port on a pike . . . well, in place of reading my pellucid prose you'd probably be skipping over some unctuous obit on the late Scalpel, Jonathan The by that self-important Gretchen What's-Her-Name whose incoherent ramblings blight these pages when I'm away on assignment. (By the way, that picture they run above Gretchie's byline isn't really her—it's just a stand-in. Our Valiant Editor is afraid that if he shows the Gretch as she really is, the *Weekly* will get popped for Harboring The Product Of A Genetic Experiment Counter To The Public Interest. Hi, Gretchikins. Kiss kiss.)

But as you have probably guessed by now, Vavash did not choose to take extreme rancor. She simply stared at me with piercing eyes and said, "You are rude, Mr. Scalpel. I can't tell if you're being rude because you don't know any better, or because you intentionally want to provoke me. Which is it, Mr. Scalpel? Are you a pugnacious little brat or some scheming Machiavelli?"

"I'm an Art Critic, ma'am," I replied.

"And does that justify taunting a woman to her face?"

"Politeness is the enemy of both Art and Criticism, ma'am. It colors true perception, dilutes strong emotion, and replaces genuine compassion. To pursue bad manners is childish; to pursue good ones is emasculation."

"Are you quoting someone?"

"Myself," I said, wondering why it wasn't self-evident. "Look, how can you people call yourselves artists if you don't read my column? Why would you let a Critic in your front gate if you didn't know that you could respect his judgement? I feel like I've just washed up on one of those islands where the local lizards have never seen a predator."

She looked me up and down once more with a critical eye. Suddenly, I had the impression she was assessing me for my proficiency in the Slap-And-Tickle Disciplines. I knew the colonies that Vavash called the Second Wave were rife with the belief that Genital Interlock could solve any problem, from How-Can-I-Show-This-Cocky-Little-Punk-He-Doesn't-Know-Everything to Oh-God-I'm-Bored-And-Everyone-Around-Me-Is-Senile. I was rehearsing my standard speech #24 ("I'm sure it would be delightful, duckie, but I only review people on one Art at a time") when Vavash shook herself and said, "You are many things I dislike, Mr. Scalpel; but I believe you have integrity. Feel free to wander where you choose."

She left in a tie-dyed swirl. Leppid, who had a toady's way of hovering in the background whenever Vavash was near, came out from behind an installation piece (a mound of ragdolls, each with a picture of Selene spiked to the chest with a voodooine hatpin) and mopped his brow, saying, "Ye Gods, Scalpel, I thought I told you to be deferential."

"You did. I ignored you."

We spent many hours touring the studio building, Leppid looming behind my shoulder, pointing out the obvious and the obnoxious, punctuating his every remark with a pudgy finger poking at my chest. For your delectation, a representative Leppidine diatribe, held in front of a *trompe l'oeil* picture of a shadow-bedecked wooden chair with a teddy bear carelessly sprawled on the seat: "See this, Scalpel? An oil painting. Colored pigment on canvas. Showing something you can immediately recognize. That *sells,* Scalpel, that sells on any planet, Fringe World or colony you want to name. Why? Because Art consumers recognize it as Art. Yesterday you were saying that Art isn't a matter of artifacts, and you are exactly right. Art consumers—my Art consumers—aren't buying artifacts, they're buying into the Human Artistic Tradition. And this Crèche stuff, it's classic. Painting, sculpture, tapestry, illustration . . . that's what Art's been, for a thousand years. People know that. And they want to be part of the greatness. So you tell me why Inter-World is so chintzy with their cargo space that they're only allowing me eight cubic meters on this next flight out. At that rate, it'll take me decades to get a good volume of Crèche's work on the market!"

Well, Precious Perusers, whatever there may be off-planet, there is a whacking great volume of work in the Crèche studios, and it is quite beyond the capacity of this reviewer to critique a comprehensive catalog. Some of it is quotidian—all the time and freedom in the Bang-Crunch cycle won't wring masterpieces from the determinedly mediocre—but much of it is high quality stuff . . . if you like being chopped in the chin with childlessness. Wham, we don't have children; whap, we *can't* have children; powee, we'll never again *see* children.

How much Crèchian work has actually found its way out to the World At Large? A tiny fraction of what is still on-planet. And on any given world, there would be at most twenty pieces, distributed over several collections. No one out there has experienced one iota of the cumulative impact of a sortie through Sterility Studio-land.

For example, empty cradles were an extravagantly popular theme, especially when embellished with some unplayed-with toy trying to look pathetic. Wooden cradles; macramé cradles; molded glass cradles with marbles embedded in them; wicker cradles fondly tucked up with bunny rabbit blankets; cradle sketches in pencil, charcoal, India ink, sepia, silverpoint; cradle paintings in acrylic, watercolors, oils, *gouache,* tempera, and several homemade concoctions that looked like crushed lava particles suspended in white glue; and this is not to mention all the collages, assemblages, and installations that managed to sneak in cradle-like objects amidst the battered packing crates and out-of-context clippings that traditionally provide the background for such works.

There were indeed pieces without obvious reference to barrenness—mirrored cylinders were very big, for example, and it didn't take someone of my keen intellect to make the connection with the stasis chests that carried the colonists to Crèche—but there was no escaping the overpowering presence of the underage absence. It was a scab they couldn't help picking, psychological vomit they had to keep revisiting.

With brief stops for lunch and supper at the refectory (bot-staffed and culinarily uninspired), I ploughed on undaunted until we saw twilight through the skylight. In that whole time, I had encountered none of the other colonists. Leppid said they were probably holding some kind of post-funeral vigil for Selene in the hut where she had lived. Considering my usual working conditions, trying to do my job while sandwiched between artists and agents grovelling, picking fights, or both, I was quite chipper to be left on my own.

Naturally, I left what I hoped would be the best till last: Vavash's studio. Several times during the course of the day

I had caught a whiff of it, a tingly tangle of herbs and chemicals with the fragrance of the back room of an alchemist's shop. When I stepped through the door, I immediately saw where the smells came from: vats of fabric dyes, extracted by hand from roots and leaves and flowers and seeds that Vavash must have brought with her and grown hydroponically over the years. Above the vats were festoons of freshly dyed yarn in long skeins as thick as my arm, cones of thread stuck on pegs, and wool bats hanging from hooks like fuzzy ping pong paddles. On the opposite wall were shelves all the way up to the roof, thick with bolts of felt and broadcloth and muslin. In one back corner, a spinning wheel stood beside a cherrywood loom with more pedals than a pipe organ; in the other, a sturdy table two fathoms long supported a gleaming new sewing machine with so many dials and levers and robotic attachments that it would probably qualify for full citizenship under the Mechanical Species Act. And in the middle of the room, Vavash had left a small collection of her work. It brought tears to my eyes.

Honored Reader, Genius is rare. True talent is sparse enough, but Genius . . . the kind of great Genius vision, where every picture tells a satori. . . . Some psychologists would have it that inside every human soul, there is Genius waiting to spring forth in strength and passion and beauty; and some sentimentalists would have it that full many a Genius is born to blush unseen and waste its sweetness on the desert air. All I know is that billions upon billions of human beings have been squeezed from wombs throughout history, but there are less than a thousand whom we can scrupulously say had Genius.

Vavash had Genius.

And she had squandered it.

Doll clothes. A tapestry hung with toys. Empty cradles.

So damned close to being a profound statement of loss or yearning or bitter tragedy, but ultimately heartless . . .

some step of emotion that wasn't there to take. Entirely new ways of combining textiles and dyes, ideas as eye-opening as pointillism or cubism or scintillism were in their day . . . but once your eyes had been opened, there was nothing to see. The visions of a human being who had stared into the depths of the Abyss, and then had decided to make floral wallpaper.

Empty cradles. Empty fornicating cradles. Vavash had the eyes of Genius, the hands of Genius, the brain of Genius. But not the purity. Not here. Not in these works.

"There has to be more," I said hoarsely.

"What?" asked Leppid.

"The woman's been working here for sixty years. She's done more than this. Where is it?"

"I think they have some storerooms in the basement here. . . ."

"Show me."

Leppid was looking at me nervously, as if I were a bomb about to go off—not a bad assessment of my mental state. Keeping fidgety watch over his shoulder, he led me through bare cement corridors to a thick metal door. "I think it's down there. I've never been myself." He tried turning the knob. "No, no good."

"Get out of the way," I told him.

"You can't go down there," he said. "It's locked."

"Nonsense," I said, looking at the latching system. It had been obsolete for centuries. "A lock is a security device. This old thing is just to stop the door from banging in the wind." I reached into my pocket and pulled out my namesake and totem, the most magnificent solidinum scalpel influence-peddling could buy. By grandiose claim of the manufacturer, it would cut through anything short of White Dwarf material.

"What do you think you're doing?" Leppid moaned.

"Vavash told me to feel free to wander where I chose."

"I'm not going along with this," the Doctoral Triumvirate muttered and stomped off. I suspected he was going to get Vavash, but I didn't care. I had got it into my head that I was being played for a fool. For some reason, Vavash had only put out her conspicuous failures for me to see. Perhaps she was trying to test my judgement after all. Perhaps she had been in a nasty mood one day and tossed together some bathetic Oh-Our-Terrible-Totless-Tragedy garbage to sell to off-planet yokels through D-D-Doctor Wouldn't-Know-Art-If-It-Carried-I.D. Perhaps someone else with hideous taste had chosen Vavash's display, and there were good and powerful works just on the other side of this door.

I started cutting. The scalpel upheld the family honor with speed and grace. In something under a minute, I was descending a long flight of steps into a darkened basement the size of a steel mill. Halfway down, I passed through an electric eye and a bank of lights turned on in front of me.

Blinking my eyes against the brightness, I saw a jungle of artworks, some packed in crates, some covered with tarpaulins, most just sitting out and gathering dust. They stretched off into a deep darkness at the far end of the cellars, where I could just make out a faint shimmery glimmer.

I walked through the silent collection, harsh overhead lamps turning on automatically whenever I approached the edge of the next darkened area. Flash, lights up on a flock of life-sized papier-mâché pygmies, some standing up, some lying on their backs, one squat little androgyne fallen over onto a terra cotta jar whose rim was now deeply embedded in its throat. Flash, and there were long vertical racks that held canvasses slid in on their sides; I pulled a few out, saw stuccoed prickles of color in abstract patterns. Flash, and an echoing aura ignited in dusty stained glass, vases striped wine red and frosty white, engraved with tall slim men wearing the sharp-edged styles of long ago, casually embracing one another.

Flash, flash, flash, then Vavash.

Unmistakable, Unforgettable. Genius.

Utter simplicity: a tapestry hung from a tall wooden arch. A sun-crowned rainbow bursting upward in joyous fountain between the legs of a prone woman. Truth. Beauty. Purity. A clamping knot of hunger untied in my chest, like the release of doves at High Festival. Yes. Yes. In the hands of someone else, it would just be hackneyed vomit, trite images done to death by the sentimentality squad. But this . . . exquisite workmanship, flawless clarity, profundity in naïveté, artless artless Art.

"Mr. Scalpel!" Vavash stood halfway down the stairs, one hand clutching the railing tightly, the other shading her eyes as she tried to catch sight of me amid the clutter.

"You've been hiding your light under a bushel, madam," I called to her.

She turned toward me and snapped, "Get out of my things." There were perhaps fifty meters between us; her voice sounded thin and shrill.

"I can't imagine why you've been keeping your best work down here in the dark," I continued. "Of course, it's blatant birth imagery, but why should that bother you? Humans have been expressing their feelings about pregnancy and childbirth since Adam and Eve. There's nothing to be ashamed of." I picked up a bulb-shaped basket made of bright ribbon woven on a wicker framework, and held it high enough for Vavash to watch me examining it. Through the vulva-shaped opening at the top, I could see an effusion of stylized flowers made of colored felt: cheerful, bubbly happiness embodied in fabric with love and spirit. "You know that this makes the rest of the work here look like botwork."

"Leave that alone!" Vavash cried.

"Why should I?"

She glared at me with a hatred clear enough to see even at that distance. "You have the sensitivity of a thug!"

"That's it, exactly," I snapped back. "Every critic is a thug, and we work for that merciless godfather called the Spirit of Art. A long time ago, old Art loaned you a wheelbarrow full of talent, didn't he, lady? But recent-like it seems you ain't been keepin' up the payments. So Art sent the Scalpel-man to chat wit' youse an' have a look-see how to get you back on the program."

"You're ridiculous!"

"If necessary," I answered drily. Vavash was still up on the stairs, bending over awkwardly in an effort to see me under the glaring lights. Her feet seemed cemented to the step. I said, "Why don't you come down here where we can talk about this more comfortably?"

"You come up here."

"Now why would a grown woman be afraid to come into a well-lit basement?" I asked conversationally. I turned my back on her and began walking toward the area that was still dark.

"Mr. Scalpel!"

"Is she afraid of mice?" I went on. "No, no mice in your standard Straight-From-The-Package terraformed ecology. Dust? No, regulation dome air filters make sure all dust is hypoallergenic. Things that go bump in the night? No, that's just childish, and there've never been children on Crèche, have there?"

"Mr. Scalpel. . . ."

The flash of another bank of lights, and there before me slept a herd of stasis chests . . . row upon row of glimmery mirrory cylinders, laid out with the care of a graveyard. The chests were less than half the normal adult size. In front of each chest was mounted a machine-lettered card. I walked among them in slow wonderment, picking up a card here and there to read: *Samandha Sunrise, April 23, 2168. Jubilo De Féliz, June 12, 2169. Tomas Vincent-Vavash, October 3, 2165.*

"So," said Vavash softly, "now you know."

She had approached silently, and now stood among her artworks, her body limp, her face old.

"I don't know anything," I answered. "Are they dead?"

"They were alive when they were put in," she said distantly. "That means they're alive now, correct? Time doesn't pass in stasis. Not a fraction of a second. Not even over all the years. . . ."

"They've been in stasis for sixty years?" I asked in disbelief.

"Some. We kept having them . . . no medical supplies, you know, no birth control or abortion. We'd try celibacy but it got so lonely sometimes. . . ."

"You just kept dropping foals and merrily putting them up in stasis?"

"Oh, it's very easy to be self-righteous, isn't it?" she said angrily. "Imagine yourself in our place. Imagine yourself with a world entirely to yourself, and being free, absolutely free to follow your Art as you chose. No Philistines to question the value of what you're doing, no political system that feels threatened by your activities, no mundane responsibilities to weigh you down.

"And then the children come. In no time, you're up to your ankles in diapers and demands for your attention twenty-five hours a day . . . no time to work, not even a decent night's rest, the incessant crying . . . and finally, one night when you're groggy with lack of sleep, and desperate for anything to make it stop, you think of the stasis chests that you have by the hundreds and it's like an answer to a prayer to tuck the baby away for the night. Just for a few hours of peace and quiet. And the baby isn't harmed— doesn't even know that it was . . . shut off. And you take to

doing it every night—you get a good sleep, you rationalize
that the child will benefit from it too, you'll be more relaxed
and attentive. And in the middle of the afternoon when you
decide you want to get a bit of work done without interruption . . . after a while, you tell yourself it's all right, the
baby's fine, if you take it out of stasis for an hour a day,
that's enough. You can play with it happily, make that little
bit of time, everything's fine . . . even if you miss a day once
in a while when you're busy, when the work's going well.
If you have a life of your own, you know you'll be a better
mother. . . .

"And you miss a day and a week and a month, and
every time you think about it, you're filled with the most
sickening dread, the most sickening paralyzing dread . . . you
try to put it out of your mind but you can't, you want to
make it right again but you can't, you tell yourself how simple it would be to plunge in and fix it, but you're just so paralyzed with the dread, you can't face it, you want it just to
go away, and you scream at a bot to get the chest out of your
sight, get it out, get it out. . . .

"And when another baby's on the way, and you swear
on everything you hold sacred that you will be good to this
one, that you'll never make the same mistake, that you'll be
so much stronger . . . I had five children, Mr. Scalpel." She
waved at the silent chests. "They're all out there. Sometimes I have nightmares that I lost count, that I really had
six. Or seven. I don't know why that terrifies me. Losing
count. What would be the difference? But the thought is so
. . . chilling . . . I don't know why.

"But. . . ." She straightened up a bit. "Stasis *is* stasis,
isn't it? The children are still fine. No harm done."

"No harm done!" I roared. "You stupid bitch! Don't
you realize what's happened here?"

"The children haven't been hurt! When we're all dead
and gone, someone will come down here, find them, and

<BINK> let them out. They'll be fine. Famous, even. They'll all be adopted. . . .''

"Do you think I care about a pack of puking papooses?" I shouted. "What have these *tabulae rasae* ever produced but drool and stool? The harm was done to your Art! You're so obsessed with your little secret here, so wrapped up in your own culpability . . . before you tied yourself in knots, you were capable of masterpieces like that rainbow tapestry. You could have produced a legacy a hundred times more important than Five-Or-Six-Or-Seven brats, but all you've given us is this facade of empty cradles and dolls and shit! At best, it's the product of plain old-fashioned guilt over abandoning your progeny. At worst, it's some shoddy con game to get pity you don't deserve. 'O woe, we're so devastated at being childless, see how poignant our Art is, buy it.' What crap!"

"All right," she replied angrily, "I know it's had an effect on my Art. Don't you think it's made me sick too? Don't you have any idea how debilitating such a mess can be? Run away, lie about running away, cover up the lie. . . . God! The feeling that there's no way out of a hopeless snarl. . . . ''

"What you have here," I said quietly, "is a Gordian knot." Which (for you culturally bereft swine who are only reading this column in the hope that I'll savage someone) was a knot from classical Greek history, a knot that was touted to be impossible to untie. "And," I went on, "the way to deal with such knots is always the same, isn't it?" I pulled out my scalpel.

"What are you going to do?" she asked, taking a step forward.

"Do you know why Art Critics exist?" I said. "Because every polite community needs barbarians who aren't afraid to cut what needs cutting." And before she could move to stop me, I plunged my blade into the silvery static surface of the nearest chest.

My intention, Dearest Reader, was to < BINK > open the chest, reveal the child within, and force a Reunion-Slash-Confrontation. Alas, stasis dynamics do not seem to be so clear-cut. In the time that has passed since the events that I relate, I have discussed stasis fields with many learned physicists, and while they are apt to hem and haw about the point, they will eventually confess that we know little more about said fields now than when we were first given the technology at the historic Coming-Out-Party sponsored by our Chums-From-Beyond. We know that the fields will cooperatively < BINK > off when touched with a standard-issue dispeller wand; we know that they will collapse under intense heat or pressure or magnetic fields; and we have recently discovered that they put up one roaring pig of a fight when you attempt to cut them with a magnificent solidinum scalpel that can purportedly cut through anything short of White Dwarf material.

Fluid silver energy flowed up the blade like a mercury cobra on a rope, swallowing my hand with a blisteringly cold mouth. I jerked away fast and tried to let go of the knife, but the nerves and muscles seemed to have stopped talking to one another in the neighborhood of my wrist and the silver kept coming up my arm. A snowfall of ice crystals cracked out of clear air around me as the temperature plummeted; it occurred to me that molecules in complete stasis would naturally gauge in at zero degrees Kelvin. Another moment and the zone of cold reached the concrete floor, riming it with frost. The floor shivered once, then groaned open in a wide cleft that snaked out underneath the field of silvery chests. Chests trembled on the edge; one began to tip in.

I tried to call out to Vavash but my throat wouldn't work. Slowly, ice in my veins, I turned in her direction. She was coming toward me, but I couldn't tell if she was moving fast or slow. Suddenly something hissed behind my back and a fist of sulfurous steam punched its way out of a fissure in the bedrock. Hot and cold met like two hands clapping together thunderously in preparation for a cyclonic arm wrestle. Then, just when things promised to get *really* interesting, something silver swept up over my eyes and < BINK > I was in a clinic, surrounded by a team of white-gowned medical types, poised to throw themselves on whatsoever wounds I possessed. Tongues clicking, they busied themselves with my knife hand. I couldn't feel anything from my shoulder down, and didn't want to.

"Don't move, Mr. Scalpel," Vavash said, her face looming into view above me.

"What happened?" I croaked.

"While I was showing you around the basement at our retreat, there was a small tremor and a minor geyser broke through the floor. You were injured. I managed to surround you with a stasis field and bring you to the Med-Center here for treatment."

"I see. Was there much damage?" I asked carefully.

"Some minor works that had been sitting around for a long time fell into a crevice," she replied evenly.

I looked at her sharply. She met my gaze without flinching. The doctors murmured about tissue grafts. I asked, "Were all the works in that area destroyed?"

"Yes," she answered.

"You don't seem to be affected by the loss."

"Mr. Scalpel, when one is forced to confront one's feelings . . . it's been forty years since I stopped doing that kind of work. It was done by a different woman. I realized that I no longer had any feelings at all . . . for the works themselves. My anxieties were just residue that had been accumulating over the years. Now that the situation is resolved, I feel cleansed. < BINK > and my stasis has been dispelled. Isn't that what you wanted?''

My mind was clearing a little from the adrenaline rush of the panic that for me was only a few seconds gone. I wondered how much real time had passed since the stasis field swallowed me. I wondered what had happened while I was silver-sleeping. I wondered if my abortive attempt at cutting open a chest had really killed all those children. "How do I know that all of the works fell into the crevice by accident?''

Vavash smiled without warmth. "If you are going to play the part of Art's barbarian, Mr. Scalpel, I don't think you can afford to worry about such niceties. Neither swords nor palette knives can indulge in the luxury of a conscience. Or are you just a spoiled young dilettante who talks about devotion to Art but runs crying at the first little harshness?''

There was a bright fire in her eyes, a fire like none I'd ever seen before; but like all fires, it was terrible and awesome, powerful and pitiless.

Why This Book Is
by
Algis Budrys

About the Author

Algis Budrys is the author of Who?, Rogue Moon, Falling Torch, *and* Michaelmas, *among other SF novels, and about two hundred other science fiction and fantasy stories since 1952. He has also worked as an editor from the same time, starting with Gnome Press. In between, he has been active as a literary critic for* Galaxy *magazine and* The Magazine of Fantasy & Science Fiction, *winning the Locus Award one year, and recently winning the award for Literary Criticism from The Friends of Literature. Since 1984, he has been Co-ordinating Judge of L. Ron Hubbard's Writers of The Future Contest, and editor of this anthology.*

Welcome to Volume VI of what *Locus* magazine calls the best-selling SF anthology series of all time. We hope you will agree with me that this latest volume once again justifies the kudos.

For one thing, it has eighteen stories in it; the twelve annual winners of L. Ron Hubbard's Writers of The Future Contest for 1989, plus six Finalist stories. That's more than we've ever had before. And it enables us to cover the field more broadly than ever before. We think you'll like, very much, the mix of stories we've presented here; we've got a little bit of just about everything in science fiction, fantasy and horror.

Then, we've got something completely different. The illustrations, which we hope you'll agree are striking, are by the winners in the first year of L. Ron Hubbard's Illustrators of the Future Contest. Twelve of the illustrations— the illustrations for the twelve winning stories—are entered in the Grand Prize judging. One of them, in consequence, will win an additional $4,000. It will also win its illustrator a letter of introduction to the art school of his or her choice. I will leave the complete telling of this to Frank Kelly-Freas, who is the Co-ordinating Judge of that Contest; I did, however, want to mention it. Along with the fact that in the Writers' Contest, one of the four First Place winners will also win $4,000 additional.

Additional to what, you say. Well, this is how the Contest works:

In 1983, L. Ron Hubbard started the Writers of The Future Contest, and it has been run in accord with his design ever since. That is, every three months all the entries are gone through, by me, and the Finalist entries then go on to a panel chosen from among our Blue Ribbon judges, who in turn pick First, Second and Third place for the quarter. And the prize money is $1,000, $750, and $500. Then, once a year, they pick the Grand Prize winner, and he or she gets the $4,000 additional. Winners in the past have been Robert Reed, Dave Wolverton, Nancy Farmer, and Gary W. Shockley. Who this year's winner will be is unknown at this writing; we save that for the Awards event, which happens simultaneously with the release of this book and therefore can't be predicted at this writing.

The Illustrators' Contest works essentially the same way, except that we have three co-winners every quarter.

L. Ron Hubbard—who passed from this life January 24, 1986, at the age of 74—was a remarkable man. He pursued a great number of careers, of which the chief one that concerns us is that of writer. In the 1930s and a fair chunk of the 1940s he sold an enormous amount of wordage in an enormous number of varied magazines, of which the ones that demand the most attention from us are *Astounding* and *Unknown,* those being the science fiction and fantasy magazines, respectively, of the Street & Smith chain.

Ron Hubbard had not specifically written science fiction and fantasy when he was brought in by Street & Smith to lend the weight of his proven byline to the young John W. Campbell, the brand-new editor. Inside of a very few years, however, he had not only furnished some of the most exciting prose either field had ever seen, he had written *Final Blackout* for *Astounding* and "Fear" for *Unknown,* arguably the most popular stories of their day . . . destined to still, after more than fifty years, be mentioned with awe and respect whenever these two genres of popular fiction are discussed.

His fiction writing career interrupted by World War II, he returned to it briefly afterward. However, he was increasingly impelled toward writing the results of his researches, a quarter of a century investigating the nature of mankind which would lead to Dianetics—and in 1950 he wrote his last piece of fiction for over thirty years.

His work there completed, in 1982, celebrating his Golden Anniversary as a pro writer, he wrote *Battlefield Earth*, and 1986 saw the launching of *Mission Earth*, his ten-volume dekalogy and *magnum opus*. All of them—eleven volumes—hit the New York Times fiction best-seller list.

So when he initiated the Writers of The Future Contest in 1983, it was a means of giving something back to the field, and of continuing his gift into the future. And so it has remained.

With this volume, ninety writers have been brought forward by this series of anthologies. They have included Nina Kiriki Hoffman, Karen Joy Fowler, Dean Wesley Smith, and David Zindell; Ray Aldridge and Robert Touzalin Reed; M. Shayne Bell, Martha Soukup, Paula May and Dave Wolverton, and R. Garcia y Robertson. We do not claim these writers would be unknown if it were not for us; we do claim that we found them and gave them a platform, in some cases years before anyone else would have. And we will continue to do so, finding new names, each year, to join with the old. That was L. Ron Hubbard's plan, and it is a good one. "An artist injects the spirit of life into a culture," he said. And "A culture is only as great as its dreams, and its dreams are dreamed by artists." He knew what he was talking about.

As always, there are some people we want to thank especially. Certainly Gary Feinberg, Ed Gibson, Sheldon Glashow, Yoji Kondo, Tim Powers, Charles Sheffield, and

Robert Welch, of our panels at the United Nations on the occasion of last year's Hubbard Awards; Hans Janitschek, of the United Nations, who presented each of the Writers of The Future judges with the award of honor from the Society of Writers at the U.N.; Gregory Benford, Algis Budrys, Ramsey Campbell, Anne McCaffrey, Andre Norton, Larry Niven, Frederik Pohl, Jerry Pournelle, Robert Silverberg, John Varley, Jack Williamson, Gene Wolfe, and Roger Zelazny.

But in the end, we all thank the Writers of The Future, who are:

James G. Bishop, David Carr, Charles D. Eckert, James Gardner, Michael I. Landweber, Jo Etta Ledgerwood, Scot Noel, John W. Randal, Bruce Holland Rogers, Michael L. Scanlon, Sharon Wahl, Matthew Wills, and David Ira Cleary, Pete D. Manison, Stephen Milligan, Jason Shankel, Annis M. Shepherd, and James Verran;

and the Illustrators of The Future:

Beryl Bush, Kevin Dzuban, Jeff Fennel, Derek J. Hegsted, Allison Hershey, Kevin Hopkins, Kelly Faltermayer, Daniel S. Oman, Peggy Ranson, Timothy Standish, Ruth Thompson, and Timothy Winkler.

Without them, there is nothing.

The Scholar of the Pear Tree Garden

by
Annis Shepherd

About the Author

Annis Shepherd is 51, and has lived all over the world. Born in India, she had a brother in the Foreign Legion and another in the safari business, and spent two long stints in Australia. The majority of her education came in various countries on the Continent. She has been a teacher at all levels, and has taught both special education and accelerated courses besides. At present she is a 5th Grade teacher in Mesa, Arizona. One of her three daughters has just been named "Miss Tucson" and will go on to the Miss America competition. She began writing at 16, in Switzerland, because she could not speak the language and was lonely; her husband got her interested in science fiction some years later. All in all, an extraordinary lady.

• • •

Annis Shepherd's illustrator is Allison Hershey.

Ikono, the Scholar, waited for
the man who owned his soul. He would come
as he always came: smiling, sure, always the
master of his world. For the man knew, as the Scholar
knew, money had bought everything.

Ikono angled his back against the curve of the chair, his
black kimono a sharp frame for the pale slant of his body.
Humming in a high falsetto, he watched the entry way.
When the door flexed open, for one brief instant he would
see the outside world without the barrier of glass or stone.
For over a century this museum had been his prison, his
only reality. For he, the Kabuki Master, was his nation's
treasured masterpiece; the New Asian Federation's defini-
tive work of living art.

Even now he was on display. In some inner sanctum in
this exquisite fortress, computers controlled and checked
his health, gauged his feelings, and supervised this protected environment. Organ banks supplied him with necessary replacements and gene manipulation provided him
with immortality. He, the Scholar of the Pear Tree Garden,
was priceless, because he was unique. He had turned the
classical Kabuki from an ancient Japanese theater form into
an artistic battle between man and the jewel insects.

The insects of Mons. Ikono knew they waited for the
same release he now sought. Their hive was their prison as
the museum was his; their art a part of him. Even now they
waited to join with Ikono—to perform before an audience of
hedonistic voyeurs.

Illustrated by Allison Hershey

The Scholar straightened, remembering his contract and the man who had offered immortalilty in exchange for wealth.

"I will ask him," Ikono thought. "I, Ikono, will ask him to let me go outside for just one hour. Just one hour to smell the air, touch the grass, feel the summer. Just one hour and I will never ask it again."

Yet Ikono had made that request each year and the answer was always the same. You are ours, and we protect what we own. But he would ask it, because to try was not to fail.

Ikono stretched out his hand, absently noting the unnatural beauty of each gene-manipulated curve. His fingers twisted rhythmically in the air, spelling his pain. Freedom, for him, was beyond price.

The sigh of an opening door and the firm step of authority broke his reverie. But too late. As Ikono glanced up, the door to the foyer closed. Freedom was but a sliver of light, immediately gone. His anger stirred, both at his dreaming and at the man who now stood before him in the glass-enclosed vestibule.

"Ikono, my dear fellow. It has been too long." The Director of the Museum of New Tokyo beamed. He gestured his inability to shake hands and sat on an antique Mandarin chair on display there.

"My lord, I greet you with thanks." Ikono bowed in trained deference, but was amused by their dissimilar speech patterns. He, with his poetical Kabuki emphasis; the other, with the hint of old British colonialist expressions, which, even after centuries, high officials still affected.

"I hear you wanted to talk to me. Something urgent, um?" Director Sakimoru's tone implied total amazement that such should be the case, yet the Scholar knew the man was prepared for Ikono's yearly request on this, the anniversary of the day the Museum had bought the Kabuki

Master's skill and beauty; had stamped, sealed, and delivered his art as a museum piece for the ages.

He had been forty then and was the flower of perfection amongst the Scholars of the Pear Tree Garden. He had borne with pride the ancient name for those who studied this classic art, and he knew it was pride that had blinded him to the cost of such a step.

"I would like to buy one hour of freedom," Ikono said. "I will return the millions of dollars you have paid me for that single pleasure."

"But you are free." Sakimoru motioned towards their surroundings. "Look about you. You have everything you have ever desired. Just as we promised when you accepted the contract. Your wish is our command—but within reason."

"I wish for so brief a taste of freedom, my lord. Isn't that reasonable?" Ikono stroked the hairless dome of his head with fingers that tensed in anger.

"Of course, dear boy, perfectly reasonable. But I have no say in the matter. You belong to the Federation. With insurance rates as they are, to take you outside, even enclosed, would be impossible. You are quite an investment."

Ikono read Sakimoru's smile. The apparent kindness did not match the indifferent gaze of the man's eyes.

"I did not make a contract that included such restrictions." Ikono spoke with gentle control. His anger was too longstanding to be stirred to action.

"One never knows the restrictions of contracts made so far in the past." Sakimoru spoke now with authority. "I do what I have to do, just as you do. Politics are such that if any malcontents seized you, the Federation itself could be held for ransom. I cannot take the risk."

The Scholar rose and started to pace, each stride slow and graceful as if rehearsed. He knew his dream was hopeless, and his hopelessness accentuated the puppetlike motions of his Kabuki training.

"I need your help, my lord." Ikono deliberately slid his voice from falsetto to bass as if he were on stage and playing to the gods. "I have given you my life, yes, even my soul, but allow me the autonomy of my art. I must be part of life if I am to imitate it."

Sakimoru shifted his heavy body, obviously bored.

"You talk as if you are an evolving artist, an innovator," he said. "I hate to disillusion you, Ikono. You are not the creator, but the created; an artifact. You are yourself complete. He paused, brushed an imaginary fleck from his jacket, then leaned forward like a father counseling a child. Stop thinking of freedom, of soul, as if they are contributing factors to your existence. Your life belongs to the Museum, the Federation. We are what makes your art possible."

"But I *am* a creator." Ikono slashed the air passionately with both arms and bent his knees to form a *mie,* the traditional Kabuki point of emphasis.

"A creator?" Sakimoru rose, the smile returning to his lips. "Let me repeat, Ikono. You are quite mistaken. You are no artist now. This is just a job. You are what we made you. And you wanted it that way, um? You set your parameters as we all do. Accept them and enjoy your life. Until next time, yes?" and Sakimoru bowed.

For the Scholar of the Pear Tree Garden, his anger was finally given focus. His rage was now a fever driving him to find an answer. Fearing that Sakimoru would read his intent, he turned his back on the world he longed for.

Not a creator! Not an artist!

Ikono, the Scholar, burned at the insult and promised revenge. A century ago, he, the Kabuki Master, was honored with the highest stage name bestowed on an actor. Danjuro XXV they called him, the twenty-fifth to bear the glory of that name. He had perfected the image of the arogoto superman so that he was synonymous with the term. Then he had done the unthinkable. He had brought innovation to an art that refused change and bowed to no rule. With his jewel insects he had turned his art from the past into the future, and had bought immortality.

Ikono strode down the halls, his rage plotting alternatives. He was oblivious to his collection of the world's art. Through massive rooms shadowed and framed in beauty, he went; through decades of the new, the strange, the bizarre, all things bought to evade his eternal boredom. No matter how palatial his surroundings, how frequent his experiments, or how much money he squandered, this place was a prison, and the prison was etched into his mind.

Ikono swept past windows that could never open for fear of contaminating his laboratory home, past glass that reflected his streamlined form and gave it meaning. His reflection was his only true companion, his alter ego who, although a shadowman and voiceless, was the only family permitted him. When he danced before his mirrors, he became everyman, yet noman.

Ikono entered his makeup room, and?

He could feel *them* watching. Them! The jewel insects.

Slow-time, he controlled the gradual turning of his body to face the great hives against the walls.

A pride haunted by terror filled him. They belonged to him, the Kabuki Master, and they were his cast of thousands. Stolen from a far world and bought with dishonor, they fed his art as they might one day, if he lost control, feed on him.

Ikono halted, turned his body in half-circle, and struck a *mie*. Ah! Out swept his arms like a lover offering an embrace. Hear me, he whispered, and knew they did. Their artistic bond was now an instinct.

Ikono approached, dream-pulled and obsessed. Was

their need to escape as strong as his? If so, did their fury match his own?

Beautiful creatures! Ikono placed his palm flat against the glass hive like a caress. Yet their very beauty was deadly. Clusters of winged bodies gathered in an array of rainbow colors, many iridescent, shifting in intricate patterns of movement between each group with hypnotizing effect. Even Ikono, who knew them so well, felt driven to watch—watch and love.

Ikono kicked out his leg, then snapped it backwards, to lunge forward onto his knees and bow in submission.

He knew the insects would kill him if they could. These alien creatures with their brilliant colors, their shimmering movement, became a splendid yet decadent living costume on his naked body. Each day when they performed the dance of death with him, each day when they fostered the unhealthy dreams of the endless crowds, Ikono felt hostage to their threat; for like the piranha of Old Amazonia, they fed on warm flesh in swarming hunger.

But you dare not harm me, hm? Ikono raised his head and looked at his beloved adversaries, crooning his sympathy. For unknown to the tourists who would shortly watch them perform, these creatures were docile as long as their queens lay peacefully on his skin. Yes, the queens, those pulsing bodies so small and seemingly frail, those factories of terror, were his to control. But to the crowds who gathered, he, Ikono, was in constant danger. For had not the brochures told them so in explicit detail?

Ikono glanced at the clock and realized that he must hurry. Decorating his entire body needed both time and patience.

Swiftly he undressed, sat before the huge gilt mirrors, and began.

And the jewel insects watched.

Here. A tanu seed placed, oh so delicately, by the corner of the eye. The centuries-old ceremony executed with precise movements, choreographed and evocative, was just as crucial to the focus of his art with no audience, as the actual Kabuki dance performed before the public. Within an hour, the seed by the fold of flesh would begin to irritate the fine skin below his eyes causing it to swell and form an exquisite shading that even makeup could not imitate.

Then. He opened vials of plant mixtures which would produce allergic reactions in different sections of his body. Touches. Here, there, light touches of the brush to give shape to the irritated patches of skin. He knew such illusions of design could have been created with paints, but only the swellings would give the designs a three-dimensional effect. Without this hint of masochism, much of the fascination with his image would be gone for the voyeurs who shortly would feast their imaginations on his craft. As a living work of art, he must show not only his body's skill in depicting pain, but his ability to overcome it.

Next, more illusions. For his art could not allow predictability. Each audience would search for that certain alteration that made his dance, his image, a creative extension to the traditional role.

Rising to his feet, Ikono walked over to his showering area. Closing the door, he set the controls. A fine spray of white powder filled the air, covering his hairless body with a luminescent impression of snow. A delicate perfume now masked the odor of his skin which would divert his insects for the time he needed.

He smiled, a slight baring of his teeth. The allergic reactions were already beginning to develop soft swirls of pink and red, like channels mapping his skin. Soon the insects would trace these paths in ever changing colors, providing a constant costume change which had taken the art of hikinuki to the extreme.

His task completed, Ikonu readjusted the controls and warm air breathed about his body, brushing the excess powder to the floor. Already he could feel the thrill of creation fill him.

Stepping out of the shower, he relaxed his neck, allowing his head to loll from side to side, stretching, stretching. His pulse started to pound and his lips went slack. He *was* a creator, and he would make them know it.

He turned. The jewel insects watched and Ikono gloried in their hunger.

"Sakimoru," he whispered in delicate falsetto. "I will create for you, you shall see."

Next, Ikono lifted his testicles and gently pushed them into the pelvic cavities. Reaching for a clear tape, he positioned his penis between his legs; a final touch to streamline his body. Asexual, now his craft would have the freedom to suggest whatever his audience desired.

Still the jewel insects watched, and Ikono imagined he could hear their mass hunger moan in anticipation—we want, we want, give! And his pleasure increased with the realization that at least these unearthly creatures had need of him. They would help him bring his art to fever pitch.

It was two hours before he could look in the mirrors with satisfaction. Once again he was amazed at the endless range of his vision and his artistic skill. If at forty he had been recognized as the master of his craft, what could one call him now? After centuries he *was* the craft. No more, no less. But was not the true and ultimate creator the craft? Yet to maintain the one, the other must exist.

Ikono bound the hachimaki around his head, the only traditional touch of costume he permitted. Its stark color, "Shogun's Purple" was the ancient name for it, created a dividing line across his chalk white face. Symbol of wealth, it accentuated the horror of his red Kumadori makeup. This illusion of luxury and frustrated desire would stir the lust of the audience to come.

Ikono was caught in his dream and his body molded the dream shape before the mirrors. Just being himself should be enough. But it was not. The world denied him privacy, denied him free will. Even the reward of youth and immortality and wealth was not enough. Could never be enough. Ikono's eyes blazed with desire.

And the jewel insects watched, and their desire matched his own.

Ikono was in position when the crowds came.

The Kabuki Master had placed the five docile queens about his body. His heart, liver, groin, back, and left thigh. The queens pulsed and glowed as they waited for their swarms to join them.

More than a lifetime of skill had been needed to train him to control his fear each time the jewel insects entered the acting arena. Here, the hira-butai was surrounded by invisible walls of ultrasound; here, Ikono would perform for the glory of his nation. There was no Hurry Door so strategically placed for a quick exit at the rear of every Kabuki stage, no hanamichi or "flower path" reaching out into the audience for escape. Here he was inside a hive of his own, looking out.

The insects of Mons came in a swarm, each group separating into bands of flowing color as they descended protectively on their queens.

Ikono felt his nerves contract, but he remained still.

The red group, ranging from deep amber to crimson, gathered about his heart as he knew they would; the green by his crotch. The fluorescent, purple, and aquamarine insects streamed to both liver and back, while the luminescent silver group swirled in pulsing lines about his thighs.

Once content that their queens were safe, the insects turned and prepared to protect their territorial rights.

Ikono angled his head so he could watch their formations and so imitate their movements with corresponding moves of his own.

He could feel the minute insect legs grip his skin with a pulsing rhythm, as if marching to an alien drumbeat. The shifting bodies, thousands of them, were surging, seeking. The groups flowed down the maze of channels created by the allergic swellings he had fashioned earlier on his skin; hungry for food, hungry for battle.

The doors of the Museum opened, and the crowds descended, hungry for an emotional stirring of heart, mind, and loin.

They came, these sightseers, eager to participate vicariously in a possible tragedy, eager to see the Scholar of the Pear Tree Garden display fear, anger, sensuality, and imagined torture in his carefully measured gestures and movements.

Men, women, children, crowded into the small amphitheater. For many, the art of dying was their cultural heritage.

Ikono saw their eyes. Round, slanted, brown, gray; eyes narrowed and considering, eyes widely set and feverish with? Hope, desire, despair, and even joy. These were the voyeurs of erotic suggestion, the parasites of his imagination and craft.

Ikono heard the slow wail of a flute rise to the strike of a gong. Then came the clappers, slow and even, warning the audience that the dance would begin. Like a subtle heartbeat they accentuated the pulse of the jewel insects of Mons.

Slowly he turned, puppet-slow, focusing on the cold marble of the niju-butai beneath his feet. Even he did not dare disturb the insects with the harshness of movement. Yet it was this deliberate slowness that accentuated the idea of possible torture.

He flexed the upward curving lines marking his forehead into a frown, red the color of courage. The touch of blue about his mouth displayed his ferocity as he smiled. He was hero and villain rolled into one, tachi-yaku and kataki-yaku with the lift of a brow or a sway of the head.

Between his thighs and across his shoulders, Ikono felt the grip of tiny feet, the brush of quivering wings, the promise of voracious mouths open and ready.

This was what he had trained for, this was why he had sold his life. Each move of his arm, each slow turn of body and leg, created an image—a kaleidoscope of rippling colors and designs never to be repeated. And they called him a product? Anger twisted in his chest, feeding his revenge.

The shuffling swarms mapping his body seemed to feel his rage and reciprocated with a rage of their own. Their wings fanned the air in a shimmer of frenzy, and their buzz became a whine that pained the ear. It was the whine Ikono heard when they fed on the carcass of a goat or calf each day.

Ikono looked out over the heads of the crowd, lost in the slavering mass dream. He looked past the faces and the glittering eyes, past works of art created in another time, another place, and searched for the man he knew would be there.

Sakimoru! Sakimoru who was now watching Ikono with the same confidence he had shown earlier that day.

See? Sakimoru's smile mocked Ikono. See, you really are the art, not the artist. The artist is dead. These people? They watch you like a painting, a performing puppet with no life of its own.

The room seemed to darken in Ikono's vision, then lighten as his anger rose. He had to be the creator still if his art was to have meaning. He had to have control, had to have freedom.

Swaying cobra-fashion, Ikono again whispered, "Sakimoru! I will create for you. Wait and see."

Like the first Kabuki Master, Danjuro I, his namesake, Ikono knew then that the ultimate effect of his craft was the image, the gift he would give to the imagination of all who saw him. And truly the gift could only be given once in a true work of art. It could not be repeated.

Ikono rolled his head, his gaze focused on Sakimoru's face. With perfect control, he symbolized with outstretched fingers the shape of a fan. The moon is setting like a falling leaf, his fingers said, and the audience called his name in affirmation.

"Danjuro."

He heard the name and welcomed it. The honor of his ancestors was his. Slowly, as the clappers intensified, he cut a *mie* and crossed one eye to emphasize the emotion of the moment. The man would indeed know that his plea had been in earnest.

Pulling the hachimaki from his brow, Ikono, the last Scholar of the Pear Tree Garden, the Kabuki Master, reached out his hand and crushed the queen that trembled over his heart.

Maddened, the red insects swarmed, bloodlike droplets glistening as their wings fanned outwards in a frenzy.

Deny him his artistry, would they? Ikono responded to the pain that streamed through his chest like fire. He arched his body, his arms beseeching a dream god to accept his passion. Clutching his chest, he raised a hand dripping with blood, a nimbus of insects about his head. A painting of St. Sebastian on a far wall was his mirror and spurred him on to glory.

Ikono struck out once again, brushing the insects about his waist in search of the blue queen. There. He found her and crushed her. Wings of blue fire whirred upwards, circling his head, only to dive in formation towards their prey.

Ikono pitched his moan in a high falsetto, keening with antiphonal repetition with the flute.

The insects were feeding now.

He could hear the dripping of blood about his feet. Yet the pain was a glory, the essence of his art. His ancestors had known how to die with grace and honor for their family, so too would he die for his honor and these insects who were his only family. He would become one with them.

Ikono plunged his hand between his outstretched legs to stir the mass of insects, a glittering trove of aquamarine and green, into chaos. Like jeweled sperm they arched away from his intrusive hand only to re-form for the attack.

As Ikono danced, his distorted gaze could see the crowds. Their mouths opened in horror, in fascination. He could hear their screams and the sounds seemed to encourage him. Children clung to parents, wives turned to husbands, but Ikono knew they would turn again to see their fears transformed to reality.

He could see Sakimoru's face. Shock had turned to fury. The man was giving orders to reluctant guards, screaming at them.

The museum doors yawned open as more guards streamed in. Through those doors, free of barriers, Ikono could see summer in action, and he smiled.

He plunged his hands into his half-eaten flesh as he fell to his knees. The darkness about him mingled with the sweat and color of blood. A multitude of incisors were tearing, tearing.

Ikono spread out his fingers and watched the blood dripping down his arms over feeding insects, and looked at Sakimoru. He saw the defeat in the slackened jaws, the hatred in the man's eyes, and gloried in it.

He the artist would be remembered.

The cameras that filmed all his dances would take his

art beyond this small arena. This audience would remember, as Sakimoru would remember.

Kneeling, Ikono bent over to complete his act of seppuku. The marble whiteness of the niju-butai was like the ceremonial cloth that would accept the purity of his courage, the artistic frame for the blood sacrifice to honor.

The torture he felt was not reflected in his face as he repeated the ceremonial rites. Only his body reflected the ecstasy of his revenge and the knowledge that his life and his art were his only real possessions.

Now, he whispered to his insects, as a barrier of glass descended to hem them in. Now I have my freedom. Now they will know I am an artist.

The whir of wings and the slice of miniature teeth was his only reply.

Under Glass

by
David Carr

About the Author

At 26, David Carr is a general assignment reporter for the Waterbury Republican, *where he has worked since June, 1988. He grew up in Wallingford, Connecticut, and while in high school there he wrote the first draft of a novel about a world where children could fly. One result, ten or so years later, is "Under Glass," which owes part of its existence to the advice of science fiction writer Mark McGarry, who worked as a copy editor for the* New Haven Register *while David was doing an internship there. Chris Feola, of the* Republican, *who also writes SF, gave him invaluable coaching on the final draft.*

• • •

David Carr's illustrator is Timothy Winkler.

The dream was Ting leaning
out the window of the bedroom he'd had on
Earth a long time ago, watching the building
across the street burn. Something had exploded against the
face of it, blowing all the windows out. Men on the roof
were firing their rifles down the street at the attackers. They
ignored the smoke rising past them. They didn't seem to
mind the flames creeping higher, one story at a time.

Luckily, his mother had left him alone for a little while.
She never would have let him watch.

After fading in and out, the distant sirens were growing
steadily louder but not as quickly as the rattle of enemy fire.
Screaming people streamed through the street.

The rooftop men's bullets were answered from a window far down the street by rapid violet sparks that made the
air crack like thunder. One of them exploded against the
wall below Ting, and the crate he was standing on shot from
under his feet, making him pitch forward over the splintery
sill. A woman in the street saw it happen. Already screaming as she tried to hurry the crowd forward, she screamed
for him, too.

He stopped breathing, and his eyes fixed on the side-
walk. But it seemed to have come no closer. A breeze moved
him down the street toward the harbor. That wasn't right.

He looked back at the bedroom window, behind him
and above him. He had fallen perhaps twice his height. The
wind picked up, tumbling him farther from home. He
bumped against the side of one building and tried to hold

on, but his fingers slipped free. The sound of the battle died away, and he floated over the heads of happy people who were unaware of the approaching firefight. The fleeing mob was gone.

His eyes flickered open on another bedroom, another world. Clothes on the floor, dim shadows of branches on the curtains. Then his eyelashes touched lightly, unfocusing the image.

He dropped almost to street level before a strong gust punted him over the harbor. He wanted to imagine himself back to the battle so he could find out how it ended, but the dream would not allow that.

Landing on the water, he did not sink. He tried to walk on it, but the waves kept tripping him up. At last, a boat passed, and he leapt into the rigging.

His eyes were fully open by then. He watched the light grow stronger in the window.

Sailors slapped him on the back and marveled at his feather weight. Their feet pressed firmly against the bucking deck, but he had to be held down.

He lost the thread of the dream as other thoughts crowded in and the light in the window turned from gray to pink.

If he was going to meet Henry for that hike into the mountains, Ting had to get up now. The more he thought about it, the harder the bed seemed to suck him under its covers, as if some of the Earth-weight missing in his dream had returned.

He dozed.

When his eyes snapped open, the last gray was gone from the light in the window. Ting got out of bed too quickly, rocketing to the ceiling so fast he almost didn't get his palms out. His elbows took up the shock, and he dropped to the floor, catching himself against his dresser.

He slipped into a pair of jeans and pulled on a blue

sweatshirt, dug a pair of socks out from under the bed and shoved his feet into them.

The house was very still. He crept to the door and opened it.

A hint of pink light from the windows in the living room showed him the end of the hall. The rail to the stairs was a snaking shadow, and the knob of the front door was a spark. There was a hint of light from upstairs, too. He heard a sound like a fish jumping: his mother cupping water from the sink to splash on her face.

Ting briefly considered going back to bed. Instead, he slipped into the hall and stretched out his arms until he touched both walls with his fingertips. He pushed backward, ever so gently. His legs trailed behind. He heard the thump of each fingertip as it made contact with the wall. Just before the stairs was an unsteady table on which his mother kept rings of keys, envelopes of seeds, baskets, spades and earrings. He folded his arms across his chest, pressed his legs together and drifted slowly past the table on the strength of the last push. He told himself he had made it.

The bathroom door popped open upstairs, and, in the light filtering down, Ting saw himself half a meter from the doorknob, his momentum failing. One kick against the banister, and he could have his hand around the knob. But the banister was creaky. He held his breath.

He thought of his dream and drifting with handholds always just out of reach.

The door to his mother's bedroom was at the top of the stairs. Looking over his shoulder, he saw her glide out into the hall, using the railing to keep her feet on the ground. For a moment, he believed she would go through the door without noticing him.

She never did look down. Somehow, that made it worse when she spoke. "Not this time, Ting."

She entered her bedroom. Ting kicked the banister and

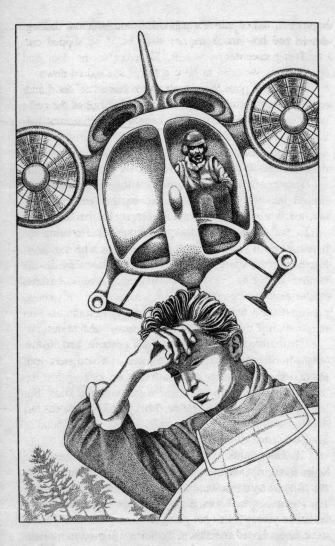

Illustrated by Timothy Winkler

the knob smacked into his palm. He thought about darting outside and how much angrier she'd be if he slipped out after being caught.

"I think we need to have a talk," she called down.

He sighed, pushed himself away from the door and went up the stairs six at a time. His palms slapped the ceiling of the upstairs hall, and he caught himself against the door frame.

She was sitting on the edge of her bed facing him, wearing a rainbow-striped terry cloth robe she'd bought at a fair and rubbing her head with a towel of the same pattern. A bead of water freed itself from one strand of her long, red hair, and he watched its leisurely descent to the floor.

He had been rude, making so much noise coming up the stairs. He was always breaking things when he moved at that pace, and she was always reminding him to slow down. But she refused to react to that. She made him wait while she finished drying her hair.

"You want to talk?" he asked.

"I'm still thinking about what to say," she said.

Finally, she folded the towel, set it beside her on the rumpled bed and looked him in the eye. "Where were you going?"

He said nothing.

"Tell me, had you forgotten that I said I had chores for you?"

"No," he said, trying to match her cool.

"I didn't think so. Listen, if I can't trust you. . . . Never mind, it's apparent I can't. Let me put it this way. I was going to have you weed for a couple of hours this morning. Just a couple. I was going to let you have the rest of the day to yourself. I'm not going to do that. Instead, I have some things I need from the City Store. I'll give you a list. You're going to get them for me."

"It's my day off!"

"From school. Not from this. Go wait in the kitchen, and I'll be down as soon as I'm dressed. We need to get you on your way so you'll be able to make it back by sunset."

He turned.

"Close the door," she said.

He slammed it.

The list was not long: corn syrup, flour, a measuring cup, a hand rake to replace the broken one, a small tarp and a jar of paint thinner. The infuriating thing was that she could have hopped in her tractor and run the errand in a couple of hours. It would take him most of the day. He sat at the kitchen table staring at the slip of paper she had given him while she left the room. Of course, once she sent him out the door there would be nothing to stop him from making his rendezvous with Henry. Nothing but the knowledge of how much trouble he'd be in.

"Do I get breakfast?" he asked when she returned with a wad of credit slips.

"You didn't look like you were going to stop for breakfast a minute ago," she said. "What were you going to do? Pick an apple, maybe? Well, do that."

Too mad to answer, Ting pushed away from the table and shot down the hall, kicking at the walls. He jammed on his shoes, which lay beside his mother's boots on a mat just inside the door, and stormed outside.

Dew splashed off the lawn. The sun was about to rise, and every tree stood out along the profile of New York Mountain. Dawn colored the barn a very bright red.

Ting wanted to stomp, but his slight weight turned his stomps into ludicrously high skips.

"And no detours!" called his mother. He looked back and saw her standing in the doorway. "I want you back by four."

He gritted his teeth. When his feet touched the ground

again, he got himself under control enough to dig the cleats on the soles of his shoes into the soil. He walked slowly toward the barn.

Each time he set a foot down, he twisted the toe in and the heel out. To free the hooked cleats from the soil, he twisted the toe out and the heel in. Normally, his footwork was good enough that he could even run, but today his concentration was shot.

Inside the barn, he kicked a trowel into the seed loft, where it knocked the back wall and a post and rang a watering can. Why didn't he just tell her to go to hell? he wondered. Well, because his home was really hers, and he had to stay on good terms with her if he wanted any peace. She held his happiness hostage.

With his hands thrust into his pockets, Ting slouched a few steps toward the corner of the barn where a familiar shape peeked from behind a stack of crates. The dirt floor was packed and did not want to give his cleats purchase, so he leapt over the crates, catching himself against a rafter, and pushed down.

He regarded his biplane in the dim light, feeling sad and a bit foolish. This morning had reminded him he could not win.

Stepping forward, he spun the plane's propeller with his hand. Every spot where the wood showed through the faded blue paint reminded him of a crash. A smile snuck onto his face.

When the propeller ratcheted to a stop, he grabbed the handle under the nose and rolled the plane outside. The just-risen sun, a slightly flattened yellow circle, shone over the shoulder of the mountain. Two fingers of light reached out along faults in the sparkling glass sky.

He thought of the clear blue, faultless sky of his dream. His friends who'd been born here envied him memories like that. He wished he remembered more.

Ting strapped himself in. He took the control stick in his right hand and, with his left, spun the small wheel on the dashboard that turned the rudder. A cottontail watched as it chewed on a leaf of his mother's lettuce.

"Good boy," said Ting, with a flat smile. "Eat it all up." When Ting put his feet to the pedals and the propeller began to beat the air, the rabbit fled in a single long hop. With a jerk, the plane rolled forward. As it picked up speed, its tail lifted, and dust rose from the thinly seeded lawn.

In his agitation, Ting couldn't keep a steady hand on the stick, so the plane weaved as it took to the air. As he pulled farther back on the stick, he gave the rudder wheel a quarter-turn clockwise. The plane cleared the fence at the border between the yard and the fields, and Ting pedaled into a steep climb, pumping his legs until they filled with hot and sluggish blood. He watched in the mirror while the woodframe house shrank into a shoebox and the fields became patches on a quilt.

He could not imagine that land cold, dry and lifeless, as it had been hundreds of years ago before the war.

Vesta had been brought from beyond Mars and used as a fortified base during the siege of the homeworld. Explosions just as violent as those that leveled Earth's capitals must have touched Vesta, but its inhabitants had wisely buried their city deep underground.

After the war, the Vestans peered down on Earth through thick dark clouds and watched the spreading rot. Like repentant murderers, they acted to save what they had tried so hard to destroy. That, at least, was the story the farmers told about the conception of their world.

Sweat stung Ting's eyes as the burn in his legs grew hotter. At last, he abandoned the climb, letting his plane fall into the arms of the wind. His anger had left him. His feet slipped off the pedals, and he watched the propeller turn without force.

As he glided, he was struck again by how green the world below was. If this really had been barren once, the City had worked a miracle here. Yet the creators of the copy were the same people who had come close to destroying the original.

Rows of trees neatly bordered the small, square farm plots, except where streams, ponds and rocky hills broke the geometry. Some of the ponds were old craters. Traces of the ancient pockmarks were everywhere the land wasn't plowed, though they were heavily overgrown.

Early risers moved about their farms, occasionally crouching to weed or tend some ailing plant.

A six-fan chopper rose noisily from the de Santo farm, its outboard props gimbaling from horizontal to vertical as it cleared the roof tops. Ting wanted to thumb his nose at it. The de Santo kids bragged endlessly about their father, the militia colonel.

The warm sun was off his right wing tip, so Ting knew he was facing north, toward wilderness. All the farms of all those the Vestans had brought here in sixty-odd years and all those of their children circled the planet's waist, and Ting's mother's farm was close to the northern edge of that band. If he just flew straight, he could be beyond his mother's reach before sunset.

But he was already tipping the stick right, making the right wing drop, and the plane swing right along a curve. When the nose came into line with a certain mountain peak, he centered the stick and played with the wheel. The breeze wanted to blow him south of his heading, so he set the rudder to point the plane's nose slightly north.

Ting put the plane into a shallow dive, getting scant encouragement from Vesta. Only when he had fallen so low that his plane's wheels scraped the tops of the cornstalks did he pedal again.

An old man yelled at him from the back porch of the nearest farmhouse. Ting shifted gears and pedaled faster.

An hour later, just as Ting settled into the dull rhythm of pedaling purposefully onward, Kelly Lang flashed by his right wing in her bright red barnstormer with the orange flames on its wings. As he strained to catch up, she did a roll, and he matched it. He shouted "hello," and they played follow-the-leader, racing between the banks of a narrow gully, scraping under a low stone bridge and slipping between two birches that leaned away from each other.

Ting began to feel he couldn't keep up with her after the energy he'd wasted on that stupid fast-climb. But at last she leveled off and let him catch up.

"Not too bad," she said. Her long black hair streamed out behind her, and a grin split her pale, sharp-chinned face.

"You didn't do anything that impressed me," said Ting.

"Oh? Then how about a nose-dive contest? Right now. That will separate the wheat from the chaff." Out of the grin, she manufactured a sly look that made Ting's heart sink.

"I don't know. I've got an errand to run, and you've got me going in the wrong direction," he said.

He didn't expect to get off so easily, but she asked, "Where are you going?"

"The City Store," he said. He looked east, and the nose of his plane swung around that way. He half expected to see Lincoln Peak, but he had not come that far. From there, he planned to follow the Muddy River south.

"I was headed more that way," Kelly said, pointing 9 o'clock from his destination and almost due north. Her expression was uncommonly serious.

"Yeah?"

"Yeah. Why don't you ride with me for a few minutes?"

"Sure," he said. "That would be great."

They flew with their wing tips almost touching. "Where are you going, anyway?"

"Oh, nowhere," she said. "I thought a picnic by a stream somewhere sounded nice. Too bad you can't come."

A picnic. He didn't believe her and thought she knew he wouldn't.

He didn't know a lot about Kelly, although he'd flown with her once or twice before, and his eyes often wandered to her in school. She was a troublemaker, he knew. Last year, when the Clemens silo went up in flames, the militia had found her and Toby Simon in the woods nearby. They said they knew nothing about it. Kelly was also famous for skipping school.

"What's going on?" he asked.

"I don't know what you mean," she said.

"Tell me. I think I already know, but tell me."

She glanced back over her shoulder. He looked back, too, and saw nothing. The wind gusted, and he almost swerved into her.

"Remember those tests they gave us last month?" she asked.

It irritated him to have her answer with another question, but he nodded. The militia had taken over the classroom for two days to administer a long series of written tests. There had been almost as many adults as kids in the classroom and no opportunity for cheating. As far as anyone knew, it had never happened before.

Kelly said, "It has something to do with that, I think. On Monday, a militiaman—our neighbor, Mr. Lee—delivered a letter to my parents, and the letter invited me and my brother to go to school in the City. We'd have to live there. Neither of us wants to go, but my folks say we can't refuse." Abruptly, her eyes grew damp.

"Wow," Ting said.

If she was right about the test, he knew why he hadn't received an invitation like hers. Thinking the whole thing creepy, Ting had purposely given wrong answers.

"I won't go," Kelly said firmly. As if to contradict her, the beat of motorized props sounded from below the southern horizon. Kelly shot ahead and dove as the chopper appeared.

"Are you nuts?" Ting cried as he chased her.

"Probably," she said.

"You're going to draw their attention by running," he said.

"At that distance, they may not have seen me," she said. "They probably saw you, though."

"For all they know, we might be on our way to a picnic," Ting said.

"Not really."

"What do you mean?" Ting asked. In his mirror, he saw the shadow of the four-fan against a brilliant white cloud. Had the pilot seen them? Whatever the answer, the chopper was heading north, as Ting and Kelly were.

The wind stole her mumbled reply, and he had to ask her to repeat it. "I left a note," she said.

"A note?"

"I hid it under my pillow. My mother wasn't supposed to find it until later."

"Why didn't you just leave a map saying where to find you?" Ting asked.

"Shut up," she said. They dipped behind a hill and flew westward along a shallow valley. The chopper was hidden from view.

"Are you coming with me?" she asked.

"If they're already after you, you'll never make it," he said.

She nodded but didn't slow down. The prop beat was growing louder. "I suppose you're not prepared anyway."

"Not hardly," Ting said, as he managed to pull beside her.

As the words were leaving his mouth, his mirror showed the chopper swooping low into the valley and banking violently. Through the glass dome in the nose, Ting could see the bearded pilot grinning maniacally. The stubby craft's fans roared within their wire cages. They were vertical, so it was flying like a plane.

Ting looked to see Kelly's reaction, and caught a glimpse of her plane slipping into the woods. At the same time, the chopper bore down on Ting, almost ramming him. Somehow he rolled out from under. The cargo door on the side of the chopper rolled open, and a second militiaman stepped onto the running board, supported by a tether and with something bundled in his hands.

The militia craft made a wide turn and came back at Ting, who didn't have the presence of mind to get out of the way, though he automatically hid his face behind an outstretched arm. The pilot yelled something, soundlessly within the glass, and his comrade threw the bundle. It opened as it fell, and Ting saw it was a net about to entangle his propeller. The throw was good, and he knew he was caught. But he dove recklessly, almost piling into the ground, and the net caught his rudder instead and streamed out behind him.

He was winded, and there was no point in trying to get away, but he ran anyway, shifting into high gear as he dashed over a woods, trying to hide among the treetops.

The net caught on a branch and tore loose, taking a thick splinter off his rudder. In a panic, he pulled up, and the chopper, which had headed off in the wrong direction, swung about after him.

Where was Kelly, who had gotten him into this? There was no sign of her.

• • •

Pedaling as hard as he could, Ting was still no more than half as fast as the chopper. Fortunately, he could dodge and weave in ways it couldn't. Every time it came close to him, its mass would drag it past. Before long, the pilot began to moderate its speed in an effort to gain more control. This might have been a good sign except that Ting felt his legs giving out. He began to imagine the scene his mother would make when the militia brought him home.

The fields they flew over now were newly broken and the houses were new or unfinished. The farm line, as the border with the wilderness was known, had to be very close. Ahead and to the west, an unplowed field gave way to acres of willow-choked marsh.

He kept thinking of Kelly. Probably some militia member had looked up from his fields, seen her pass overhead, run to his chopper and intercepted her. It should have happened to Ting by now.

The chopper was gaining on Ting. For the last few minutes, the militia pilot had been reacting perfectly to his every move. Suddenly, the roar of the fans redoubled, and the chopper rushed him. If it hit him, he was dead. But it veered aside at the last moment, and Ting dodged another net. By the time the militia pilot got the chopper turned around, Ting had gained a substantial lead.

As the marsh rolled under him, he tried again for some treetop concealment. But he still saw the chopper when he looked in the mirror, which he guessed meant its pilot could see him. He inhaled the aroma of decaying plants and swore. Where was the rest of the militia to head him off? Then he saw the second chopper coming up behind the first.

A pond of drifting colors split the tree cover. Ting dipped his plane into the cavity, and the helicopters disappeared from his mirror. He banked hard to the right, toward a gap in the wall of trunks. His propeller chopped a hanging frond as he entered the natural tunnel cut by a thick, slow-moving stream. He stopped pedaling. Without warning, the stream gave way to soggy earth, and the trees closed in rapidly. Ting made a series of reflex twists and turns, but as he banked to avoid one trunk his right wing tip tripped on a jutting root and tumbled the plane abruptly into a muddy pool. His head cracked against the dashboard and seemed to spin in queasy circles as the plane settled upright.

He wiped mud from his tearing eyes. His forehead was unbloodied, but he felt the blood throbbing beneath the skin there.

The air was full of wobbly balls of muddy water, some the size of grapes, others as big as melons. The branches overhead were wet and dripping. Ting watched mud drops slowly sink to the surface of the pool and melt in.

The first chopper passed to the west and kept going, though it seemed to have slowed. It would turn back in a moment, Ting was sure. The second one passed overhead, and it, too, kept going.

Ting's wits began to come back. Nothing seemed to be broken, not even his ringing skull. What if his trick had worked, and the militiamen still thought he was going north?

One chopper did come back, and it passed close by. But Ting and his plane were well camouflaged with a coating of mud, and the chopper went away. Its roar sank under the buzzing of insects.

For a while, Ting didn't feel like moving. He peered through the branches, looking for pursuers, and breathed slowly. Then his back itched, and he began to squirm. The next thing he knew he was kicking his shoes into the nose of the plane, cuffing his pantlegs and climbing over the side. Something live wiggled out from under his left heel. He walked to the front of the plane, hating the ooze between his toes, grabbed the handle under the propeller and heaved until the wheels came free. The mud gave him traction to walk it to a bank of packed mud. He reached out to a branch and steadied himself before pulling it the rest of the way out.

He was sure that a leech had fastened itself to the inside of his left knee, but nothing was there when he looked.

His stomach growled. It was after his usual lunch time, and he'd had no breakfast.

The bank was actually a thin bar separating the muddy pond from a larger and surprisingly cleaner one. He had been that close to finding more maneuvering room when he'd crashed. Of course, if he'd made it, he might have been in the open when the militia arrived.

He stripped, draping his clothes over a branch, and dove into the clearer pond to scrub the mud off his face and out of his hair. He was back out in a hurry, still thinking of leeches, and returned to the water's edge to rinse out his muddy blue sweatshirt. It was cleaner but too damp to wear when he was finished, so he dressed in his jeans, which had been dirty to begin with, and his undershirt. He hung the sweatshirt over the back of the seat in his plane and considered the fact that the choppers hadn't returned to flush him out. It was time to leave, if he could.

At first, he thought he would take off along the bank. But it was too easy to see himself struggling into the air too late to avoid the trees. It was a while before he saw another possibility and decided it was worth a try. He climbed back into the plane and slipped on his shoes. The propeller turned reluctantly. Dirt and water blew back in Ting's face, and he held up a hand to ward them off. The plane rolled forward. When the wheels came to the surface of the clearer pond, they tried to roll on it. But the water caught at them and the plane pitched in nose-first. It threatened to flop over on its back but instead toppled to the left, making the wing on that side stab in and touch bottom. The plane rocked back and floated.

Ting had hoped the plane would act like a boat until it got up to speed. But it moved sluggishly in the water. When he pedaled too quickly, the nose dipped. When that happened, the propeller chopped the water, sending shock waves back to his legs, and refused to turn at any speed.

In frustration, he tried the same thing again, pedaling even harder. A sheet of water slapped his face as the propeller bit into the pond. When he gave up pedaling, the plane's tail splashed into the water and the nose reared high. The moment almost escaped him before he thought to pedal again, frantically this time. The plane lurched up and forward. The tail came free of the water with a loud sucking noise, and the plane twisted through the grabbing branches. Startled birds rose all around it.

He flew south and then east, and the choppers that he saw did not chase him. By the time he saw the tower on the horizon, it cast an endless shadow against the falling sun.

The tower was round, golden and partly transparent. Sometimes it was possible to see the shadows of enormous rooms migrating up or down its center. The City Store was a dome joined to the base.

Ting walked in with his hair cemented in odd curls by particles of clay. Inside his shoes, the mud between his toes was still damp, and he itched everywhere as if covered with insects. They seemed to be devouring his privates.

The store was vast, with great, arching plastic rafters holding up the ceiling. The floor was smooth, but magically sticky. Every other time he had been here, there had been a small crowd loitering just inside the entrance. Today, he saw no other customers, just a stooped clerk restocking the hardware shelves. The man was one of Ting's people. Only once had Ting seen a Citizen here, and that was many years ago.

Ting jumped and touched down gracefully atop a stack of seed sacks.

"You there!" shouted the clerk, getting to his feet. A splotch the color of bruised strawberries covered the left side of his bald head.

"I'm looking for flour," Ting said.

"You can do it from ground level," the man said, glaring. His left eye twitched. "Flour is there by the wall."

"Thanks," Ting said, as he dropped thirty feet and pushed off in a shallow bounce.

"And slow down! This isn't a playground," called the clerk. But Ting didn't slow down much.

He moved more cautiously on the way out. He had put the items his mother had asked for in a sack and slung it over his shoulder. The sack tried to wiggle free every time he rounded a corner. He could see himself tripping, letting it fly across the room.

"I told you to slow down," said the clerk, coming over to attend the register.

"Please, sir," Ting said, letting his weariness show. "I'm in a big hurry. If I don't get out of here, I may not make it home before dark."

"Where's home?"

"Daleville."

The clerk nodded as he fed Ting's credit slips one by one into the register. At last, it spat out the change.

"Get going," said the clerk.

Ting slapped the sack back onto his shoulder with a grunt and hurried out the door. He ran recklessly across the lawn, stumbled to a halt beside his plane and stuffed his purchases into the space behind the seat. When he took off, the sun was low.

So Ting did not do loops or barrel rolls, plunging dives or straight-up climbs. He flew straight and as fast as his tired legs would carry him.

As dusk was deepening into night, he knew by the fading landmarks below that he would not make it. But there was one other destination he could try for, and he turned south.

As night came on in earnest, the world disappeared entirely, except for the lights shining from the windows of houses below. No stars shone through the dark glass above. He wondered where Kelly was and whether he would have been smarter to head north and try to find her again.

At the same time that he was mad at her, he took a guilty pleasure in having helped her. What kind of life she would have in the North, he didn't know. Many others had fled there. Some said the militia caught them all, but there were also stories of outlaw colonies.

He spotted a square of yellow light shining from the open doors of an addition to a barn. Knowing whose barn it would be, he descended. The ground rose up too fast for how tired he was. With shaky reflexes, Ting hopped his plane to the left of a boulder and got his wheels on the dim driveway. The plane skidded sideways, and the tail came perilously close to ripping into a flower garden. Ting jumped over the side and dragged his feet until the plane stopped, then he ran toward the light in which McManus was silhouetted beside a wide-winged, delicate craft he called a "pedal-glider."

Only when McManus called "Whoah" did Ting realize he was running up too quickly. The gray-haired man whose face now emerged from the shadows moved too late to intercept Ting, who caught himself against a table. The table toppled, and a flying screwdriver broke a glue jar on a shelf on the far side of the workshop.

"I'm really sorry," Ting said from his resting place on the floor.

"You'd better be," McManus said mildly, as he hobbled forward. His right leg wouldn't bend. "What's wrong with you?"

"I've had a really bad day," Ting said.

"You're a mess," McManus said. They righted the table, and Ting began recovering the tools that had spilled from it.

"I had a crash. In a swamp," Ting explained. He shouldn't have said it was in a swamp, but surely McManus could tell just from looking at him.

"A swamp?" McManus chuckled. "I'm sorry. Doesn't seem funny to you, I guess. Well, how'd you manage that? Your own recklessness, if I know you."

"That's about right," Ting said. He wondered again where Kelly was.

"Sooner or later you'll learn. What are you doing out so late?"

"Trying to get home. But the sun wouldn't wait for me."

"You want to call your mother for a ride?"

Ting nodded.

"Fine," McManus said. "First you need to go tie your plane down before it blows away. We don't need two disasters tonight."

Ting went outside with the flashlight McManus had handed him. The sky was black now. He tried to remember what stars had looked like. It made him think of the night he and his mother had ridden on the back of a truck out into the country to meet the space ship, which his mother had called the Charity Ship. The sky had been full of stars that night, but his memory of them grew dimmer every year.

Crickets sang to him as he pushed the stakes into the ground. He tested the lines and walked slowly back to the workshop.

McManus was cleaning up spilt glue. It had dripped down from the shelf onto his desk and the pages of a book. Ting had seen only five books in his life on Vesta, and two of them were sitting on this desk. One lay closed at the right edge. The other lay open at the center with snotty glops stretching across the drawings of ancient aircraft. As

McManus wiped a dry cloth over the drawings, a little ink came up with the glue.

"I'm—" Ting stammered.

"I know."

"I'm really sorry."

McManus tossed the rag into a bin without looking at Ting and led the way out, across the lawn and into the house. As they came through the front door, the plane maker pointed to the telephone on the wall at the far side of the living room.

"Hello, Ting," said Mrs. McManus, coming in from the dining room.

"Hello, Mrs. McManus." Ting crossed his arms awkwardly in front of himself as he remembered his silty hair and clothes. The room around him looked just-cleaned.

"He's been getting into trouble again," McManus said. "Could you guess?"

"That's always my assumption with him," she said, smiling as she slipped into the kitchen.

Ting shot an embarrassed look at McManus, who responded by pushing him gently toward the phone. The press of the man's palm on Ting's shoulder conveyed forgiveness as words couldn't have.

The boy dialed and allowed fourteen rings. "She's not there," he said.

"Maybe you dialed wrong," McManus said.

Ting tried again. Still no answer.

"Do you have any idea where she'd be?" McManus asked.

"No," Ting said.

Mrs. McManus poked her head into the room. "Are you staying for supper, Ting?"

Ting looked at McManus. McManus said, "We don't know what's going on with him yet. He just tried to call home for a ride, but there's no answer. I suppose I'd better take him over there and see what's going on."

"Is your mother a member of the militia?" Mrs. McManus asked Ting.

Ting stiffened.

"No. Why?"

"They were up to something today, I think. I saw a lot of choppers. More even than on most weekends when they're out drilling. If it was important, she may have decided to help them out."

"Wouldn't we have heard about it?" McManus asked.

"You always say no," she replied scornfully.

"Not always."

"Most always," she said. "Anyways, I hope you get it sorted out, Ting. I'll keep something warm for you, Earl."

Ting followed McManus out behind the barn, and they mounted a four-fan adapter on the hood of his tractor. When they were inside the cab, McManus started the motor, flicked on the headlights and pulled back the stubborn lever that engaged the fans.

"Noisy damn thing, isn't it?" he shouted. "It kills me that this is the only way I get to fly these days. I'm trying to rig up a way to work the pedalglider with my arms."

"Can't they fix your leg?" Ting asked.

"I don't like doctors. Bad example to you, I guess, but there it is."

"That's not the real reason," Ting said.

McManus shrugged.

"It's not doctors you don't like; it's City doctors," Ting said.

"I try to be as independent as I can," McManus said. "And I don't like doctors. Never have."

"How can you claim to be independent? They tell you you're a farmer, so you're a farmer, even though you could make planes day and night if they'd let you," Ting said.

"That's enough."

"Tell me how I'm wrong," Ting said. "We're practically slaves!"

"You know nothing about it."

Ting gave up. He should know by now it was pointless to bad-mouth the City around his elders, especially those who remembered a harder life on Earth. But it pained him to think of McManus sandwiching time in his workshop between blocks of other labors that clearly brought him less satisfaction. Customers brought him a donation from their harvests to apply toward his quota, but it never seemed to go very far.

They were coming up on New York Mountain. Home was just on the other side.

"If you'd been shot at a few times, you'd understand," McManus said unexpectedly.

Ting just looked at him.

"If you'd stayed on Earth, someone would try to kill you just for pocket change once or twice a year. This would seem like heaven."

Ting thought of men firing rifles from the roof of a burning building. Was that what the old man meant?

The tractor had crossed the mountain now, and the helicopter blades beat the air more gently as the craft descended. In the down-tilted headlights, Ting's home appeared out of the darkness.

"Where have you been?" Ting and his mother asked each other when they met at the front door. Ting reflected her anger with a set jaw.

Determinedly, she calmed herself and insisted, "You tell me first."

"Spoken like a true mother," McManus said, as he followed Ting inside.

"You stay out of this," she said. Though she affected to make the words only mock-stern, they had a hard edge.

"I was over his house, asking what I should do about my missing mother," Ting said. He met her eyes, cocking his head to the right. "Your turn."

She almost smiled at his willfullness. "You know Kelly Lang?"

"Sure," Ting said, as smoothly as he could. His heart thundered. He'd been afraid she'd ask him why he was so dirty, but she didn't seem to have noticed.

"Well, Kelly decided to go north today," she said.

"Kind of young for that, isn't she?" McManus asked. He had just remembered to take off his hat and was folding and unfolding it absently.

"I don't know that it's a matter of age," she said. "It if were, you'd have run off by now, since you're certainly old enough. You and Mrs. Claus could make toys at the Pole."

"Not a bad idea."

Ting waited for his mother to say something about a second runaway, but she didn't. The militia pilot who'd harried Ting must have mistaken his plane for Kelly's.

"Did you catch her?"

His mother and McManus exchanged a glance, and Ting saw they knew who he was cheering for.

"Yes, we did," his mother said.

"Better her own people than the police," McManus said gently.

Ting said nothing, but he noted the cutting look his mother gave the plane maker.

"Kelly was silly to think she'd have a chance at freedom," Ting said. All he could think of was how she probably would have made it if she hadn't taken those few minutes to fly with him and how nothing ever turned out the way he wanted it to.

"Even the City people aren't free, Ting," McManus said. "Not if freedom means being able to do whatever you want."

McManus stayed for coffee, though he said he couldn't stay long.

"Thank you for keeping an eye on him," Ting heard his mother say as he was washing up for a late supper.

"Oh, you have to keep a close eye on him too, I'd say,' McManus replied.

Ting's mother whispered something.

"I don't know," McManus said.

Obviously, Ting had not escaped suspicion, though he hadn't quite been caught.

"I feel bad for the Langs," his mother was saying downstairs.

"Why's that?" McManus asked.

"The silly girl had just gotten a scholarship of some sort. They were going to make a Citizen of her, I guess. You should have heard her mother brag. But with all the trouble Kelly's gotten herself into. . . . Well, it's just too bad."

Upstairs, Ting wished his mother could see the expression on the face in the mirror. He winked at himself and went downstairs to eat.

The Illustrators' Contest

by
Frank Kelly-Freas

About the Author

Frank Kelly-Freas is Co-ordinating Judge of L. Ron Hubbard's Illustrators of The Future Contest, and Illustration Director for this series of books. His honors and awards in the field of science fiction and fantasy, alone, are too numerous to list. Since 1950, he has been a premier illustrator in this field, and in many others.

He approaches his work with a twinkle in his eye, and he discusses it lightheartedly, most of the time. Do not let this fool you; he is deadly serious about illustration, as the following essay will leave you in no doubt.

How do you get in the Illustrators' Contest, and how good are your chances? Well, the important thing to remember is that you stand as good a chance as the next woman or man. Maybe not right away; there are differences in experience and acquired skill. But sooner or later—sooner than you think, probably—you're going to be competing right up there with the best. Meanwhile, there's no time like the present to start entering. What have you got to lose? And you have quite a bit to gain; the steady discipline of entering, and perhaps a critique, at least, of your work.

The next thing is that there's no entry fee, and never, at any time, do you compromise any of the rights to any of your work.

The third thing is just because you don't speak English, if you don't, doesn't mean a thing against you. We all speak Illustration, and that's what counts.

Finally, don't sweat it—just draw.

In return, here's what you get:

A chance at $500, first of all. Send in three unrelated drawings of your own choice, according to the instructions given in the rules, and every three months there'll be three co-winners, who get $500 apiece. That's yours no matter what.

Then you'll get, in the mail, a story. It'll be one of the winning entries in L. Ron Hubbard's Writers of The Future Contest, and you'll have thirty days in which to illustrate it.

Illustrate it well enough, and you'll win $4,000 additional, plus a letter of introduction to the art school of your choice. The letter of course will be signed by some pretty high-powered names in the field of Illustration.

And, your illustration may also appear in **L. Ron Hubbard Presents Writers of The Future** at an additional payment, from Bridge Publications, Inc.

Then, you'll be invited to the Awards event. It's in a different place each year. Most recently, it was at the United Nations, in the Trusteeship Council Chamber.

So, I suggest two things. One, look carefully at the illustrations for this book. You'll see a wide variety of styles; we don't favor one over the other. But there's a certain sureness of hand that is common to all of them. That's important, I think, and I think you should strive for it in your own work.

Two, I suggest you listen closely. . . .

Ever since I took on this job and began attending s-f/fantasy art shows all over the country, I have been raving to anyone who would listen about the incredible amount of talent Out There. . . .

I still am.

There can be little doubt that intentionally or otherwise (probably otherwise; we don't usually seem to be that smart) we have reared a generation of youngsters as hard to pigeonhole as it is to manage. One thing about it is certain; these young people are as highly visual as they are visible, and their imagination is as creative as it is sometimes hard to fit with existing notions of right and wrong.

The most surprising characteristic of these young artists is perhaps their independence. If one is fortunate enough to be supported by a rich aunt, artistic independence comes easy. But for those of us who have to depend on our skills and our wits to continue eating regularly, it seems wiser to apply some fraction of our abilities to supply the presumed needs of the mundane world. One of the more satisfying ways of doing so is through applying our talents to illustration of one sort or another. You would expect this new breed of young artists to be flocking to market with their portfolio stuffed with samples of their story illustrations, no?

No.

Incredible as it sounds, only about one out of four of these marvelously talented and creative people is even interested in becoming a professional illustrator.

To us who find visual storytelling, communication of nonverbal concepts, and in general visual interpretation of the written word, to be the most exciting aspect of our art, merely Doing Your Own Thing seems singularly unrewarding. And of course seeing one's own work in print—knowing it is to be seen by thousands of people rather than the relatively few who go to art galleries—tends to be highly addictive.

I am presently occupied in trying to develop a whole new school of American illustration, making a practical social and economic use of that superb body of artistic talent developing Out There. Naturally it's a bit frustrating to find that potential illustrators are a small portion of that group.

On the other hand, from the viewpoint of the would-be illustrator, this isn't a bad thing at all! Competition is stiff at best—and to find it reduced by a factor of three can be very helpful. . . . As Kipling advised the artist who complained that nobody understood his problems ". . . be glad that your Tribe is blind."

The illustrations herein will give you an idea what our new colleagues can do. And let me point out that the runners-up are so good that judging was a heroic job, with the edge frequently being a fraction of a fraction. Imagine what these illustrators will be doing after a few years of honing their skills in the market!

So pass the word on to your artist friends. The competition is tough—but there's not nearly as much of it as you might expect.

And it's fine company to be in! So, here's the address:

> L. Ron Hubbard's
> Illustrators of The Future Contest
> P. O. Box 3190
> Los Angeles, CA   90078

You'll find the rules in Page 412 of this book. What more do you need?

NEW WRITERS!

L. Ron Hubbard's
Writers of The Future Contest

A Contest for New & Amateur Writers

AN INTERNATIONAL SEARCH FOR NEW AND AMATEUR WRITERS OF NEW SHORT STORIES OR NOVELETS OF SCIENCE FICTION OR FANTASY

No entry fee is required
Entrants retain all publication rights

☐ **ALL AWARDS ARE ADJUDICATED BY PROFESSIONAL WRITERS ONLY.**

☐ **PRIZES EVERY THREE MONTHS: $1,000, $750, $500.**

☐ **ANNUAL GRAND PRIZE: $4,000 ADDITIONAL!**

Don't Delay! Send Your Entry To:

L. Ron Hubbard's
Writers of The Future Contest
P.O. Box 1630
Los Angeles, CA 90078

˙C O N T E S T   R U L E S˙

1. No entry fee is required, and all rights in the story remain the property of the author. All types of science fiction and fantasy are welcome; every entry is judged on its own merits only.

2. All entries must be original works of science fiction or fantasy in English. Plagiarism will result in disqualification. Submitted works may not have been previously published in professional media.

3. Eligible entries must be works of prose, either short stories (under 10,000 words) or novelets (under 17,000 words) in length. We regret we cannot consider poetry, or works intended for children.

4. The Contest is open only to those who have not had professionally published a novel or short novel, or more than three short stories, or more than one novelet.

5. Entries must be typewritten and double spaced with numbered pages (computer-printer output O.K.). Each entry must have a cover page with the title of the work, the author's name, address, and telephone number, and an approximate word-count. The manuscript itself should be titled and numbered on every page, but the author's name should be deleted to facilitate fair judging.

6. Manuscripts will be returned after judging. Entries must include a self-addressed return envelope. U.S. return envelopes must be stamped; others may enclose international postal reply coupons.

7. There shall be three cash prizes in each quarter: 1st Prize of $1,000, 2nd Prize of $750, and 3rd Prize of $500, in U.S. dollars or the recipient's locally equivalent amount. In addition, there shall be a further cash prize of $4,000 to the Grand Prize winner, who will be selected from among the 1st Prize winners for the period of October 1, 1989 through September 30, 1990. All winners will also receive trophies or certificates.

8. The Contest will continue through September 30, 1990, on the following quarterly basis:

> October 1 - December 31, 1989
> January 1 - March 31, l990
> April 1 - June 30, 1990
> July 1 - September 30, 1990

Information regarding subsequent contests may be obtained by sending a self-addressed, stamped, business-size envelope to the above address.

To be eligible for the quarterly judging, an entry must be postmarked no later than Midnight on the last day of the Quarter.

9. Each entrant may submit only one manuscript per Quarter. Winners in a quarterly judging are ineligible to make further entries in the Contest.

10. All entrants, including winners, retain all rights to their stories.

11. Entries will be judged by a panel of professional authors. Each quarterly judging and the Grand Prize judging may have a different panel. The decisions of the judges are entirely their own, and are final.

12. Entrants in each Quarter will be individually notified of the results by mail, together with the names of those sitting on the panel of judges.

This contest is void where prohibited by law.

Copyright © 1990, L. Ron Hubbard Library. ALL RIGHTS RESERVED.

L. Ron Hubbard's

ILLUSTRATORS
OF THE
FUTURE
CONTEST

OPEN TO NEW SCIENCE FICTION
AND FANTASY ARTISTS
WORLDWIDE

All Judging by Professional Artists Only
Frank Kelly-Freas, Co-ordinating Judge

$1,500 in Prizes Each Quarter

No Entry Fee   Entrants Retain All Rights

Quarterly Winners compete for
$4,000 additional ANNUAL PRIZE
under Professional Art Direction

L. Ron Hubbard's
Illustrators of The Future Contest
Box 3190
Los Angeles, CA 90078

CONTEST RULES

1. The Contest is open to Entrants from all nations. (However, Entrants should provide themselves with some means for written communication in English.) All themes of science fiction and fantasy illustration are welcome: every entry is judged on its own merits only. No entry fee is required, and all rights in the entries remain the property of their artists.

2. By submitting work to the Contest, the Entrant agrees to abide by all Contest rules.

3. This Contest is open to those who have not previously published more than three black-and-white story illustrations, or more than one process-color painting, in media distributed nationally to the general public, such as magazines or books sold at newsstands, or books sold in stores merchandising to the general public. The submitted entry shall not have been previously published in professional media as exampled above.

If you are not sure of your eligibility, write to the Contest address with details, enclosing a business-size, self-addressed envelope with return postage. The Contest Administration will reply with a determination.

Winners in previous quarters are not eligible to make further entries.

4. Only one entry per quarter is permitted. The entry must be original to the Entrant. Plagiarism, infringement of the rights of others, or other violations of the Contest rules will result in disqualification.

5. An entry shall consist of three illustrations done by the Entrant in a black-and-white medium. Each must represent a theme different from the other two.

6. ENTRIES SHOULD NOT BE THE ORIGINAL DRAWINGS, but should be large black-and-white photocopies of a quality satisfactory to the Entrant. Entries must be submitted unfolded and flat, in an envelope no larger than 9 inches by 12 inches.

All entries must be accompanied by a self-addressed return envelope of the appropriate size, with correct U.S. postage affixed. (Non-U.S. Entrants should enclose International Postal Reply coupons.)

If the Entrant does not want the photocopies returned, the entry should be clearly marked DISPOSABLE COPIES: DO NOT RETURN. A business-size, self-addressed envelope with correct postage should be included so that judging results can be returned to the Entrant.

7. To facilitate anonymous judging, each of the three photocopies must be accompanied by a removable cover sheet bearing the artist's name, address, and telephone number, and an identifying title for that work. The photocopy of the work should carry the same identifying title, and the artist's signature should be deleted from the photocopy.

The Contest Administration will remove and file the cover sheets, and forward only the anonymous entry to the judges.

8. To be eligible for a quarterly judging, an entry must be postmarked no later than the last day of the quarter.

Late entries will be included in the following quarter, and the Contest Administration will so notify the Entrant.

9. There will be three co-winners in each quarter. Each winner will receive an outright cash grant of U.S. $500.00, and a certificate of merit. Such winners also receive eligibility to compete for the annual Grand

CONTEST RULES

Prize of an additional outright cash grant of $4,000.00 together with the annual Grand Prize trophy.

10. Competition for the Grand Prize is designed to acquaint the Entrant with customary practices in the field of professional illustrating. It will be conducted in the following manner:

Each winner in each quarter will be furnished a Specification Sheet giving details on the size and kind of black-and-white illustration work required by Grand Prize competition. Requirements will be of the sort customarily stated by professional publishing companies.

These specifications will be furnished to the Entrant by the Contest Administration, using Return Receipt Requested mail or its equivalent.

Also furnished will be a copy of a science fiction or fantasy story, to be illustrated by the Entrant. This story will have been selected for that purpose by the Co-ordinating Judge of the Contest. Thereafter, the Entrant will work toward completing the assigned illustration.

In order to retain eligibility for the Grand Prize, each Entrant shall, within thirty (30) days of receipt of the said story assignment, send to the Contest address the Entrant's black-and-white page illustration of the assigned story in accordance with the Specification Sheet.

The Entrant's finished illustration shall be in the form of camera-ready art prepared in accordance with the Specification Sheet and securely packed, shipped at the Entrant's own risk. The Contest will exercise due care in handling all submissions as received.

The said illustration will then be judged in competition for the Grand Prize on the following basis only:

Each Grand Prize judge's personal opinion on the extent to which it makes the judge want to read the story it illustrates.

The Entrant shall retain copyright in the said illustration.

11. The Contest year will continue through September 30, 1990, with the following quarterly periods (See Rule 8):

    October 1 - December 31, 1989
    January 1 - March 31, 1990
    April 1 - June 30, 1990
    July 1- September 30, 1990

Entrants in each quarter will be individually notified of the quarter's judging results by mail. Winning entrants' participation in the Contest shall continue until the results of the Grand Prize judging have been announced.

Information regarding subsequent contests may be obtained by sending a self-addressed business-size envelope, with postage, to the Contest address.

12. The Grand Prize winner will be announced at the L. Ron Hubbard Awards event to be held in the calendar year 1991.

13. Entries will be judged by professional artists only. Each quarterly judging and the Grand Prize judging may have a different panel of judges. The decisions of the judges are entirely their own, and are final.

14. This contest is void where prohibited by law.

Copyright © 1989 L. Ron Hubbard Library. All Rights Reserved.

"...as perfect a piece of science fiction as has ever been written."

— Robert A. Heinlein

An extraordinary novel featuring the inspiring career of an extraordinary hero - **FINAL BLACKOUT** is the action-packed epic adventure of a man re-building a war-ravaged civilization and willing to pay the price for what it takes.

ONLY $16.95 HARDBACK
FREE SHIPPING!

GET FINAL BLACKOUT
by master storyteller
L. RON HUBBARD
TODAY!

Available at bookstores everywhere

TO ORDER CALL TOLL FREE 1-800-722-1733
(1-800-843-7389 in CA)

Bridge Publications, Inc., Dept. WOF6, 4751 Fountain Ave., Los Angeles, CA 90029
Copyright © 1989 Bridge Publications, Inc. All rights reserved.

READ
BATTLEFIELD EARTH

Battlefield Earth
A saga of the year 3000

THE #1 NATIONAL BESTSELLER

L. Ron Hubbard

Internationally Acclaimed New York Times Bestseller
Saturn and Tetradrama D'Oro Award Winner

It is the year 3000. Earth is enslaved by an alien race called the Psychlos. Johnny Goodboy Tyler battles against incredible odds to unite mankind in a last desperate fight for freedom.

"...think of the Star Wars sagas and Raiders of the Lost Ark, mix in the triumph of Rocky I, Rocky II, and Rocky III and you have captured the exuberance, style and glory of BATTLEFIELD EARTH."
— THE EVENING SUN

Voted one of the all time favorite science fiction and fantasy novels in the Waldenbooks 1986 XIGNALS Reader's Poll.

ORDER YOUR COPY TODAY!
CALL TOLL FREE
1-800-722-1733 (1-800-843-7389 in CA)

OR WRITE TO:

Bridge Publications, Dept. WOF6, 4751 Fountain Ave., Los Angeles, CA 90029

"The Best-selling SF Anthology of All Time."

— LOCUS

L. Ron Hubbard presents

WRITERS OF THE FUTURE®

VOLUMES I, II, III, IV AND V

Enjoy these award-winning science fiction stories selected by famous authors! Order your copies today!

"...packed with raw talent...a must buy..."
— Fantasy Review

ORDER THESE VOLUMES WHILE THEY LAST!
Volumes I&II: $3.95 each;
Volume III: $4.50;
Volume IV: $4.95;
Volume V: $4.95.
FREE SHIPPING!

ORDER TODAY!

Bridge Publications, Inc.,
Dept. WOF6, 4751 Fountain Ave.
Los Angeles, CA 90029

CALL NOW!

1-800-722-1733 or
1-800-843-7389 in CA

L. RON HUBBARD

AUTHOR OF 23 NATIONAL BESTSELLERS

"REMEMBER how you felt the first time you saw STAR WARS? This book will do it to you again." — ORSON SCOTT CARD

If you liked the adventure of the Indiana Jones sagas, the excitement of Lethal Weapon and the sinister drama of Batman, you'll love MISSION EARTH, the blockbuster by master storyteller L. Ron Hubbard.

"...a big, humorous tale of interstellar intrigue in the classical mold. I fully enjoyed it!" — Roger Zelazny

50% Savings!

BLACK GENESIS

THE INVADERS PLAN

10 volume hardback set:

~~$189.50~~
$99.95

Mission Earth ®

The biggest bestselling Science Fiction dekalogy* ever written!

Start your adventure TODAY! Order all 10 hardcover volumes for only $99.95 (a 50% savings). Single volumes $18.95 hardcover. Paperback volumes 1 to 8 currently available. Volumes 9 & 10 paperback release during 1990. Paperbacks also available wherever fine books are sold. $4.95 paperback

ORDER DIRECT FROM BRIDGE PUBLICATIONS, INC.

Dept. WOF6, 4751 Fountain Avenue, Los Angeles, California 90029
CREDIT CARD ORDERS CALL TOLL FREE:

1-800-722-1733 (1-800-843-7389 in CA)

FREE SHIPPING. All orders shipped within 24 hours.

Copyright © 1990 Bridge Publications, Inc., All rights reserved. MISSION EARTH is a trademark owned by L. Ron Hubbard Library. 2703901681

*Dekalogy: A series of 10 volumes.